The Joseph Communications:
the Fall

Dedicated to the Earth and Mankind

The Joseph Communications:
the Fall

Michael G. Reccia

with thanks to:
Jane, David and Tony
and
Maria Luisa

Published by Band of Light Media Limited © 2012

10 Sparrable Row,
Briercliffe,
Burnley,
BB10 3QW
United Kingdom

www.josephspeaks.com

ISBN: 978-1-906625-05-4
First Edition July 2012

Printed and bound in the UK by Biddles,
part of the MPG Books Group, Bodmin and King's Lynn

Contents

The long, hard road to the Fall
an Introduction

Where am I?

To be more precise, *what* am I?

I appear to be a 'consciousness'. Nothing more than that. No form. No substance. ...I think, therefore I'm... *what*, exactly?

I begin to remember. I've voluntarily vacated my physical mind and body so that they can be used by someone else – by the discarnate spirit *Joseph* – and he's just returned to the sphere inhabited by himself and other members of his 'group soul'. He's vacated the premises in effect, leaving an empty house.

Yes, that's right... *I remember now*... my body is around here somewhere... Ah. *There* it is. My eyes are tightly closed. I vaguely sense arms and legs, fingers and toes, eyes and lips – but I can't move them. After what seems like an age someone gently touches my arm. It feels as though the fingers are actually penetrating my insubstantial, ethereal flesh. It's Jane, by my side as always. I know I'm close to my body but it also feels like I'm teetering on a high, rocky ledge, about to fall. Yes... I'm falling.

Falling.

I open my mouth and gulp in a lungful of air.

I'm back.

After a few minutes I force my eyes open. They're heavy. Uncooperative. On a couch opposite me I can see David and Tony peering at me, a look of concern on their faces. Jane hands me a glass of water. I hold it, stare at it. It's fascinating. I can see the glass, the water, but at the same time there appears to be nothing there – it's simply a pattern of Light energy. And that's nothing too. Eventually it becomes substantial enough to my altered senses to allow me to take a sip. 'Was it all right?' I manage. 'Did we get a chapter?'

...Going into trance is not a pleasant experience for me. I'm nervous beforehand, because there are always those unspoken questions lurking at the back of my mind: Will I come back afterwards? Will I be able to get back into my body? Will everything *work*? I suffer *afterwards*, too. There inevitably follow two or three days of intense fatigue, a day of irrational anger and irritation, and a day of acute depression (my vibrations, having been 'set free' and accelerated into bliss during a trance session, have to slow again in order for me to live in this world as I'm supposed to, and the shock of being dragged back down into this sticky, heavy atmosphere always brings my psyche low as it struggles to adjust). In total, following each session, there's at least one full week ripped forever out of the calender of my life – a week when I'm neither here nor there, so to speak; a man with a foot in both worlds, master of neither, able to do little other than gradually recover.

So, *why do this*? Why do I and Jane and David dedicate so much of our lives to the exacting and debilitating procedure of bringing through *Joseph* and making his messages for humankind available to the world?

Because, in a world gone stark, staring, raving mad; a world that likes to pretend it is less violent and more civilised than it has ever been with regard to its savage past, what Joseph explains and suggests is vitally important – *essential* – to us all, for the liberation of our very souls and an end to physical and mental torment, and for the future and restoration of the planet we're ravaging and destroying minute by minute, by our actions and, more importantly, through our thoughts and beliefs. In the introductions to his other books I've already covered in detail the story of how I initially took on the task of bringing through *the Joseph Communications* as a result of a 'chance' remark from my now-departed spiritual teacher, Joan, and how what began as a series of clairvoyant communications (I had previously worked as a conventional spirit medium for many years) eventually deepened into trance transmissions, allowing me to take myself out of the picture completely so that Joseph could bring through much more information during those times when communication took place. I won't, therefore, tread old ground here.

Instead I'll ask you to consider our situation from your point of view. If you had, for whatever reason, been given the ability to bring into the world advanced, enlightening spiritual information from a highly evolved and benevolent source in contemporary language, information that, if heeded and acted upon, allows the individual to live a more fulfilled, healthier, happier life; information that finally and fully and absolutely and *wonderfully* explains who and what we actually are, why we are here on Earth, what we are truly capable of and what, unless we work to change things *now*, we are rushing headlong into, could you in all conscience do anything else but access and deliver that information? And, having brought through the Communications from higher dimensions, which of these options would you then choose in all conscience – to hide them under a bed and pretend the sessions had never happened or, instead, and despite being 'plain, ordinary folks' with plain, ordinary lives, to seek to move heaven and Earth daily in order to get them out into the world and *actually make a difference*?

We had no idea when Joseph's first book, *Revelation: who you are; why you're here*, was published that there would be other books no follow – and that each book, although it could be read independently of the others, would expand upon the last, building into a constantly unfolding, enlightening and informing narrative – we simply knew that we were the humble custodians of something very special.

We were a little surprised then, when Joseph, having explained the 'spiritual mechanics' of ourselves and of the world in *Revelation*, went on to deliver a second volume – *Illumination* – this time chronicling what could be done to change humankind for the better and to restore the planet, and also explaining why, exactly, that change was necessary. A third book, expanding on the first two, was to follow, offering possibly the most comprehensive account ever written of what to expect once we leave this world behind physically – *Your Life After Death*.

Intriguingly in all three books a thread could be glimpsed running through and behind the narrative in the form of a term gradually introduced at first but which would gain greater significance and be mentioned with increasing frequency as time went on. That thread, that term, was *the Fall*.

Joseph regularly alluded to some kind of cataclysmic event that had taken place aeons ago in our dim and distant spiritual and material past, an event that had produced an Earth that had been changed and diverted away from its original purpose and form in some way, intimating that humankind on this planet had been around for far longer than we supposed, and that we are, each of us, not only unconscious contributors to the world of war and torture and power-seeking and lack we walk today, but also unwitting cultivators and perpetuators of this sorry state of affairs.

It became obvious that Joseph's Communications were leading to a full and extensive examination and explanation of the Fall, and that this communication had an urgency about it – a need to be brought through as quickly as possible. Shortly after the last words of *Your Life After Death* had been uttered, therefore, we began to sit together again to allow *Joseph* to dictate the contents of the book you are now holding. I, personally, had begun to feel the intense pressure and responsibility of bringing through such a book many months before a single word of it had ever been delivered. Its implications were so enormous that, as with the other books, we simply *had* to capture and record every word with unerring accuracy, a task made all the more daunting by the fact that, throughout the project, we knew there would be direct opposition to this information being accessed and made public from the Field, that negative, sentient, all pervading thought-field projection of mankind that has its own, very specific agenda – that of keeping things in this muddled, violent world *exactly as they are at present.*

Indeed, during the course of these Communications we would find ourselves and our endeavours 'attacked' at every opportunity. Loud arguments would erupt inexplicably between passers-by outside the house during communication, severing the link and bringing proceedings to an abrupt close. Atypically late postal deliveries would send heavy parcels crashing through the letterbox onto the floor, again temporarily severing the delicate connection, wrenching me out of trance and causing us all to suffer from acute headaches for days afterwards. During a public trance demonstration at which Joseph invited and answered questions from the audience a barely disguised hostility and anger was unwittingly directed towards him from a couple of attendees, opening a conduit for negative energy that resulted in weeks of disturbance and trouble for Jane, David, Tony and myself. Delivery of the final chapter was interrupted by negative energies that prowled the boundaries of our little circle of Light, with me being pulled out of trance by the lack of available spiritual energy several times, and us having to regroup following a hot, calming drink and a time of peaceful meditation, in order to bring the book to a successful conclusion.

To make things even more stressful, when we were midway through the book Joseph intimated to us that the need for *the Fall* to be in the world as quickly as possible had increased, leading to our decision to sit for communication not once a month, as we had been doing until that point, but *twice*. This ultimately enabled us to complete the Communications some seven months earlier than we would have done if we had followed our original schedule, but the consequence for me of this accelerated timescale was confinement to a murky, not-quite-here existence during which my spiritual, mental and physical energy levels were drained almost to zero, with me at times wondering in all seriousness whether I would, in fact, live to complete the task at hand. As you can see, I'm relieved and delighted to be able to report, with a wry smile on my face, that I did.

With Joseph's words here in physical form there then followed a busy period of preparing the book for print, during which I allowed myself the luxury of reading it for the first time. 'What's that?' you say... reading it for *the first time*? Well, *yes*. You see, the other members of our group, being present, naturally knew what the book contained but I, having vacated my physical body and mind to allow *Joseph* centre stage during the Communications that constituted its contents, had no idea of what had been said, and deliberately avoided asking the others for information in case I absorbed some knowledge that would subconsciously influence and colour future transmissions. What I discovered upon that first read-through was the most astounding spiritual manuscript (I'm allowed to say that because I'm only the messenger – only the 'instrument' as Joseph calls me – not the originator of the words). Contained within this book is an explanation of why things are as they are here, what caused things to be this way, and the simple yet committed steps that need to be taken in order to lift us out of the current status quo on Earth. Each of us, when reviewing *the Fall*, felt humbled by the enormity of its revelations and the simplicity of its message, reassured by the way that every fact and explanation made perfect sense and related backwards and forwards to every other piece of information in this book and the others, and even more determined to spread *The Joseph Communications* as far and as wide as we possibly could during our lifetimes.

Joseph's delivery is presented here as it happened during the times when we sat together for communication. Where breaks in transmission occurred for whatever reason those are indicated in the text. In instances where Joseph fished around in my mental dictionary for suitable words to better describe certain concepts those strivings for clarity have also been left in. At the conclusion of each chapter Joseph would also invite questions from Jane, David and Tony concerning the issues he'd just raised. As these, too, are packed with information and Joseph's characteristic attention to detail, and as they expand on the themes covered in this book, they have also been included. As for introductions, Jane is my hard working partner and my rock; David is the closest of lifetime friends and fellow spiritual seeker/member of The Band Of Light (Joseph's title for us, not ours); and Tony is our staunch supporter and friend whose generous spirit has made possible the creation and distribution of our books, and who sits in on the Joseph sessions whenever duties at his Healing Sanctuary allow (explaining his absence from certain sessions).

If *the Fall* resonates with you as it has with us, please, for the sake of humankind, for the sake of future generations and for the sake of this planet, recommend this work to those colleagues, friends and family you feel are ready to access this information. The one fact that Joseph has impressed on us during this work is that the time to change things, the time for action, is *now*. There's no point putting things off until tomorrow, because, as you'll discover by the end of this book, unless we use our todays wisely, there are only a finite number of tomorrows left.

Michael G. Reccia
June, 2012

'The Field' – a brief explanation

If you are new to *the Joseph Communications* and have not read *Revelation, Illumination* or *Your Life After Death,* the first three books in this series, allow me to qualify the term 'the Field', which Joseph refers to at points throughout this book.

When referring to 'the Field' Joseph is describing the conscious field of thought-energy we, as spirits on Earth, are surrounded by and live within. Every second of our lives we project our thoughts and beliefs as to the nature of reality into this energy field. The Field is actually created and maintained *by us*, but we have lost sight of this fact. As a result of us forgetting this, which is in itself as a result of 'the Fall', the Field is not operating as it was originally intended to. It was supposed to serve us, but at the moment we, in effect, serve it. It exhibits, and seeks to perpetuate in us, a negative charge and outlook, and, because of this and its disconnection with God-Light, is maintaining itself and us via a finite and dwindling amount of energy. The Field in its present state, and therefore also we as human beings existing within it, cannot last much longer. Joseph urges us to re-energise the Field with God-Light and, by doing so, to transform it and take control of it once again for the betterment and continuance of humankind and of the planet.

Chapter One
In The Beginning

Joseph: A book starts at the beginning; a program starts at the beginning; a drama starts at the beginning ...a very good place to start, *the beginning*. And so, to open this examination of why you are as you are at the moment we must, relatively speaking, go back ...and back ...and back ...*and back* to *the beginning* and to a time before you existed as you do now – but not *before* you existed, because **you *always* existed**. You existed as an aspect, a facet, an opinion, a point-of-view of the Divine, of God. You existed encompassed by God, existing within God, but I have to take you further back than that in order for you to understand – to a time when the matter and space that you are surrounded with did not exist; when you existed simply as a *potential* – an individual potential wrapped around by the all-encompassing, all-embracing concept of God.

In the beginning there was *no thing* (and you can reference 'no-thing' in my first book [*Revelation*]); there was no thing; there simply ...'was' is the wrong word... IS. There simply *IS*. **In the beginning, before all things, there was simply a state of IS;** and that state of IS was and is the consciousness of God, the expression of God, the expression of what IS.

The IS felt within Itself a *desire* – not a *need* because God does not have needs – a *desire* to examine aspects of Its being; to express aspects of God's being and to give... not *separation*... but a *form* to parts of Itself. And so, as a result of a desire to

16

express and examine aspects of the Whole, there was the first movement – before that time there was no movement; there was simply the IS.

Imagine you have a rope and imagine that that rope is made up of separate fibres bound together to form the rope. Imagine, as an analogy, that God is and was the 'Rope' and that there came a time when the Rope wished to express and focus on the individual 'fibres'. Those fibres were always part of the Whole, always part of the Rope, but could be examined, if so wished, as individual fibres within the body of the Rope. This is what the Divine sought to do in the beginning but you must understand that this is not the beginning of God – **GOD IS!** This timescale I am talking about is to do with the beginning of *your* cycle, because we are examining who *you* are, where *you* are and where *you* came from.

At the beginning of this particular cycle, the IS decided that It would examine the various fibres that made up part of the Rope that is the IS. (I hope I am expressing this sufficiently well for you – I always knew that this book would be the hardest one to bring forth because the concepts that we are dealing with do not translate *easily* into the dimensions of where you are.) An aspect of the IS decided to examine the fibres within the Rope that made up that aspect of the IS and, in order to do that, It loosened the bonds within the Rope. It gently untwisted the Rope until the fibres became apparent as individual fibres but still within the bounds of the Rope. And, when the fibres had been sufficiently loosened, the IS placed part of Its consciousness into each fibre.

This is not creation as you understand it; this is divination – a desire to see things through different viewpoints. It is not creation at this point; it is simply a positioning of energy within the Whole to give the illusion of separate consciousness to the 'fibres'.

The fibres that were then observed by the Whole began to regard themselves as a separate viewpoint from the IS... began to regard themselves as individuals... but not 'individuals' as you understand the term because, at that early point in the creation of the area of space, time and matter that you find yourself in, there was a conscious link to the IS from the fibres. In other words the fibres *knew* that they were the IS and at the same time were reflections, mirrors and aspects of the IS, but always contained *within* the IS. There was a consciousness that was unlike your consciousness at this time; there was a glorification of being; there was an acceptance of the Whole and the All being the individual – and the individual being the Whole and the All. **And these fibres or beings that were made self-aware could be described as *angels*.**

From God came an angelic stream of consciousness and the angels were Light as God is Light – or the expression and movement behind Light. The angels were Light and at the same time that the fibres or angels were given being ...*creation began.* Creation of this physical universe you find yourself in began, and it began as God's Creation, yes, but as a generation away from that as the creation of the angelic Light or the fibres that came from the IS. The fibres, being equal to God in their examination of being, had a desire to create; there was a desire to *bring forth* as God has brought forth His children, in effect, by disentangling the fibres from the Rope. The fibres themselves then had a need to create.

The fibres used condensed Light (not as condensed as the Light you find yourself in at the moment) in order to give form to their expression.

You are living in a universe composed of Light.

So, from the IS you have the fibres or angels that are still part of the IS; the angels in turn then loosened the area of influence around them (or the edges of their being) and condensed the Light in the area that they created. Let me try and explain – as they loosened the edges of their being, they mingled those edges one to another ...to another ...to another to form an area of creation. They donated something of their own essence – the edges, if you like, of their Light-sphere or aura, which they mingled together to create matter through slowing the rate and condensing the Light at the edge of their auras. They were aware of themselves as individuals but also as part of the IS. They consciously chose to donate some of their Light into a pool of potential that they could manipulate by their thoughts, wishes and dreams...

...and the next sound that you hear is:

BANG

...because, as they condensed the Light from the edges of their being, **creation began.**

Your scientists say this and that about the Big Bang, but the Big Bang was created by the angelic fibres of the IS deciding, *in love*, to create a playground, to create an area within which they could examine certain aspects of themselves because they were not all alike. Each fibre of God is a potential, a different potential of the IS, and the IS takes joy in multiplicity, in examining different potentials within Itself and different reflections of Itself. The angelic beings that were created within the Rope when It was loosened were all different and all had something different to contribute through the condensing and slowing down of Light into the matter universe they were creating in order to experience themselves.

So behind the Big Bang was a *wish*; the 'word' was a wish and the word was made Light. There was Light; there was the Big Bang and the angelic fibres segregated themselves each according to their potential. Certain of them became in charge of construction – the construction of form within the matter universe that they had created. Certain of the angelic fibres became concerned with the sweeping away of form that did not please, that was not perfect and was not the wish of the angelic group. Certain of them became concerned with how form looked and an investigation into the potential of matter to bring forth exciting opportunities for the angelic forms to investigate and to experience.

As these thought-processes, examinations of self and generations of potential took place within the hearts and minds (and those are only analogous terms) of the angelic beings the universe formed, because behind the physical universe is an angelic framework. **Thought produces form.** And the IS watched and experienced with joy as the angelic fibres within the Rope created and examined physical form simply by wishing to do so. What I am trying to explain is that, behind the physical universe, there is a matrix of thought and what you perceive to be aeons of time – wherein planets and stars are born, worlds cool and solidify, and areas of space change and are attracted or repulsed by certain forces in the physical universe – are the hard-matter reflections of the thought-processes of the angelic group that governs, creates and maintains this physical universe.

Some people reading this book will be appalled at the *suggestion* that the physical universe came about through angelic creation and not God-Creation, and to those of you I would say: examine what has been said earlier in this chapter. The angelic forms came forth from the IS and are a part of the IS. Therefore, that part of the IS that is the angelic forms created the universe. There is *no conflict*. There is no conflict with your religious upbringing; there is no conflict with the creation stories that you have. Creation came forth from God, from the IS, but simply as the IS first bringing forth a concentration on aspects of Itself, which then decided to create a sphere within which they could experience and bring greater glory to the IS by sending back to the IS their experiences.

So the physical universe that you are in began as a wish to bring to the IS greater glory through the angelic beings that manifested as a result of the IS wishing to examine aspects of Itself. The point of this chapter is to break away your conception of the universe as being an expression of matter that may or may not have a spiritual purpose behind it. I want to turn that on its head and show you that in the beginning, and *now*, **the universe was and is a creation of spiritual will and thought-process** – not the other way round.

What you comprehend and see as being real and solid is an expression of angelic thought and creation that is stable. You have a hierarchy of being, of purpose and of the bringing forth of new states: you have the IS, from the IS comes the angelic form and from the angelic form comes *this particular universe* – and I say 'this particular universe' because there are other expressions of the IS but we shall examine them at a later date. It is this particular expression of the IS that concerns you because, from your point of perception, you are living within it. But not totally within it because, as with the physical universe being an expression of the motives of a spiritual group, *you* are the expression of a spiritual truth, and what you perceive to be you encased in matter is actually a projection from the spiritual truth that is you that you have shifted your consciousness into and believed to be true.

And the IS looked upon... here we get back to biblical and religious teachings... the IS, through His angelic expression, looked upon the condensation of Light that had become the physical universe and it was good.

It was good!

...Because at that time it *was* good, and we shall examine in the future how most of it is *still* good – it is only the particular region of time and space that you find yourself in that is not so good.

The building blocks of the physical universe are particles of condensed Light. I wonder if you dare say that to your scientists – to look no further for the secret of creation than to *condensed Light*, a slowed vibration of Light-energy that gives an apparent form and is manipulated by the minds, the will, the dreams and the harmony of an angelic group. Look no further than particles of condensed Light because particles of condensed Light are what the angelic group that oversees this physical universe use to give form to matter. To simplify things it is a process of first imagining and then giving form to those imaginings by grouping particles into the illusion of solid matter.

As I deliver this first chapter through Michael, I am sitting on a chair but the chair doesn't exist, Michael doesn't exist, the room doesn't exist as anything more than an illusion that takes form through condensed particles of Light adhering to each other governed by the wishes of an angelic group to be clustered in a certain way.

I find this more tiring than any of the other deliveries so I must, at this juncture, end this particular section, but I will, as normal, ask for questions from the group and you will forgive me if I exit at a time when I cannot maintain contact any longer. Are there questions?

Tony: Do we, as part of that universe that was created or manifested through thought, also have the ability to create as those angels created the universe? Does that pass down to a limited amount? Do we, as individuals on Earth, have the ability to create?

Joseph: We will examine next in detail how you arrived and how the expression of God as an angel was and is perfect and, therefore, there is no division between the angels who manifest the universe and yourselves and no difference except in outlook.

The nature of the IS is to bring forth potential and examine it joyously, constantly and for ever and ever; to bring forth potential; to look at possibilities and to make possibilities whole; to examine them and then to either perpetuate them or let them go. That potential is translated into the angelic forms and then translated, as we shall see, to yourselves. We shall also see that the physical universe is not only apparently (because we are dealing with matter that is not really there as a solidity) outside of yourselves but that physical universe is also *inside* of yourself; that you are each a physical universe and you each have the potential, not only of the angelic forces that create and destroy matter, but of the IS that is behind those angelic forces. It is a vast subject and one that we will examine in depth – that is the purpose of this book. Does that answer your question for now?

Tony: Thank you so much.

Jane: Joseph, when you said we could say to scientists that matter is *condensed particles of Light*, could you use the word 'energy' for 'Light', because scientists seem to talk about energy? Is Light energy?

Joseph: They talk about energy because they do not understand the nature of Light and they see everything as a vibration, which is good because everything *is* a vibration, but it is a condensation of God-will that gives form to the Light and the matter that you see in this Universe. What I am trying to do with that statement is to say: 'Look no further! You are looking for complexities; you are looking for something that has a name, something that is difficult and something that has to fit in with your complex view of how the world works. The answer for the scientist is simple and when the scientist relaxes his iron-like grip on what he considers to be true then he will realise what is really going on. And what is really going on is that Light, (which is in itself an expression of the IS and the unseen), is the basis of all Creation. Light reacts in different ways dependent on the thought-process that is put on to it and is applied to it.

Light can be many things but it is always Light: the piece of coal that you pick up is Light; the sky that you look at is Light; the complex forms that you make in order to express your technology are Light because there is nothing else within this bubble of physical universe you find yourselves in. **Light is the building block of all matter and all creation** within this sphere; there are other means of creation but they, too, are based on Light. Imagine children's building blocks, which you can put together to make many forms, but at the heart of the many forms is the identical building block; it is just put together in different ways to create different pleasing forms to the eye. The building block of the physical universe is the particle of condensed Light, which, through the thought-process of the angelic group, is grouped together in different ways to give the illusion of different forms, but if you were to have a 'spiritual microscope' you could examine every form and see within it that identical building block. Do you see that?

Jane: Yes.

Joseph: That is what I am trying to convey to the scientists… to *relax their complexities*, and in relaxing their complexities they will see through the illusion and discover that the building block of the physical universe is a condensed particle of Light.

David, is there a question from you?

David: You talk about this physical universe being created by an angelic group, which is part of the IS and, at the same time, to use the Rope analogy, the IS is unravelling in a different way elsewhere to create maybe another universe – how can you know that from your point of view?

Joseph: Because we are taught by angelic beings. We *are* angelic beings ourselves but at a certain level in our completion of the cycle that takes us back to God (which in our case is not completed yet) we are visited by the purity of angelic forms that have not been corrupted, displaced and locked in by the effects of what we are about to discuss later in the book – by the Fall. As we free ourselves from the restricting illusions around us, we have access to those who talk to us and demonstrate to us – just as we talk and demonstrate to you our more enlightened viewpoint (I hate the term 'enlightened' because it seems arrogant but it *is enlightened* because we have divested ourselves of much of the physical matter around us so we can see a truer path). Because of our increased vibration we are, therefore, allowed to discuss such things with messengers. On Earth you regard guides as messengers (and to an extent we are) but we have messengers who talk to us, who come and go from the IS, who are filled with a joy that you cannot know until you divest yourself of the illusion of physical matter, and who talk to us of different aspects of the IS and who also *are* different aspects of the IS.

We sometimes experience visitors from the IS who are joyfully different from the visitors from the IS who govern this physical universe. It is like seeing different expressions of colour or sound, and we see them as potential. Sometimes they come to visit because, unlike us at the moment, they are free to come and go from the all-embracing IS; they are free to experience different expressions of reality. They come to visit us to show us the potential in other areas of the IS but there are so many other areas of the IS. **The IS is infinite;** God is infinite as you say quite rightly. Infinite! And, therefore, expresses infinite potential, and there is an infinite desire and an infinite joy in examining different viewpoints, different playgrounds, different constructions of matter, different examinations of the IS expressed as the fibres of the IS. At times we have access to different fibres of the IS from different parts of the IS but all parts of the IS exist at once. You see the difficulty of expressing this in words, but if you were to consider the IS or God as a 'Hub' from which stretches different pockets of reality, which are all part of God but are all very different, then perhaps that gives you something to anchor on to via a physical mind – it is not how things are but it is an analogy that works.

Does that answer your question?

David: It does, yes, thank you.

Joseph: I must leave Michael; I have tired him greatly. Thank you for the opportunity to begin this great work. I have no idea how long it will take us and we must at all times make sure that the flow of consciousness that I bring fits into the flow of consciousness that you find yourself in and that I am delivering a narrative that is coherent and linear. Therefore, we must feel free to confer more than we have done with the other books to make sure that we have the 'timeline' right (which is not a timeline at all!) with regards to a book that explains the greatest mystery that has vexed philosophers and religious people for thousands of years:

Why is the Earth as it is?

Why is humankind as it is?

Why does it not change?

THE PATTERN OF CREATION

Chapter Two
The Pattern of Creation

Joseph: Last time we talked about the angelic expressions of God and the way in which they projected an illusion within which they could *experience*, within which they could look at different aspects of their creation and enjoy an interplay one to the other – all wrapped within the illusion of individualism. For 'individualism' throughout this book I would like you to substitute 'point of view' because **you, Reader, are a point of view of God** – nothing more. That does not belittle you but it positions you within Creation; by 'nothing more' I mean that there is an affiliation with God; by 'nothing more' I wish to make you *more* than you appear to be on a physical level; and by 'nothing more' I am taking away from you those things that separate you, through your physical mind, from acknowledging being the part of God that you are.

You are a point of view, and the angelic expressions that inhabit the physical universe are points of views, but not the *whole* point of view. I have to demonstrate today that the angelic forces remain angelic forces within the embracing being of God. What was and is projected into the physical universes is a point of view or a 'part of view', if you like, of those angelic forces. In other words the whole angelic being (that is itself a point of view of God) is not projected into the physical universe; only a *part* or a *dream* of that angelic being forms or is given 'birth to' in the physical universe.

You are an expression of an angelic being that is an expression of God. Yes, you have individuality in that you think from a certain point of view but you are then a point of view of a greater being that is also a point of view of a greater being.

Let us talk about creation and why creation is as it is. At the point (and we are talking metaphorically here) at which the angelic beings decided that they would project part of their consciousness into a dream that was 'solidified' as it were, at that point there had to be a form to the dream they wished to project aspects of themselves into. That form could only be based, as the highest honour and highest respect, on the principle of God that they realised they were a part of. So this particular physical universe and others are **based on the principle of God being the dot within the circle.**[1]

This should explain again to your scientists why, no matter how far they look outwards from the Earth and no matter how far they look into matter through their microscopes, they see *the same pattern* – the dot within the circle. The dot within the circle is an honour to God; it is a rejoicing of God; it is saying that everything that is brought forth into the physical universe is of God because there couldn't be anything else *originally*. So the planets, the moons and the galaxies are based on the principle of the circle, and the dot within the circle emanating out that projection or illusion but only to a certain point. The illusion is held by the dot, is encircled by the dot and encompassed within the dot. So with a planet, for example, there is a core to the planet and a core to its growth, and with a moon or a galaxy there is the same thing and, ultimately, the same thing applies to the universe. Even though that universe is expanding, it remains the circle with a dot at its centre – with God at its centre, with creation from angelic forces at its centre.

And so the pattern of creation is embedded into your own cells; is embedded in the world that you live on; is embedded within the physical universe that you see; is embedded within what you call 'black holes' and is embedded within pulsars and quasars and other types of stars that you have not yet come across and are not able to understand. Wherever you go and however far you go you will always find the dot within the circle – it is the building block of the universe; it is the way that things are created on a God-level and on an angelic level.

There is a shift in consciousness at the point when it is decided that physicality should be experienced, and so at that point there comes forth physicality via the creative capabilities of God channelled through his angelic forces. Physicality – something to mirror yourself against, somewhere to have an experience or an adventure in – only relates to a point of your being and only relates to a projection from the Whole, as the angels themselves are a projection from the Whole or from God.

Limitless possibilities, limitless scenarios and limitless adventures – that is the form that angelic creation takes. In this book we are only concerned with *this* particular universe and ultimately with this region of space and the alterations that were made to this region of projection of creation long ago that has resulted in the planet that you find and the way that you view and act out your lives. Limitless possibilities, however, it has to be said, exist in other universes and within the wishes, dreams and creative hearts of the angelic forces that bring forth matter into a constructed state. Matter can be described as a malleable dream, a soup of potentialities, a state that exists within *a part* of the minds of the angelic hosts, ready to be tapped, moulded and shaped into different realities – all of which honour God and all of which can sustain life, which is a projection from the angelic forces but not the whole of the angelic forces.

In different 'areas' different types of reality and different potentialities were and *are* being created, but always within the dot within the circle principle (although, actually, everything takes place within the same area, which is no area at all – confusing isn't it!). This physical universe you find yourselves in (or think that you are within) is a certain aspect of those realities, is one of those realities, is one of those potentialities constructed so that part – only part – of what you are really can play, can examine the vastness of God's potentiality and can understand more as a viewpoint.

The angels and you (who are part of the angels and *are* angelic beings) seek to grow. You seek to become more than you are and seek to understand because, as a viewpoint, you are part of the Whole but cannot see or channel the Whole. You can channel aspects of the Whole but not the totality of God, which is infinite in its potentiality, infinite in its ability to create new scenarios and infinite in its wonder – simple and yet infinite.

This region of space or 'projection' was created (as others are, have been and will be created) in order to allow the angelic beings responsible for this area of Creation to experience and to project part of what they are into what you would describe as 'physical matter' so as to allow those aspects of what they are to discover truth, potential and more about God. *Every* region of physical space exists to allow its occupants or 'points of view' to discover more about God and to celebrate God. When you talk of 'worshipping God' in your churches that aspect of worship is askew. Worshipping God means appreciating what you are and – by appreciating what you are and looking upon it – discovering more about it and being in a state of wonderment, excitement and growth.

The whole purpose of the physical universes is to 'entertain' projections from the angelic hosts (and, therefore, projections from God) so that those points of view, in being entertained, can absorb more information about the workings, grandeur and glory of the Whole – of God.

To take that to its logical conclusion: God created the angelic hosts and the angelic hosts then projected themselves into physicality: **God is appreciating God**. The whole process is God examining God. *There* is an answer to your meaning of life.

…What is the meaning of life?

The meaning of life is to appreciate God.

…To appreciate the God that you are; to appreciate the God that is around you and to look everywhere and to see God and, in seeing God manifest in physical matter and in so many diverse forms, to glory in what you are and to channel and project more of the Whole through yourself. **You are God reflecting God and your purpose is to appreciate that.** Your purpose is to grow through appreciating that, through seeing the God in everything, through seeing the pattern in everything and through enjoying and loving the life that you have – not as something that will be taken away from you, obliterated and blotted out, but as part of an infinite experience of experiencing and discovering joy through experiencing.

Initially in this projection or region of being you were joyful and you were aware of why you were here but I do not want to get too far ahead. In this chapter I wanted to make the reader aware of a very important thing: that the meaning of life is to appreciate what you are and to appreciate that you are an aspect of God – a never-ending aspect of God that can never be damaged, can never be obliterated, can never be diseased and can never be pulled down into a state of depression, because such things originally did not exist as creation of this area was brought into being.

The other expressions of life that you see around you are *equally* projections of God channelled through angelic projections into physical matter – so the dog, the cat, the bird, the tree, the mountain, the stream, the moon, the Earth, the stars and the spaces between the stars are all projections; they are all part of the sentience of the angels and, therefore, the sentience of God. **Every aspect of being around you is alive, is part of God and exists to celebrate God** – as you, truly at your heart, exist to celebrate and to experience the wonder of God.

Later on in this book we will examine why forms are diverse and why God, expressed through an angelic filter, expresses Himself (or Itself) as so many different things. This is perhaps one of the most difficult chapters because this chapter is supposed to (and I hope I am doing this) explain the nature of creation. Creation is a dream; creation is a projection; creation is a wish; **creation is the expression of form via a wish to express the individual in appreciation of the Whole** – a complex thing to get across but nothing more than that.

Again I look at science; I dabbled with science a long time ago but science seeks to make everything so complex and so rigid, and in order to understand God-science you have to have a more open view than science has at the moment on your planet. You have a missing dimension and the dimension is *vast*. It is like an ant trying to describe a mountain from its viewpoint – the viewpoint of the ant is so small and the mountain is so vast that the ant cannot see the top of it. Science has to allow the spiritual aspect to infiltrate into its machinations: the understanding that the scientist is part of God, the science that he or she is examining is part of God, and that creation is not complex but is a projection, an illusion and a temporary set-up to allow experience. The scientist is having an experience by examining his small view of science but it is the wrong experience – it is a limiting experience.

Physicality was set up to allow projections of God (i.e. you) to have ever more rewarding experiences as you bring to God (who tastes what you taste, hears what you hear, sees what you see, says what you say) ever more expansive experiences of whatever He, She or It is – mirrored back through you to the greater glory and greater potential of Creation so that you channel back to God your experience and understanding, which enlarges God's experience and understanding and evolves the Godhead into more areas of Creation and more areas of projection.

So you are vitally important, but your viewpoint has to be the correct one in order to fully experience and enjoy the life that you have been given without the fear of death, without the fear of violence and without the fear of depreciation of the human body and mind.

Let me see if I have covered the areas that I wish to cover; have I sufficiently explained the nature of physical creation? Does this make sense to you?

Tony: Absolutely, you have put it beautifully, Joseph. It is amazing!

Jane: You say that the pattern of physicality is based on the circle but a lot of things are waves – such as light waves and sound waves; is that also based on the circular pattern because a wave on a graph looks like a sequence of alternating semi-circles?

Joseph: Frequencies have a part to play within the spectrum of creation: frequencies maintain or take away the illusion; frequencies allow form to be perceived and to perceive; frequencies within the dot within the circle of creation are the filter by which the unseen appreciates itself and others as the seen and focused.

They are set up, as you know, by the circling or vibration of the dot within the circle. Every aspect of Creation has a sound, has an energy, has a projection, and everything seeks to project. God seeks to project; the angels seek to project; you seek to project (but you do not know it) and what you perceive of as frequencies is that volition to project emanating from the unseen into the seen and, because vibration also is alive, there is a purpose to vibration that *changes*.

Again science looks at particles and says that one moment a particle is there and the next it is not. That is because the vibration that that particle is an expression of has changed its volition at that point, has changed its 'mind' as it were (although mind is totally the wrong word), has changed its perception and is experiencing somewhere else and being something else. So the scientist sees, through the microscope, the particle disappear from one area and reappear in another area because the vibration has changed its perception. Vibrations are also impinged upon by your perception, by your volition and by your wishing to be in a certain state or in a certain place. Your thoughts actually impinge on the vibrations and wave-forms around you but the wave-forms are expressions of God. If you put out your hands now, I will attempt to demonstrate and allow you to feel the tingling of the vibrations against you. Can you feel them? Can you feel the energy that is all around you?

David, Jane, Tony: Yes.

Joseph: This is because there are many of us here allowing you to do that but that is your natural state – to reach out, as it were, (and not just with your mind and your hand, which is part of your mind) and to say: 'I appreciate you; I can manipulate you!' Feel that energy! Feel also the wave – feel that the energy is tingling because it is oscillating and it is oscillating with potential. And potential is about being in one place and experiencing, for example, this room but *at the same time* (which is the other part of the wave) experiencing *what might be*, considering where you want to be next, and then you fall back into this reality. So you have this reality at the bottom of the curve ...potential at the top of the curve ...this reality at the bottom of the curve, which is vibrating at such a speed that it seems to you that you are only here but, as you are here, part of you is appreciating and considering what comes next. *What comes next!*

At its highest God-expression, *what comes next* is glorious. Unfortunately, at the moment (and we must obviously talk about this as this is the purpose of this book) for most people on Earth the bottom of the wave is appreciating being here but the top of the wave is appreciating being *in a worse state*. So, rather than appreciating this life for the joy it should be and at the same time approaching and creating the next life and its potential (and by next life I mean the next physical expression) you are appreciating this life at the bottom of the curve, and at the top of the curve are using your ability to scan potential to consider what is going to go wrong next. You are linking the two so that the energy that should flow based on this level of vibration and then a heightened level of awareness (that keeps you stable, keeps you well and keeps you full of energy through the natural balance of that vibration) is polluted. The bottom of the wave keeps you here but the top of the wave also keeps you here, which is why your life seems so small by comparison to the potentials that I am describing today. Does that make sense?

Jane: Yes.

Joseph: Is there anything else?

David: Just from the point of view of the readers of this book, who obviously think about physicality, I can see them rapping their knuckles on a table and saying that it is solid and physical. From your point of view, Joseph, the surroundings that you live in, do you refer to those as *physical*?

Joseph: We refer to them only in that they are useful to us; we refer to them because we are used to having a physical framework within which we can express ourselves. The ultimate state of God (as we have discussed in other books) is no-thing. **No-thing!** God is beyond the physical senses that you have and is beyond the physical mind in that God, as a state, is no-thing – so simple as to be 'no-thing'. From God issued forth the angels; from the angels issued forth physical life. Physical life has to have a reference; that is part of the experience and the aim of Creation is to *experience* – simply to experience, to gain experience and to examine potential.

There has to be a frame of reference but, as you say, the frame of reference can be all-embracing to the extent that it blots out the ability to see past the illusion and that is the difference between our reality and your reality. As you know, because of what I have said to you in the past, our illusion is much more flexible than yours in that we can bring forth and parcel away the reality around us according to our needs. Also we can put away that reality and enter the no-thing to experience a well-being and an order that allows us to make sense of the illusion when we re-enter it, and also to order it in the best way for our potential as we evolve through the gradations of vibration and oscillation towards escape – as you will see.

Of course we surround ourselves with beauty and it is right that we should do so (and it is what you should be doing on Earth at the moment) but we are not locked into that beauty to the extent that it blinds us into believing that it is the ultimate reality. We know better – not because we are superior to you but because we have grown and, therefore, have more information available to us to know and experience in a better and more fulfilling way than you do. We are not slaves to the 'reality' (which is not reality at all) around us.

Our wavelength compared to yours is one of a different frequency, which is why you cannot normally see us, and is a wavelength thus: *the bottom of the wave is our reality, which is a refined level of oscillation, and the top of the wave is not only an anticipation of potential but a creation of that potential and a knowledge that that potential is linked to God.* We more directly experience God than you do. It wasn't supposed to be that way and we are leading to this in this book but we first have to set the stage. What I am doing is setting the stage to say: 'Here is the stage; you are players and I will now go on to show you that there is a play on that stage but it is not the original play; it has been infiltrated by those that have rewritten the script but, nevertheless, it is a play.'

Is that a sufficient answer, David?

David: Yes. I was trying to get round the idea that even the physicality we feel we see on Earth really is a very limited view of physicality; it actually extends a lot further out, as it were, and is more ethereal.

Joseph: It is! Your reality is an anchor; within that oscillation that you tap into and are a part of (because you oscillate) you exist on two levels, but you are supposed to have access to *both* of those levels simultaneously. In an ideal world and in the ideal world that was originally created you were supposed to be able to dip into this reality to experience this reality but simultaneously have your eye on the greater reality. In other words you knew this was an illusion and could see past it when you wanted to and for whatever purpose you wanted to.

At the moment the vibration on Earth, linked to the physical body and mind that encapsulates the spirit, is compressed; is two beats of the wavelength, but the bottom one and the top one are hardly separated. So you touch the base-level, which is your reality, in one beat, and in the second beat you touch, yes, your potential, because you cannot help but do that, but your potential is limited by you believing that the bottom beat is your reality. You look at your reality, you see it to be wanting and the top beat within which you create your future potential is one of despair, is one of lack, is one of imprisonment within the bottom beat. The variance between the top and bottom of the wave is very, very small and, therefore, you succeed only in bringing to yourself more of what you believe to be true from the bottom beat which is the state of your world at the moment. Do you see that?

David: Yes.

Joseph: Does that then answer the question?

David: It does actually, yes, thank you.

Tony: Can I ask one further to that on the same theme? Does that mean that we limit ourselves by our thoughts?

Joseph: Absolutely, you limit yourselves, but you limit yourselves **absolutely**. Because you are an expression of God everything that you create – you create perfectly; everything that you believe yourself to be – you believe yourself to be absolutely perfectly. And the reader will say: 'How can that be? I have this illness. I have this problem in my life.' But the problem in your life that you are contributing to and which others are contributing to is a perfect expression of that problem. It is a perfect problem! The pain you have is a perfect pain; the depression you have is a perfect depression; the illness you have is a perfect illness because you are creating it and you cannot but create perfectly.

What you have to distinguish between is your ability to create perfectly and what you create, and there has to be a turn of the mindset and a turn of the creative ability towards: 'I will create a perfect day *perfectly*; I will create a perfect world *perfectly*; I will create perfect health *perfectly*.' Whatever you do, you create perfectly because you are God but you are polluted, you are masked and your vibration has been brought down because of the effects of the Fall that this book is about. Does that make sense?

Tony: It does; we have to learn how to think perfectly.

Joseph: You have to learn how *not* to think! It is the thinking that has steeped you in the illusion and caused your problems in the first place, as we shall see.

Before I leave you, which I must because I have drained Michael dreadfully again, I have to tell you that you also have in the room with you today (and allowing you to feel the vibrations) the gentlemen that Michael calls the *Big Indian* and the *Persian Gentleman*.[2] As we have said, we are working together on this book and many of the 'characters' [*smiling*] – they will enjoy that – that you are familiar with will be working on this book. It is a book that needs to be as plainly put out as possible and we need, within the privacy of this room, as many of my colleagues, brothers, sisters, family, loves (because I love them all and they love me) as we can in order to get things right.

38

[1] Joseph gave us the 'dot within the circle' as an ancient symbol of God in his first book: *Revelation.*

[2] The Big Indian and the Persian Gentleman are our names for two of the guides who work with us.

Chapter Three
The Physical Universe

Joseph: We have discussed creation and have touched upon the bringing through of the unseen into the seen, and today I would like to talk about the *purpose* of this. Having set out this great theatre of possibility, I would like to ask the question: '**Why? What is it about?**' It is one of your basic questions: 'Why go to the trouble to create a physical universe?'

...And the answer to that lies in exploration of what can be and what could be.

The angelic reference points (that until the physical universes were created were simply that – reference points within the greater sphere of God-energy) were given the imperative and the request that they *explore*. Explore *what*? ...Always to explore *themselves*.

To condense their reason for being into a couple of sentences, **the physical universes exist so that the unseen can become the seen and can explore itself from *within* by experiencing what appears to be *without*.**

So the matrix of physical matter was brought forth at the behest of the Godhead working through His angelic children in order that those children might go out for a 'time' into the physical universe and, by doing so, explore possibilities – always with the intention of growth and of adding more to the Godhead.

It is as simple as that! And away from this area of space and this encapsulation of time the rest of this physical universe and the rest of the other physical universes exist simply to allow God through His facets (which are also God) to explore themselves. Note that I say: 'to explore themselves' and not 'to explore what is *outside* of themselves' because if you place yourself within a physical matrix your first inclination would naturally be to explore what is out there – *but there is no 'out there'*. The physical universes can be likened to a mirror because they reflect what is *within* God's children or God's angelic facets. The purpose of physical matter and physical scenarios – differing landscapes, differing climates and differing expressions of matter – is to allow the soul or angel to view itself, to view others and to realise different things about itself. And in realising different things about its capability and potential to then take those realisations and enhanced viewpoints back to the Godhead to enrich the Godhead so that *new* expressions of potential can be brought forth from the Godhead.

Initially the Earth was a globe of exploration, a theatre ...and I almost want to say: 'a night at the cinema' (that may seem a very strange thing to say) – somewhere where the angelic facets of God could come to enjoy the unique scenarios of this particular globe. Now, we are in a complex area here because each particular globe or planet has a number of characteristics that enable those who inhabit that globe for a time to explore certain areas of self. In other words, as a broad canvas, one globe may be set up to allow the spirits inhabiting it to learn about consciousness; one globe may be set up to allow spirits to learn about selflessness; one globe may be set up to allow spirits to learn about creation in physical matter. It is no coincidence that the planets that you see in your solar system are set up in a certain way because each one *originally* had something to offer as a sphere of potential to those spirits who were passing through it.

The Earth had a set of characteristics (and I must be careful here; I must give you the exact reason why the Earth was originally as it was) – **the Earth, paradoxically, was to do with the transmission of spiritual energies and the realisation of spiritual potential with regard to reaching out to others**. Isn't that a travesty of what the Earth now is! But the Earth, as it is set up at its core and in its matrix, is *still* that planet and still offers – second by second, minute by minute, day by day – that potential to its inhabitants who are so compacted into physical matter at the moment that that is the furthest thing from their minds ... and their minds are the furthest thing from their hearts.

The Earth was set up as a sphere within which the individual's approach to spirituality and the individual's ability to transmit those spiritual energies to other beings, to the matrix of the Earth itself, out into the physical universe and through physical matter to God could be learned, examined and practised – that was its original intention. That was why, in the beginning of the Earth's consciousness, it was set up.

But before we examine the far history of the Earth in a time when spirits who visited the Earth were semi-corporeal (that is the nearest I can get to it: a blend of physical atoms and spiritual atoms. All atoms, you must understand, are spiritual [and here again I am in strange territory] but atoms with a physical spin and atoms with a more spiritual spin, that is how the inhabitants of the original Earth were made up... of those two rare and delightful elements) and before we examine how the spirits who came here lost that blend, lost the memory of being part of the Godhead and lost the intention with which they originally came to the Earth, I must tell you that every planet and the universe itself is (as I have said) to do with *potential*. I must tell you that there are angelic beings in other physical forms on other worlds and in other universes that are fully aware of that fact because they have not blundered into a mindset that has imprisoned them and separated them from their original intention.

So [*laughing*] your delightful and quirky interpretation of beings on other planets being hostile towards you, seeking to invade, to overcome you and bend you to their will is a travesty

42

and is, in fact, a projection of your *own* aims and core beliefs sent out beyond this Earth. I must put things in a linear order but you can see how dangerous you are in your current mindset and that is why you are prevented from going out further, either physically or spiritually, into this particular universe where your thoughts pollute. You are allowed to pollute the Earth and pollute yourselves to a certain extent but you are not allowed to pollute the greater universe. You would be like a spreading disease or a cancer were you to send out your intentions and beliefs into physical space and beyond this physical solar system **and that is not allowed.** How it is not allowed I will tell you later but I digress again.

I wish to give you some idea of life in a physical universe without the confines of the Fall and the situation that you have set up for yourselves on Earth. The universes (– *universes plural*) are teaming with life. First of all the planets are alive and the stars are alive but the space between is also alive because they all issue forth from the creativity of the angelic hierarchy working on the imperative of God to bring forth physical form. But quite apart from the planets themselves being alive many, many worlds are inhabited; from the point of view of your scientists and most people on Earth this is going to sound a nonsense but: **no world is wasted.** Consider that, if each world is created as a theatre of experience and a theatre of experience from *within*, why would any world be created that is not part of that pattern? Why would there be any waste? There is much waste on Earth but in spirituality and in true creation there isn't.

I want to impress upon you today that every world, every star, every piece of space, every comet, every meteor and every black hole (or what you describe as 'black holes' but are in fact something completely different) has been set up with a particular purpose, and that purpose is always to allow the blend of physical and spiritual life (that exists outside of the Earth) to experience and to discover its potential – but always its potential *within*. So there is no waste and you will say: 'Well, we have planets that do not appear to support life,' but they *do* support

43

part of the pattern of creation …and just because *you* cannot discern life there doesn't mean that there is no life there!

The universes team with life – they can't team with anything else because the whole of Creation is one organism – and that life exists to experience. We have to understand the concept of God as *An evolving Everything*, and that might sound strange to you, that God today is less than God tomorrow – allow me then to substitute the word 'change' for evolution. We have said in other books that God is Love and God is Light …but God is also *Change* and that core ability to change is totally integrated with God. God moves, God evolves, God *changes* and, at the core of God, change is as important as Love and as important as Light. **God is ever-changing**; God is not a constant in the sense of you thinking of a great edifice on Earth that you say will be there for a thousand years. Yes, God will be there for a thousand years – God will be there for all time and beyond all time but God changes, wishes to change and has a purpose in changing. God loves to bring forth more God, more change, more possibilities and more potential but always in a positive way – never to harm, never to subdue, never to cause pain but always in the name of 'Love', in the name of 'Light' and in the name of 'Change'. It is only here on Earth that the focus has become skewed towards violence and harm through change; change here for the most part means harm, violence and power-seeking, but not in the rest of the universe and not in God.

So, God is Change and God desires change through His angelic forms and through the universe, and **the universe's *physical* purpose is to change and the universe's *inner* purpose is to present potential**. Out of the physical universe and out of the discovery of potential through living in the physical universe come greater universes, greater understanding and greater exploration. You, as the angelic beings you really are, are *limitless* in potential; you will always discover on your inner journey that there is another secret chamber, that there is another area of yourself that you have not discovered before. You can never reach the sum total of yourself because there is no sum total. **As you change, God changes ...providing you with more potential and more experience** – that is the nature of Creation and the nature of God and it is something that I don't feel has been expressed correctly in words before. It is so difficult to do so; not only are you dealing with abstracts but you are dealing with beyond and deeper than the abstract, and yet it makes perfect sense to me and I have to try to make it make perfect sense to you.

Before we examine what went wrong on Earth, I am setting up a picture of the way the universe works, and it has been compared to the inner workings of a watch, to clockwork and to a great machine but also to randomness too, as if it is all by chance. It is not all by chance – it is all by *change* and the universe and the change that you see around you are things that need to be welcomed.

To sum up: the original intention and the intention that is still there with regard to the Earth is to allow you to explore your spirituality in a physical universe – that is the key to this planet. Other planets are set up for different reasons to allow the people who inhabit and who visit them to explore other aspects of being and other un-trodden corners of the journey to the centre of the soul. The whole physical universe and physical universes are interlinked; everything that you see as chaos in space and everything that you see as destruction, and the birth and death of stars, is actually part of an intricate, interwoven matrix that needs every other part of itself to function properly. The destruction you see is not really destruction; the births and deaths of stars are not really births and deaths – they are the coming into prominence and the dying away from prominence of certain vibrations that allow clusters of souls to experience in a certain way at a certain time in order to bring change to themselves and change to the Godhead.

That is the backdrop of the universe, and within this particular physical universe you have a boundary, and within that boundary or 'no-fly zone' you have the Earth. And you have trapped, within this area of reality, the souls who visited the planet originally with the purpose of discovering more about themselves and the physical universe spiritually. They became trapped – we are building up to that and will examine it later.

I have been talking about a very difficult concept – do you understand the concept?

David, Jane, Tony: Yes.

Joseph: In understanding the concept can we then, through our usual conversation, extrapolate on that and can I invite questions?

David: Joseph, could you expand on and explain our spirituality on Earth in a physical context? What does that entail? Does it mean juxtaposing our physicality with our spirituality?

Joseph: It is certainly a balance of the two that was the original intention of coming to the Earth. It is to do with spiritual physics and the long-term potential of each soul to operate in a God-like manner *totally*. There is a hierarchy to the angelic nature or angelic projection from God that you really are – which is talked about in Bibles and holy books and there is a truth to it. There are angels who are closer to God (not closer to God in locality but closer to God in *ability*) and, because there has to be change because God is Change, there has to be a progression within the angelic beings who visit the planets they have created, and that progression involves understanding how the physical universes are brought into being.

The physical universes are brought into being through the desires of the angels who have grown closer to God and who understand how creation is brought forth. The primary purpose of the Earth plane was to teach angel 'children' (not children in that they had to grow up and become adults but children in that they were new creations of individuality or new reflections of God) and was to bring those delightful spirits here to allow them to examine the method of bringing forth physical matter through the opportunities that the planet had to give to them.

That was the original intention so, if I am answering your question correctly, the reason for the Earth presenting opportunities of investigating that blend of physical matter and spirituality was to allow the souls that visited it originally to *grow*, to grow in terms of being able to create their own universes eventually and to do that in a delightful way whilst having an adventure on the Earth and taking in the effects of the opportunities that the Earth presented to them at that time to teach them. Not to sit them down behind a desk and have a teacher there saying: 'This is how you bring forth physical matter,' but to teach them through experience and through the gentle, loving centre of the Earth. Have I explained that sufficiently?

David: Yes. What you are saying is that the newly formed individualisations are exploring themselves; they are exploring their own abilities and part of that is done on a physical plane on Earth.

Joseph: There is also the question of why form needs to be physical. It needs to be physical at its extremity from God in order to give a backdrop against which souls can measure themselves, and that is the only reason for the physical spin on atoms – as opposed to the more etheric and spiritual spin on atoms that you experience in other realms that are non-physical. So there is a need for physicality, but not physicality as dense as the physicality you have on Earth at the moment. The reason for physicality being so dense on Earth is because of the adjustment that came to the Earth and its surrounding area via the wishes of the children who came here and skewed their lesson. I have talked in the past about an 'experiment', and it *was* an experiment, but an experiment that has brought forth the wrong result. Do you understand that?

David: Yes.

Joseph: It is an overload of the physical and of that side of the balance, which we will talk about, but it needs to be in the context of what went wrong. There is a need for physical matter and for a physical matrix; it is to do with this distance analogy that I have given with the angels, who are more experienced, being closer to God. 'Distance' is the wrong word but, as you come out further from the Godhead to experience, the matter becomes denser – and needs to be denser because you are experiencing at a distance. You experience at a distance for a purpose: to understand that dense matter, how to deal with it and how to create it …but always infusing it with your spiritual side. Does that make sense?

David: Thank you.

Jane: Joseph could I ask a question about the density of matter, because with us being in this sealed off, no-fly zone and because we have compacted matter more than it should be, when we look out into space at the rest of the physical universe what are the elements of those planets and stars made of? What is it we see?

Joseph: You look through a glass darkly. What you see, even with your telescopes and probes (because they are made and infused with your own dominant vibration) is a reflection of yourself and so you see the heavier elements of Creation but you do not see Creation as others see Creation. You see it polluted; you see it as though you are looking through smoke because you imprint *everything* that you perceive with your own identification vibration. This is a very good point because we have been talking today about everything outside allowing you to explore what is inside and being a mirror – everything! So, whatever you look at on Earth or outside of the Earth is coloured by your dominant vibration. You know on Earth that two people can look at an object and have a completely different reaction to it. The object is the same but their reaction to it is different and is 'reality' because the only reality *ultimately* is the reality from within.

As a group of spirits you have created for yourselves a dark and dim view of reality because there is not much Light in it, so what you perceive outside of yourselves is coloured by that perception of reality, and you see the universe as a threatening place when it is not; you see the stars and the suns as violent bodies when they are not. You project – because you are creating and you are God – you project what you believe to be true onto those things that you see outside of yourselves ...and what you believe to be true is fuelled by the pollution of the Field and your error in the past. Your view of the universe is not the view of the universe of someone living in another sphere that has not been polluted by an experiment that has gone wrong. Do you see that?

Jane: Yes, but I just wondered if the other stars and planets had elements like iron or carbon; do they have something equivalent that is not as dense as our iron and carbon?

Joseph: If I was to take an element of carbon and give it to someone who lives in an enlightened world, they would see delightful atoms spinning around in beautiful harmony; they would hear a beautiful song from those atoms of carbon; they would see particles that have within them the potential to become something else so easily by the application of will to them. If I was to give the atom of carbon to someone on Earth they would see an atom of carbon, they would see restriction and they would see the potential of carbon only to be carbon because their view is compacted, so they project a compacted view onto that carbon and they see it only as carbon. The person who is living in the enlightened world sees it as carbon, but also sees it as potential, sees it as beauty ...sees it as God.

Do you see how blinkered your view of things is? And you mention carbon and you mention iron but they are only terms. They are terms for groupings of atoms that you recognise and those groupings of atoms exist beyond this sphere of influence, but beyond this sphere of influence those groupings of atoms are worth *so much more* and do not have name-tags. They can be carbon today and another element tomorrow; they can be a wish and a dream, which is what they really are. Your view is condensed so your expectation of what you see is similarly condensed because all you see is a reflection of what you are in your souls. Do you see that?

Jane: Yes, but do the elements still have those basic blocks?

Joseph: They are neither basic, nor are they blocks: they are groupings for a time for a purpose. It is as though you could create a wall of bricks in front of you – a moment ago there wasn't a wall and now there is one. This brick you could name 'carbon' and this brick you could name 'iron' and this brick you could name 'space' and this brick you could name 'a tree' ...but they are only those things whilst you create them and they are, at heart, the same thing – which is no-thing. They are potential and you bring forth from potential that which you need and that which you observe [*laughing*] and this is a wonderful illustration of why you were here in the first place to discover this but you have skewed and compacted it.

In order to understand the limitlessness of spiritual potential you need to shake free your perception of things. It is not an atom of carbon and yet it is – it is an atom of carbon but it is also a dream. It is also no-thing; it is something that has been brought out of the no-thing so that for a time you can experience it, but when it is no longer required what is it? Is it an atom of carbon when you are not looking at it? It is only by you segregating it and compacting it that it becomes what you wish it to be but in spiritual reality it is no-thing; it is a temporary arrangement of atoms brought forth by those who are like you (but haven't become trapped) in order to experience a certain set of physical realities. Do you see?

Jane: Yes, I do. Thank you.

Tony: Further to that, Joseph, are we then exactly the same as that carbon; are we put together as the angels' dream? Have we been brought into being?

Joseph: No, you are the dreamers. You are the dreamers and the physical body that you see as being so solid is only a temporary vessel that encases your soul and, as I have explained in other books, there is you and there is perceived reality, which in reality is no-thing. You are not no-thing; you are the I AM. There is the I AM and there is the no-thing and from the no-thing, via the I AM, is brought forth form, but you are not that form.

Again, this is something that will come up but you mistake yourself – the I AM – with the form that you project temporarily and believe that you are that temporary form. You, therefore, fear death when death is a concept that you have brought forth. Death does not exist because you are the I AM – the I AM does not die and the I AM is not born. All that is born and all that dies are projections of reality, which are projected by you the dreamer.

In order to experience you need to have a theatre within which to experience; you need to have a backdrop against which you can measure yourself but that backdrop and that theatre is only a mirror to show you what is actually going on within yourself. **You are not the backdrop!** This is something else that you believe on Earth, which is part of the problem of the Fall: you believe that you are the flesh; you believe that you are the backdrop; you believe that you are not in a theatre but in a be-all-and-end-all reality and you are not – nor are you that reality. You believe that you are that reality; you believe that you are the kidneys, and the brain, and the hands, and the feet. Those things are only there as an expression of you to allow you to experience the reality that you find yourself in at this time (which is also an expression of you) and neither the hands, nor the feet, nor the kidneys, nor the brain, nor the expression of reality around you is *real*. It is a dream and you are the dreamer – but the *permanent* dreamer; you cannot die because you have never been alive in a *physical* sense. You cannot die, you cannot end, and all that can end is the expression of reality that you place around yourself. Do you see that?

Tony: So as the dreamer we can create the reality around us... but is there a limit to that?

Joseph: There is a limit in that you have limited yourselves, but there is no limit outside of that limit you have placed on yourselves as a reality. So you have to break through the 'reality' which is not a reality, that says to you: 'I cannot possibly do that.' You have imposed that set of limitations on yourselves but they are not real. Your existence is limitless; your ability to experience is limitless; your potential is limitless and goes on... and on... and on but you have gathered it around yourselves and said: 'No, this is all we are capable of. This is reality. This is what we are.'

In forgetting your God-core, through fear you have invested in what you see around you, which is originally what you created and, because you believe you cannot connect to that God-core, you have to believe in something else and so you believe in *this* being reality and it is not.

Tony: Thank you, Joseph, it is very helpful. Can I just add one little bit and this is personal to the group: we all feel that our reality is constricted by time and we are all very busy – is that an illusion and something that we have created or is it a 'right' level of busyness?

Joseph: You are part of the matrix of the Earth and part of the matrix of souls that inhabit the Earth, so you have imposed on you a certain viewpoint of society, time, capability and age – all of which are illusions. I do not belittle your efforts because you have to negate the effects of the millions of souls that are around you who believe not as you do – so it is difficult.

All you can do is connect to us as often as you can and ask to be shown on any given day what is relevant and what isn't; what to put your energy into with a view to expanding the spiritual message that you are attempting to punch through this reality with and what is not important with regard to expanding that message on that day.

It is the same for the souls that are outside of this area of reality that is influenced by the Fall – you go within, and by going within, you will be able to discern what is important and what isn't important, which way to go, which door to close and which door to open. The answers are not outside of yourself, and remember that we are working with you and we understand your frustration. We understand how it is difficult to influence others because others are influenced by the Field to a greater degree than you are. There will always be the inertia from other people to a certain extent because they are being fed by this reality that they originally created that tells them that they are getting older but, at the same time, tells them that there is all the time in the world in which to do things.

Allow us to lead you, allow us to guide you, and we are aware on a day-to-day basis of the frustrations because we experience them ourselves and the false starts that you seem to be coming up against. Remember that this is a major, major, major *change in thinking* that you are trying to pour out into a 'polluted bowl of liquid' as it were; you are trying to put a dye into that polluted bowl and initially it looks as though that dye is submerged but when we have enough dye then the liquid will change its colour. Do you understand that?

Tony: Yes, thank you.

Joseph: I must leave because I have drained Michael once again. I feel exalted that I am able to bring through information but I also feel sad that I have to do it at such risk to his physical being. The reason that his physical being becomes so exhausted is because of the amount of drag of the Field on his body when the Light from a higher sphere comes into it. If that were not so and I were communicating to you from another world where you were open to the possibility of me communicating with you, I could communicate with you all day ...and all night ...and all day ...and all night, but the pull of this particular area drags and tears at his physicality to the extent that I have to exit otherwise he would become ill.

Chapter Four
The Nature and Influence of Colour

Joseph: I should like to talk today about the nature and influence of colour on the original construction of the Earth and of planets that have not been affected by the localisation of the Fall.

God expresses creation through coloured rays, and colour rays interpenetrate and layer to produce aspects of reality. At the beginning of this planet's tenure and being, the world was a very different place; it was principally a place of colour and the colours that you see now are but pale imitations of what actually lies *within* the construction of the planet. The angelic forces that created this world did so by manipulating atoms of physical matter and also by manipulating coloured rays that contained within them those atoms.

Construction in those days was a very different process than the heavy sequence that you see now in order to arrive at something in physical form. Here it is difficult to explain but construction was a matter of **intent given form through directed thought and the use of colour-charged atoms.** Each planet was first created as a sphere of intent and the Earth was created for very specific reasons, to allow certain circumstances to play out during a visit to this sphere and, through those circumstances, to give to the Whole certain colours and certain tones.

My emphasis on colour is an attempt to describe the issuing forth of angelic intent, the inhabitation of angelic beings within an area of angelic intent, and the bringing back of messages and experience to the Godhead through the medium of colour. In other words, the physicality was created through manipulation of colour – the experience was quite literally 'coloured' whilst the beings that chose to visit the Earth were here. Then, in order to enhance the Godhead, the results of that experience were directed back to the Godhead as coloured rays because **the angelic beings that you really are communicate principally through coloured rays.** You are used to communicating through speech, through hearing, through touch and through the other physical senses but the angelic thought-process manifests itself as bursts of colour.

So, before the angelic being detaches itself, as it were, from the Godhead in order to experience a sense of individualisation and to bring back to the Godhead the results of having experienced that individualisation, the purest form of angelic 'be-ing' is invisibility. It has no being in the sense of perceivable form, but the angelic being can express itself through the bursts of colour that it brings forth. If you were to view an angelic being within the Godhead (and by that I mean not individualised but operating within its original placement) you would see not a being but bursts of colour, and those bursts of colour represent the thoughts of the angel. Then, as there is a 'distancing' from God in order to experience in physical reality, those bursts of colour are used to create physical matter. And those bursts of colour were used originally to create the Earth.

The Earth in its original form (and that form is still held within the heavy, degraded shell that you exist within and on) existed and exists as a crystalline sphere of colour, as a sphere that reflects intention, because all experience is a reflection from an area of being. The original intention of this planet and of every planet that you see was and is to confine experience to an area of reflection so that the beings existing within that bubble of experience give out into the experience, and rays of intent that are manipulated by the wishes of the individual are reflected back into that individual and then carried back to the Godhead. It is a complex notion to put into physicality because I am trying to translate something that is essentially crystalline (and more etheric than that, even) into a heavy-matter world.

The planet was a sphere of experience; it did not have the weight and the solidity that it has now and, were you to look at it from space and see it interacting with angelic beings as they originally existed here, you would see a kaleidoscope of colour as the wishes of the angelic beings interacting with the wishes of the other angelic beings within the sphere 'bounced off' the edges of the sphere of intent (which is transparent) and were transmitted back to those beings in order that they might experience certain sets of circumstances. So you would see from space, not the blue-green sphere with clouds you see at the moment, but a sphere of influence that would look like a wonderful, coruscating jewel that is constantly changing, and every area of that sphere would have patterns of colour scintillating against other patterns of colour.

That was the extent of physicality. In the beginning the angelic beings residing within the sphere sought nothing more than to experience at a level that was slightly more physical than the level that they had come from – which was complete integration with God. Therefore, compared to what you see now, the world was a very abstract place; it was an 'artistic', creative place where you would exist within thoughts of possibility, where you would experience reality that was not as dense as this chair [*reference to the chair Michael is sitting on*] but was a dreamscape of changing thought. The delight at that time was not only the joy of bringing back those thought-potentials to God but also the delight of interaction, the delight of seeing from the illusion of individualisation an integration with others who were undergoing the illusion of individualisation, and co-existing with them in certain patterns of thought.

There was an absolute delight in joining together and creating new patterns, new expressions of colour, new expressions of creation, and *contemplating* them. Because the angelic beings visiting this planet at the beginning would spend sometimes thousands of years (if we were to try and measure the period within which they existed here) joyously looking at potentials; joyously constructing and deconstructing thought-patterns to test them to see if they were worthy of further exploration; to examine aspects of physicality and aspects of spirituality; to contemplate, from an illusive distance from God, what it meant to be individual and what it meant to be the Whole; and to consider what individualisation was and to consider what the Whole was; to contemplate the meaning of existence on different levels of existence ...and to bring back those promptings and musings to God.

There were not, therefore, trees, animals or souls with human form at that stage; there was simply – I suppose you would call it 'gaseous' compared to the solidity of the Earth at this time – a *gaseous* state of being and encapsulation, a sphere within which possibility could be examined.

This, you might think, is a far cry from the Earth that you see at the moment with its jagged rocks, trees, rivers and seas, and its friction that tears it apart, but at its God-heart the planet is still the same sphere of potential. It is as though the beings on Earth have taken this beautiful jewel and encased it, sealed it up and imprisoned it, and the crust that you have built (and we will discuss how you did that at a later stage) is subject to cracking, displacement, degeneration and entropy, but the core of the planet is an unchanging sphere of potential. But you cannot access it because of the brittleness and rigidity of the crust that you have placed around that sphere of potential and the crust that you have placed around yourselves.

You are still capable of using colour in the way that you did at the beginning of this physical area of your universe and the life of the Earth but, as with most things spiritual, you don't believe that. But when you meditate, when you connect with God and when you talk to us these patterns of colour still exist within and around you, and the aura that is talked about so much in spiritual books is the ultimate example in creation of *as above – so below*. As the Earth is in reality an aura of possibility around you, as beings encased in heavy physical matter you now contain the same sphere of potential and colour around you in auric form. It is the same thing; it is a harking back to those days at the beginning when you used colour to influence this world and allowed it to influence you in order to influence the Whole.

This Earth is now encased in heavy physical matter; its colour potential is confined and your ability to relate to it and to affect it is encased. You have the colour sphere of the Earth and the sphere around you that is the aura, which is also an encased colour sphere, and the two *should* interact but don't because only with a few souls is that potential realised and tapped into. And, of course, there is the Field that surrounds and penetrates heavy matter, which also surrounds and penetrates to some extent the aura and prevents you functioning as you once did as the angelic being that you are in influencing and tapping into the sphere of potential that is in reality the Earth.

I have talked about a gaseous state but you can also liken the Earth to a liquid state or an ever-changing palette. This is what it should be and this is why your continents shift; they are reacting to the inner potential and mechanism of the planet that was there originally. The planet seeks to shift and to change and your earthquakes are a reflection of this. Yes, they are caused by the Field, but they are also a scream from the Earth to say: 'I am not as rigid as this; I am not as inflexible as this. I need to move. I need to change. I need to flow.' And this is also true of the individual – of the angelic being that you really are.

The angelic being that you really are needs to flow, to change, to examine potential and to bring through different aspects and possibilities of reality but it cannot do so because it, too, is encased in heavy physical matter. The most long-lived of you are those who have discovered something of this spiritual truth, whose molecules are less rigid through examination and immersion in this spiritual truth than those who simply believe in physical matter. The flowing of energies of colour rays from the Earth and in the individual allow the Earth to continue and allow the individual to continue. But in most cases the heavy matter that surrounds the soul eventually restricts it to the point that the spirit inhabiting that heavy matter must move on – only to be drawn back into a similar existence again ...and again ... and again. It is restriction that causes you to live for the short period that you live; you are supposed to live for far longer than you do but it is restriction of flow and of that liquid state that slows you down and eventually compresses you to the point where you have to escape because there is no more potential left. You cannot exert any influence on the Earth; you cannot exert any influence on your own aura, so you must move out of the 'dwelling' – only to move back in if that is your desire.

The communication that is taking place this morning is based on coloured rays and it is the same mechanism occurring that is allowing communication that was used originally to *create* because **creation is communication of potential; it is communication of possibility.** At its heart all communication between angelic beings (and you are angelic beings) is examining potential and evolution of possibility, and so your most mundane conversations hold within them at core that examination and questing for immersion in and contemplation of possibility. The words that you speak to each other on a daily basis are also heavy matter; isn't it true that your core emotions are only reflected darkly in what you say to people? And this is because your communications as an angelic being are actually coloured rays but your coloured rays cannot be seen at the moment because of the effects of the Fall and so you condense them. They are encapsulated within the sound vibrations that you give out in order to draw attention to yourself and to communicate with others.

I am suggesting that you, the reader of this book, please contemplate that all communication is, at core, a desire to express the need to immerse yourself in fluid possibility, the need to examine reality and potential and to bring through new potential. All communication at source, as the angelic being you are, is colour – coloured rays that manipulate and change the sphere of influence that you live in. So your aura, which is a sphere of colour energy and potential, is encapsulated by heavy matter; your communication is encapsulated by heavy matter; your sight is encapsulated by heavy matter. Were you to look into this world *psychically* you would see its crystalline basis; you would see the energy that is inherent in every form, but again you are immersed in heavy matter to such an extent that all you see is that heavy matter reflected back at you.

So you are imprisoned: you are imprisoned in that you feel you cannot create as you once did and don't understand how you once created; you are imprisoned in your speech and your communication because there is heavy matter surrounding the core intention of your words; you are imprisoned in your sight because you cannot see the glory that is right in front of you because of the effects of heavy matter and your eyes only operating physically at a frequency that harmonises with the heavy matter around you. Your senses, then, are imprisoned, but each of those senses has within it the spiritual equivalent – and the spiritual equivalent exists to allow you to be a limitless conveyor of possibility and constructor of reality through the use of coloured rays.

When you refer to God saying: 'Let there be Light!' ...it was actually *you* who said: 'Let there be Light!' (as we have examined earlier in the book). But a better analogy would be: 'Let there be colour! Let there be colour to bring forth reality! Let there be the interplay of coloured rays and spiritual atoms to create reality!'

It is our hope that eventually there will be that interplay of Light and colour again so that the world and physical matter is re-infused with the energy and potential it once had. It is stuck; it is like having a slide show where the slide-projector sticks at one slide so you have all these wonderful slides that you cannot access. For example, it might stick at a slide that shows a garden and you believe that that garden is all there is. But it is only one slide that you have created and imprisoned yourself in, and to either side of that slide there are other slides that show other wonderful vistas, landscapes, creatures and colours beyond imagination, but you cannot access them because that one slide is stuck. The purpose of this communication is to explain, eventually through the subsequent chapters, why it is stuck, but also to open your mind to the possibility of there being other slides and to repair the machine so that it becomes what it once was.

Quite a complex concept this morning but I wanted to explain how your world came to be and the etheric quality of this planet at its source and its core – not the rock charging through space that is the reference point of this Earth that you recognise from photographs from space and say, 'This is where I live.' That is not what the Earth really is; it is a wonderful sphere that reflects back to you, as angels, the possibilities that you contemplate in glory of God, in glory of being, in celebration and joy – and that has to be established. The origin and purpose of this Earth has to be established so that we can then move on from why the Earth you see today is not the Earth that I have just described – it *is* in essence but you cannot access it.

I think that this chapter can be better illuminated through any questions you have at this stage regarding what I have just said.

Tony: I would like to ask a question and I think I am trying to clear my own thoughts on the huge amount of information you have just given us. Rays of colour are a part of how creation happens and the energy from colour is a tool that angelic beings can use to create; we as humans are stuck and surrounded by dense matter that limits our ability to use those rays of colour – are there spiritual exercises we can do to make us more flexible to be able to see, use and manipulate that colour in a way that we don't at present?

Joseph: To use an analogy, it is like having a stain in front of you that needs to be removed. Imagine that you are looking through a reflective pane of glass that has become badly scored and stained and prevents you from seeing the beauty outside of yourself and that beauty reflected back into yourself. What we want you to do, and are giving you the tools to do, is to remove that stain; and you remove that stain not *by adding to* the stain. At the moment you add to the stain: you seek to remove violence with violence; you seek to remove power struggles with other power struggles. You have to remove the stain by infusing it with Light; you remove the stain by wishing it away, by infusing it with the Light that I have taught you (hopefully) how to use in the meditations in the other books, and then you see through the pane of glass where the stain was to the reality that once was.

The use of colour is a natural tendency of the angelic form. The colour itself is an expression of the intentions or wishes of the angelic form; it is the movement of intent from an individual given form. You recognise each other at present by the coalescing of heavy matter into a form that is constant – that is how you recognise each other. You are looking at the surface but beneath that surface there is the angelic form, and the angelic form is no form at all, but the *intent* from the angelic form has a characteristic that can be recognised by other angelic forms – and that characteristic is the expression of colour. So the expression of colour is a natural result of a process within the angelic form, which is the contemplation of and examination of potential ... and that potential is creation.

The angelic form contemplates; the angelic form asks, 'What if?' and that *what if* is then given a form outside and around the angelic being. If that form is considered worthy of contemplation by the Whole and a worthy addition to the Whole then it is solidified somewhat and is brought into being. And it is brought into being by the interplay of coloured rays, expressed from a number of angelic forms who have contemplated certain potential realities, and who then bring those into *actual* reality in order to experience within them and bring to the Godhead the *consequences* of living within that reality for a time in order to enhance the Godhead.

Certain realities are brought through, examined and found not to be worthy or of little potential interest and they are then dissolved again through the use of colour. They are eradicated and wiped out – as that stain will be wiped out by the projection of Light. Other realities are found worthy, of interest, and good for both the evolution of the individual and of the Whole and, therefore, their matrices become part of the knowledge of how to bring through reality that is applied on many different levels. It is a trial and error situation but in the case of the Earth it was a trial that became a huge error ...and we will examine how that error occurred.

Does that make things any simpler or are they then more complicated?

Tony: Thank you. I understood parts of what you said and there are parts where I will have to listen again to what you said from the recording but, yes, I do basically understand.

Joseph: It is because of the personal stain (that is a terrible way to describe your recognition point, as a 'personal stain', and I mean no offence by that and it applies equally to every human being on Earth) and because of the filtering effects of the heavy matter that your soul is surrounded by that there is such a struggle to understand what I am trying to put across. That filter that you are used to seeing through makes what is beyond, behind and at the core of that filter difficult to understand. Do you see that?

Tony: I do.

Joseph: It is that which prevents what I am saying from seeming simple and it is as though I am explaining a complexity when in effect I am just helping you to remember the natural order of things. But you can only remember the natural order of things according to your ability to see through the illusion that has encapsulated you.

Is there another question, please?

Jane: Could I ask a question about form, because it sounds as if the angelic beings are in this sort of nebulous, coloured gas just examining potentials – do they put those potentials into some kind of more solid form so they can experience them?

Joseph: That is an excellent question and it is a point that I should have touched upon and the point is this: originally when certain potentials were considered worthy of further examination within the confines of the planetary sphere, they were then brought forward. It is as though you are selecting a film from all the films in front of you and you take out a particular title and decide to play it to see whether that film is something that you wish to see through to the end. So at certain times, by consensus of all the individuals involved in creation within this sphere, certain potentials from those limitless possibilities will have been put forward as worthy of investigation as a *structure* rather than a projection. Everything is a projection but in this case we are talking about giving, as you have said, solidification of matter for a time to examine whether a potential is worthy of incorporating into the 'manual of creation'.

…'Gaseous' is only an analogy …at its purest it is in an *abstract* state… from which potentials are examined and, by consensus of the majority, not in any political way but in a spiritual way in that the majority of minds are sufficiently interested to investigate a certain potential, that potential is brought forth but within the confines of the sphere of potentiality that we call the Earth.

At its beginnings the Earth had many forms and many forms were investigated. There is neither the energy nor the resources to examine those within this chapter today but, yes, many forms were brought forth. I do not want to pre-empt myself by going into the reason why this form is the 'stuck slide' but we are working towards that in a logical sequence to explain what once was and then what happened; and what is and how we can get back to where we should be. Do you understand?

Jane: Yes, I do. Thank you.

Joseph: One final question!

David: Joseph, in the past we have talked about the Lower Astral, the Earth plane and spheres above that – are all those actually contained within this original Earth and when you talk about finally 'escaping' – what we are doing is getting back to the state where the Earth is as it was so then we can shut it down and go off and do something else?

Joseph: The intention is to bring each soul back to its original template, and the spiritual spheres are a gradual cleansing and restoring to that state. Originally, as the spiritual beings that you really are, there was no need for that filtration process in order to get you back to your start point. Originally you would examine potential but also move in and out of that potential as the observer and creator of that potential to examine its merits or otherwise, but always aware at that point that you were an angelic being, that you were part of God and at any time could move your volition back into the Whole to enjoy that viewpoint or back into individuality to enjoy that viewpoint.

Our purpose is to free souls from a particular matrix that has become stuck and is running out of energy. Yes, there is the need to move on, but that need to move on is a personal consideration for each soul once it has been restored to its angelic consciousness. In other words, certain souls will choose to move on and certain souls will (we hope) look at the Earth and say: 'Well, we are back to the beginning! We can now have a look at potential within this sphere *safely*, having learned from the experiment that went wrong. We will not repeat that but we will use this area of potential again and honour the sphere that we have created and give it joy once again by allowing it to fulfil its role as a sentient being.'

So, the answer is: *yes*, souls will come away from the Earth but souls will also be able to revisit the Earth in its purest form – not to become locked in and not even to view the Earth as it is at this point, but to view the Earth as it is *at its core*, as a sphere of potential, because, ultimately, the whole of this physical universe is a series of nested spheres of potential. Your accessing and creation of potential as angelic beings is absolutely limitless but you have limited yourselves to one area or bubble but within that bubble you can create all things and outside of that bubble you can also experience and create all things. It is bringing the bubble back in line with the rest of Creation that is the task and also, of course, freeing those souls and the planet from the stuck slide that is causing (...I don't want to say 'anti-potential', although that is a term that seems fitting) – is causing a loop of disintegration and re-integration around the same process loop and is causing the same scenario to be played over ...and over ...and over ...and over ...and over again. Do you see that?

David: Yes.

Joseph: When you began this journey and when I began this journey, you could little have understood the magnitude of the information that we seek to bring through, and the book that we, as the soul group, are dictating at the moment (as I think you can see) will be one that will be available to all but will only be understood by perhaps a few. It is hoped that the other books in the series have enough instruction in them to liberate souls but only for those that are ready will the book that we are currently dictating make sense and resonate. Would you agree with that?

David, Jane, Tony: Yes.

Joseph: This is why there is an order to the sequence of books; this is why you have the very great potential to interest people with the current book [*reference to* **Your Life After Death**] and I wish you to know that we are working, sitting, projecting, seeing that book delivering that message to everyone. Part of what we are doing is dictating this book and the large part of what we are doing is infiltrating the Field and, on beams of Light, delivering the *need* for that book into people's minds – not to interfere with their free will but almost like an advertisement to say, 'Here is the book; here is something that is of great value to you – do you desire it?' and to put that thought into the minds of so many people.

I must vacate the 'premises' now or there will be very little left to work with.

Chapter Five
The Production of Form

Joseph: Good morning to you all! We are taking a moment to adjust the vibrations; there is a depletion in this room and we are generating Light-energy to give you the means to deliver the communication. Last time I talked about potential and how planets were first perceived of as potential in angelic minds, and I would like to talk this morning about form and the production of form.

I suppose you could say that angelic minds worked and *do* work, because creation is on-going, like a council in that they join together with the purpose of creating opportunities for experience. When likely opportunities have been visualised sufficiently, it is decided by a section of the angelic host that those opportunities should be brought forth from the dream state, as it were, or the pool of potential, into some level of reality. So a council that has approved a *particular* project will separate itself in mind or creative activity from the rest of the angelic host to focus its thoughts and creative abilities on the particular project that it has in mind.

It then has to bring what is in mind into form, and so there is a joining together of those individuals (that are already one, of course, but also share the illusion of individuality from the Godhead and from each other) and there is a coming together of purpose and of visualisation in order to bring forth matter outside of and around themselves for the purposes of experience.

In the case of the solar system and of the Earth, the intentions of the angelic host controlling and bringing forth this area of reality coalesced into bubbles of opportunity that you call the planets or bubbles of potential and self-contained spheres of experience.

Initially with regard to this solar system, the planets were brought through in a more etheric manner, and we will discuss later in the book how they were then dragged down to how you perceive them in their present state of heavier and darker matter. In the beginning they were etheric and, were you to see projects being formed by an angelic council, you would see the tiniest sphere appear from a point of no-thing – as the universe appeared from a dot. But within this particular physical universe that exists around you, you would see a dot begin to have *being* – a dot of Light-energy which, with regard to the *physics* of the physical universe that has also been created by the Godhead and by angelic hosts, would appear to grow in size and relate to the size of other objects within this physical universe. The vision would coalesce …and coalesce …and coalesce and would expand …and expand …and expand, and would be given the illusion of solidity.

All this takes place via the minds of the angelic hosts simply by them agreeing as a unit that certain areas of possibility that they have projected are a good thing to bring forth into physical matter so that they can be visited by angelic hosts in rarefied physical matter in order for those angelic hosts temporarily encased in physical matter to experience, to learn and to add to their abilities. So they grow together in thought and they say: 'Yes' – it is as simple as *yes*. *Let there be Light* is really: *Yes, we agree to this* and, in agreeing to it, there is a bringing forth of solid matter from the agreement of the project and from the actuation of positivity put into the project. So you would see each of the planets and the solar system beginning as a dot of Light that would expand, would grow and would be given form.

Each planet originally was different (as they are now) and each planet, if you could look at it with angelic eyes, was a crystal sphere – some with very delicate, etheric crystalline forms and some with heavier crystalline forms, as was the Earth and Venus. Mars was slightly lighter in crystalline identity than the Earth and Venus. If you were to look at the planet as it was originally planned to be and brought through in intention, you would see beautiful colours; you would see planes and higher levels. Mountains exist as an expression of higher form – you won't have realised that or considered it but higher ground exists as an expression of the desire to have some areas in which you learn certain aspects of spirituality and other areas in which you learn elevated levels of spirituality within the same sphere that has been brought through by the angelic host. What I am trying to explain is that, built into the planet are opportunities for growth as the angelic hosts encased in physical matter pass through it. So you have planes that represent one area of opportunity and higher ground that represents more developed, more etheric (how difficult to put this concept into words) opportunities for advanced growth with regard to the mechanics of the universe and of spiritual reality.

The Earth was originally an area of planes of crystal energy and was prepared by the saying 'yes' by the angelic host to an area where angelic individualisations of God could come and experience physical matter – but physical matter more closely related to spiritual intent than physical matter is at the moment. The physical matter that you find yourself in now is a far more *dense* concentration of physicality than the physical matter that the planet and the solar system were originally made of ...and *still are made of*, because the solar system, the planets and the universe are the production and on-going desire of a dream via the angelic hosts. The original form of the Earth is still here behind and through the perception of the planet that you have now. We are not yet at the stage to talk about what went wrong but, as a result of things going wrong, the planet that you see now nests, as it were, the planet that once was the original intention for the Earth. This is also true for the solar system, because the effects of the Fall contain this particular solar system *within a limiting sphere*.

Not only has the Earth been masked from its original crystalline state but the other planets in the solar system have also been affected. I have to tell you that, on a different level of perception, there are other planets within this space, and that you are not alone in the planets that you perceive in the solar system – there are two 'brethren' or two other planets that actually exist on a different level of perception and have escaped the effects of the Fall. Although the solar system is encapsulated within a sphere that represents the impingement of the Fall on the physical matter in this area, there are two planets within that sphere that remain unaffected. I want you to know that they exist and that they have an effect on the experiences of the occupants of Earth at this time – just as the other planets in the solar system have an effect on certain karmic opportunities being learned by their position within the sphere of experience that has been darkened by the effects of the Fall.

And so the angelic host originally brought through a series of spheres (you call them 'planets', we call them 'spheres') and at that time there was no need to put on a spacesuit, get into a spaceship and travel between the spheres in that way. Travel between the spheres was a matter of desire of certain experiences, so you could go from Saturn ...to Jupiter ...to Mars ...to Venus ...to Earth ...to Mercury ...to *all* the planets in the solar system simply by desiring to experience a certain set of circumstances so that you could enhance your spiritual understanding and capability in the construction of ever-greater universes and planetary systems. This is the basis behind why the spheres were created in the first place – in order for souls to experience so that they can pass through them and enhance their understanding of themselves, of each other, of God and their ability and understanding of how to create.

The solar system was positioned in a certain way so that there was a specific path through the planets or spheres of experience open to the souls who wished to go through that experience. It was positioned in a certain way so that as the spheres revolved around each other (within the greater sphere that was a sphere of Love created by the angelic council) they would, by their pull and attraction, create opportunities of experience for the souls visiting them. This is why your horoscopes have some basis in fact and I want to lay down *categorically* today the fact that there is **a mechanism at work in the solar system** and in all solar systems, in all galaxies, in all universes, and that the revolution of one sphere around another is to enable, via the attraction and repulsion of molecules of physical matter, certain opportunities to be set up for souls who are travelling through those spheres at that time.

The purpose of the Earth and of the planets originally was to act as points of entry on an adventure for souls visiting them, but that adventure was pre-destined with regard to what those souls required in order to add to their experiences. In other words the souls did not just visit the crystal beauty of Earth to sit on a plane or to look out from a mountain but, in complete volition and acceptance of this, they agreed to come here so that the movement of the spheres could unfold an adventure for them and could unfold opportunities for them to learn about physical matter, about existence in physical matter and about the evolution of physical matter. That adventure is still there today and is the *pure basis* and the original intent of karma – not for karma to act as the scales of justice, not for karma to be something that causes suffering and restricts spiritual growth through the suffering that it puts around a soul, but for karma to be an adventure and an opportunity to learn. It is the pollution of the original intention of karma that results in the accruing and dispensing with of certain experiences that you experience now as souls passing through physical matter.

Karma, at its root and core, is the invitation to and movement through an adventure so that experience can be gained.

What kind of adventure? Was it originally an adventure that involved lions and tigers or conflict, capture and manipulation by other human beings? Not at all! Not that type of adventure at all – it was more an adventure of experience via physical senses

73

and contemplation via spiritual ones; an invitation to experience the opportunities of the crystal plane in a million ways; to experience it and to understand it; to go through 'school', if you like, in the preparation of future universes, solar systems, planets and spheres of activity. To look at the plane and to see the plane but also to see, beyond and within the plane, all the aspects, all the potential and all the opportunities that that plane has to offer; and the same with the elevated places, and with the roof of the sphere – the sky – and with the depths of the sphere ... what lies below the plane. A very different adventure to the ones that you have today and an adventure dictated by love, by the volition to learn and understand one's craft and to become more than one was before one visited here.

There is a certain amount of pollution when viewing the other planets that exists within this 'sphere of confinement' (I suppose you could call it now) in that originally, from the Earth and from the other planets you were visiting, you could see the other worlds as beautiful, shining, crystal jewels ahead of you in the 'heavens' or distance between spheres. It is not possible to do that now because the effects of the Fall make distances seem greater, make colours seem muddier, and you are perceiving the planets through the eyes of souls encased within the effects of the Fall and not seeing them for the crystalline beauty that they have.

Also, your perception of the other planets that are beyond this solar system is muddied by the dulling effect of the vibrations of the Fall that are contained within the sphere that also contains the planets in the solar system. So you are not seeing *accurately* when you look out into the night sky or when you look out through telescopes or through tracking stations because all those things have been constructed on the level of reality that has been polluted by the effects of the Fall. You look out to space and see wondrous things (as you think) but those are only shallow echoes and masked interpretations of what glories you should be seeing when you look out to space ...and indeed, when you look at each other. When you look at the planet, each other and the neighbouring planets of the solar system you are not seeing the *true* representation of what was there and is *still* there.

And when civilisation has been wiped out in the past, via its own dependence entirely on the vibrations that exist as a result of the Fall, once the effects of civilisation have been taken away the planet has shone through as what it originally was *and is* – and will do so again if steps are not taken. What we intend is for that crystalline energy to shine through *present reality* without the need for civilisation to be removed so that the planet can breathe again and can pulse at its correct vibration. The end of civilisation has happened before and we hope and we pray (as you know) that it won't happen again.

The discussion that we have had today begs the question: **is there still an angelic council responsible for the maintenance of the planets within the solar system?** And the answer to that is: *yes.* It is the same angelic council that created the solar system in the first place and, therefore, you see that that angelic council is not affected by the Fall; it is outside of the effects of the Fall. It is the angelic children who visited this solar system subsequently once it was formed, who have become trapped in the effects of the Fall. There is, at this very moment, as I communicate this information to you, an angelic council maintaining the planet and the solar system as it should be, as it has been from the moment of its inception and as it will be …until such time in the future when its construct is considered to have been entirely successful in educating souls. Then it will be reabsorbed into the surrounding matter as the angelic council let go of their vision of what the solar system is and let go of their desire for souls to experience this particular set of values in order to learn.

Such complex concepts but I hope we are filling in some of the blanks so that the whole will make sense. Can I invite questions on what is a difficult subject, please?

Tony: Joseph, you say that the angelic council will stay in council until there is a successful outcome of the original dream – is that the same for everything? Is it a law or rule that works not only for our world and our universe but also works in the microcosm as it works in the macrocosm? Does it work in *our* dreams – do we have to get a *yes* and, like a council, hold something until we get a success?

Joseph: You have to want something to be. The angelic council only spends a portion of its time in maintaining what it has created; it is not that there are great angels sat around a table maintaining the solar system. There is the equivalent of that in a spiritual sense but those angelic beings are also creating in other areas. But part of their being is maintaining this area of space as it originally was and as it really is behind the effects of the Fall until such time as *universally* the concepts that have been brought forth in this solar system are no longer required or felt to be of use. From the no-thing has been drawn form with the intention of that form evolving those who visit it on a physical level, and whilst there is purpose in that form being maintained as it is at the moment it will remain.

But gradually a vibration will reach the angelic council that maintains the solar system that is a *feeling* – a feeling that that area of creation has been examined, has been used and is now no longer of use in its present form. It will at first be a vague feeling that then becomes a *knowledge* within the angelic council, and the minute that that happens universally – that matter is dispersed or set free. 'Set free' is a better term because those molecules have been held together by the wishes of the angelic council in a certain form. Once the matter has served its purpose, it is set free and the molecules disperse and can be drawn in by other angelic councils to be used on a physical level to create *different* levels of experience.

You, because you are an angel, operate in exactly the same way at your core in that, at any given moment, you are saying *yes* and *no* to a million different things. It is as though you are looking at a computer screen with a binary code on it and there is a: one, **zero**, one, **one**, zero, **one**, one, **one**. Minute by minute you are saying, 'I believe myself to be in a certain form'. Let us take that as one of the examples: 'This is the way I look. This is the way I feel' – yes, **no**, yes, **yes**, yes, **no**, yes, **no**, yes, **no** …and your desires are constantly examining whether you believe yourself to be in one certain way or another. The strength of how you appear to yourself depends on the number of yesses and nos at any one minute. But that is only one particular aspect of what you are capable of creating because every other dominant theme in your life is approached in the same way: yes, **no**, yes, **yes**, no, **no**, yes, **no** – and you are creating a balanced view according to your view of every aspect of your life.

And every other soul is doing the same thing, which I think must show you in some small way why the Earth is as it is and will make sense of the preceding books in us saying that you need a certain number of souls to change and to be able to put Light into the world before the world can truly change. You need to put yesses in amongst the nos; you need to balance and then you have balanced creation. When you have balanced creation, the original intent of this area (God's original intent and the angel council's original intent) becomes apparent in your conscious mind, allowing you to make binary judgments based on an original set of values. Does that make sense?

Tony: Absolutely – thank you so much.

Jane: Joseph, could I ask a question about the formation of the planet? Originally it was this etheric crystalline form but then after the Fall it became heavier matter… I think, according to science, the planet was formed from exploding stars and all the gravity pulling the debris into a sphere – was that process necessary to form a planet in a heavier matter way?

Joseph: What you perceive as the attraction of debris to form a physical planet is in effect the effects of the Fall. It is the attraction of heavier, un-dispersed matter towards the core of intention for the Earth that was changed (as we shall see) by the travellers who were passing through this particular journey. On a physical level they pull to themselves a heavier vibration of matter. So your scientists are correct when they say that this sphere was formed by debris attracting debris through the laws of gravity but what they don't realise, cannot understand and will not accept is that the planets *were already there* before that happened and that what you are seeing is a physical manifestation of the effects of the Fall. I don't want to use the word 'crystallisation' – it is sort of a 'de-crystallisation'; it is an attraction of heavier thought, of chaos and of thoughts and creation weighted in one way only that clump together.

This again is a good question because this is what is happening now – you clump your thoughts together and the equivalent of the planet attracting mass in terms of weighty matter happens all the time on a psychic level. You are attracting heavy thoughts; you are attracting the clumping together of your thoughts of violence; your thoughts of disease, your thoughts of lack. I must refer to Tony here[1]: this is what happens in conventional healing because you have souls who mistakenly draw to themselves heavy thoughts and heavy matter, who gather round a patient and agree that that patient is ill …and clump around that patient more of the perception of them being ill. This is what conventional medicine does and so it is imperative in healing that doctors and nurses keep an attitude of the patient as being well. If they wanted to truly heal, they would see each patient (no matter how dire the physical circumstances of the illness appear to be) and would say, 'No, that is not the truth. I am treating this patient by treating this illusion with further illusion but the core of my being believes that this patient is well.' Then there would be attracted to that patient vibrations of health, vibrations of God-health, vibrations of God-balance. Do you see that? Do you see how doctors and nurses, by their very attitude, attract more of the same to patients?

Tony: I do.

Joseph: I feel that that will be a revolutionary thought for you – that the very people who care (and I am not decrying what they do) actually bring more attention to the illness to the patient and, therefore, accelerate the illness. In true healing conditions, doctors and nurses would see that patient as being perfectly healthy. They would treat the physical symptoms as though they were treating in a dream but their core being, their meditation, their perception of that patient would always be that that patient is well, is healed and is healthy.

I diversify, have I answered your question?

Jane: Can I just ask something further: if it is only our solar system involved where did the heavy matter debris come from – because otherwise there is only our sun that could have exploded to supply it?

Joseph: The debris came from your own thoughts. Remember that you are creative beings and so the debris that you see and the matter that you feel to be real is as a result of your own thoughts. You have put greater permanence into physical matter than should be there and that greater permanence, which is an illusion, is there as a result of the Fall. We are not quite at the point in story yet where we have explained the Fall, but be patient because all will be revealed – as I hope with each subsequent chapter that things are being revealed. Do you see?

Jane: So it just came from within our solar system?

Joseph: Your view of the solar system and the matter beyond is skewed. You are trapped within a bubble of illusion and within that bubble of illusion your creative abilities have been used... not in the wrong way but in a baser, heavier way than they should be. Therefore, the heavier matter has been created by you because you are perceiving through a level of illusion that is heavier than the one that you should be existing on. That is why we return to uplift you through the various spheres to your original creative viewpoint ...and your original creative viewpoint allows you to see the solar system and the surrounding space as it really is. Do you see that? Does that make sense?

Jane: Yes.

Joseph: We are dealing with extremely complex sets of information; I will invite a further question but I do want to end this by... [*Long pause*]

I am sorry... communication is broken. [*Further long pause*]

...I experienced a jump in my own transmission of the communication. Is there a question from you, David?

David: I was just going to point out the analogy of man trying to communicate with the rest of the universe via radio waves and how that represents a very narrow band of vibration.

Joseph: Indeed. The radio waves are a heavy form of communication; they do contain information but it is heavier information, and it is the etheric waves and spiritual waves that will allow man to *eventually* communicate outside of this particular pocket of energy. But not at the moment because the denseness of the bubble created by the Fall will not allow the escape of the current communication methods used. Of course, true spiritual communication allows you to be at every point at once but you are not able to do that in your present state.

Ahead of you there is an option:

Ahead of you there is the taking away of current civilisation, a period of stasis and then a regeneration into this area so that you can try again...

...Or ahead of you (if you use that choice of yesses and nos to say: **YES** to Light, to advanced spiritual thinking and to Love) is an opening out and a discovery of what the solar system and the surrounding universe really look like.

You talk about ascension for the planet but it is ascension for *people* that needs to take place, and ascension is universal –

THE PRODUCTION OF FORM

ascension has to come to all. When you reach the spiritual spheres you will find that you can escape and can go further, but you will always have an eye to those who are left behind because they are part of you and you will not truly rest until everyone has ascended. It is as though you need to shrug off this heavy matter to remember who you are and that is the purpose of our communications.

I am sorry but conditions have not been perfect this morning but I hope that I have brought across a sufficient amount of information to fill in another blank with regard to how the book is building to an explanation of where you were, where you are and where you are going.

Is there anything else that anyone wishes to ask, please?

David, Jane, Tony: No.

Joseph: In that case I will close, and I close with a prayer for peace for you all and I close with a prayer that we can maintain communication through the efforts of the Field to close down communication. There have been on the periphery of the circle this morning certain circumstances that would have broken in had we not held them at bay. As a result of holding them at bay it has reduced the amount of time available for communication but, had we not held them at bay, then some harm would have come to you.

---

[1] Joseph is talking to Tony in his capacity as a psycho-therapist and Founder of The Sanctuary of Healing.

Chapter Six
The Birth of New Consciousness

Joseph: Having spoken about the formation of the planet, the next step would be to talk about how consciousness is brought into that sphere in order to experience.

The angelic host are one – as you are one now – but within that one of the angelic host there are many aspects or facets of the one. It is a degree of individualisation that is lesser than the degree of individualisation you are experiencing at this time in physical matter but, nevertheless, it is a degree of individualisation. What makes it a lesser degree of individualisation is the fact that, within the angelic host, it is *known* that the individualisation is only a facet, whereas here on Earth you see individualisation as a barrier between yourself and others so that you become a 'universe' in your own right and do not acknowledge that you are part of the universal that is around you.

When a planet is created via the methods that we have talked about earlier, it is then decided that a certain number of facets of the angelic host will visit that planet in order to experience what the planet has to offer in terms of *expansion* of experience – because all Creation exists to expand consciousness; to push limits; to examine new fields of influence; to allow the individual and the Whole to grow and to evolve. The universe's creation is a constantly evolving concept so that each planet is literally 'brought to mind' (as we have said) in order that the experiences that the new planet can offer will help those facets to grow and to evolve spiritually and creatively, and bring back to the Whole a new angle on creation and new possibilities.

Each planet is set up by the angelic host or council with a particular set of circumstances built into it that will allow certain areas of each facet of the angelic host that visits it to evolve. Within the angelic host there then takes place a 'quietening' of those members of the host who have decided, through free will and volition, that they wish to travel through the landscape of that particular planet so that they can evolve themselves and bring back to the host the fruits of their experience that will allow the host and the Godhead to also evolve. So a number of facets of the angelic host are quietened and put under the supervision of other members of the angelic host.

It is like separating a number of sheep (a bad analogy, perhaps) and taking them into a particular field where they can still see the other sheep but are cordoned off and watched over by sheep dogs to see that they are kept together and no harm comes to them. What a bad analogy – it suggests that there is nothing more than a sheep-mentality to the angelic host and that is totally wrong! I am trying instead to give you a picture of how certain facets are not divorced from the Whole but are taken to one side through their own volition. Perhaps you could say that they go into another room within a great university and for a while a notice is put on a door that says: 'Quiet! Experiment in progress!' And all those who are beyond that door are sheltered from the goings on of the whole university until such time as they have gone through the experience that they have chosen to enter into.

So, a number of facets of the angelic host are brought into a quiet time so that their thoughts are concentrated on the 'journey' at hand – much as you, when going on holiday, would forget about the everyday work, the house and the finances for a time and instead concentrate solely on the holiday ahead because that is where your interest lies. Then, having become quiet, a portion of the makeup of each facet of the angelic host is projected and sent as a beam of volition into the arena of the planet that has been prepared for the purposes of a specific evolution. And that projected concentration of attention and consciousness of each facet takes the best form in order to experience the aspects of that particular planet. It is solidified somewhat so that the portion of each facet of the angelic host can be given sufficient 'locomotion' to experience the physicality (or solidified thought) of the sphere in order to evolve through the experiences the planet has to offer – in this case we are talking about the Earth.

On the planet-side of that beam, the portion of consciousness of each facet of the angelic host is clothed in a concentrated but temporary solidification of thought that gives the appearance of physical form – both from outside of the facet and from the inside, so that portion is given a further sense of individuality, and becomes a citizen of that planet for a short time in order that it might progress, experience and evolve as it moves through the landscape (not 'landscape' as in trees and mountains but landscape as in the 'matrix of opportunity' that the planet has to offer the evolving portion of the facet of the angelic host).

Please understand that in perfect circumstances (as they originally were on Earth) the angelic facet and the personality on Earth are in constant connection so that the personality on Earth, whilst enjoying the illusion of individuality from the facet that it really is, is still aware that it is part of the facet. Similarly, the facet of the angelic host that has projected the beam of concentration of life-force and energy towards the Earth is aware of the facet being animated on the planet.

Whilst the projection is on the planet and enjoying the illusion of individuality, the rest of the fragment of the angelic host that remains within that 'room' can now project other areas of itself back into the 'university' beyond that room. Having accomplished the task of projecting part of itself into the planet's landscape, it can also to a certain extent enjoy the other aspects of its being and consciousness that it had before it entered that room. But it remains in that room because it is important to have contact with the part of its consciousness on Earth so that part on Earth can experience, through moving through the landscape and opportunities of the planet, and can pass back those experiences along that beam to the fragment of the angelic host so that that facet of the angelic host can evolve.

It is like having a child in another country that is in constant contact via a mobile phone, but it is more than that, obviously, because the feedback from the aspect of the angelic being on Earth is far more sensual and all-embracing than a simple telephone call. It is like having a child away from you who is reporting back and there is communication between that aspect of the angelic fragment and its projection or child on Earth so that, if the projection on Earth is unsure how to act in certain circumstances, dialogue can go backwards and forwards to say: 'Well, perhaps we should try this or perhaps we need to experience that.' In ideal and original circumstances there was communication between the angelic fragments and their children on Earth.

Then, at the end of a period of time, which is determined by whether there is anything more to be gained by experiencing certain aspects of the planet, when nothing more can be gained by travelling through that particular set-up the projected beam of consciousness from the fragment of the angelic host is pulled back to itself from the Earth. There is a dissolving or loosening of the belief in the projection or shell that surrounds the child of the fragment of the angelic host that is on the planet so its cohesion as a physical being is lessened and relaxed, and once it is relaxed there is a retraction of that child back to the angelic fragment.

Here there is another miracle of creation because, having experienced individuality as a projection into the planetary landscape and having gone through a set of circumstances where it is conscious of itself and communication with its angelic parent, when it returns to the angelic parent – it is part of that parent ...but it is also **an individual as an angelic being**. Another analogy: as a result of having gone through this act of separation, communication and re-integration, creation brings forth further angelic individuality because, from returning 'children' from a planetary sphere, you have **the birth of new angelic beings**.

You can see how the mechanism is set up for evolution of experience but also evolution of consciousness and the peeling off of consciousness into further beings whilst still retaining that link to the Whole. You can see without me saying too much at this point (because we will go into it further) that there is a type of parenthood and a type of birth that is undergone in angelic realms and that what you witness here on Earth with the production (as you see it) of further individuals through birth – is a solidification of a process that goes on, on a God-level and on an angelic level.

And so originally the Earth was set up – as all planets are set up – to permit experience, to further growth and to promote the further expansion of angelic consciousness, whilst at the same time enhancing the consciousness of the angelic hosts who are putting their time and their projection into that particular planet. Those angelic hosts, having retrieved their children, that then set out on their own journey in visiting further spheres, then re-integrate or go out of that 'room' into the 'university' and introduce, as it were, in *great joy and great bliss* to those others in the university their children – the products of their thought and the birth of their thought into further individualisation, which it must be stressed is not really individualisation but an extension of the Whole into further facets.

And so it was with the Earth at the beginning; that was the function of the Earth and that *still is* the function of the Earth ... **except things went wrong** and I must explain how things went wrong the next time we meet.

What we have talked about will be revolutionary to your readers: to suggest that angelic beings 'give birth' is not something that has been put before the people of Earth previously or in other texts. I pray and hope that I have explained it in sufficient detail without making it too complex, but I would invite questions to clarify anything that you feel has not been explained sufficiently to this point.

Jane: Do we, each of us, still have some kind of link to our angelic parent, even though we have got lost on the way? Is there still that link?

Joseph: The link is always there, and that link to God and to greater self is what we are promoting through the other books that we have put out. There has been a loss of consciousness but not a loss of the link, and we are aiming to have you rediscover that link and your core. It is not a new concept; it has been with you, but buried and masked, for millennia and it is time *now*, at this important point in the evolution of the Earth and your civilisation, to remind you of that.

So the answer is, yes, most definitely that link cannot be otherwise. If you consider the laws of the universe and the ways of creation – **everything is linked to everything else** *always*. Your specific link to your angelic parent (or your *over-soul* if you want a common term that is used in other books) is always there.

Another question, please!

David: When you talk about the angelic host fragmenting, is that what we understand as reincarnation?

Joseph: Reincarnation is something that will come up in a later chapter. The fragmentation is an example of the ability of the angelic individuals and the host to create and, having created and prepared vistas, to then project parts of themselves into those vistas. What I hope it explains better than anything else in this chapter is the need for heavier matter and the purpose behind heavier matter. Heavier matter is the solidification *temporarily* of communal desire to set up a matrix of circumstance within

THE JOSEPH COMMUNICATIONS: THE FALL

which experience can be gained. You can see physical matter as the temporary holding together of projected thought, and that is the nature and necessity of physical matter – **the temporary holding together of thought** so that a landscape can be created through which projections of the angelic fragments can experience and bring that experience back to the Whole.

Reincarnation is a repeated pattern and is a repeated pattern *here* because of the effects of the Fall. If you consider what we have said in this book thus far, if you have passed through a landscape and have gained all there is to gain by being immersed in that landscape, what benefit is there to revisiting that landscape? None at all! None at all – particularly when there are so many other projections of experience waiting for you and for your children. Why come back to visit and go through exactly the same circumstances when you have already learned from them and absorbed into your being their implications? Reincarnation is a peculiar aspect of the Fall, which we will explain as the narrative unfolds. Does that make sense?

David: Yes. So originally, to use your room analogy, a fragment of an angelic host would project into the sphere of a planet possibly once or maybe more than once?

Joseph: If you have an angelic host then an angelic 'host' by the name itself suggests a great many individualisations, so a number of angelic fragments or facets would decide to come into this particular room to project part of themselves into the planet's matrix. Having moved out of the room with their children into the Whole, there are others who then wish to come into the room, others who wish to project and others who have not yet gone through those experiences.

Without diversifying too much from the narrative that we are trying to get through to you, I have to tell you that in that university there are other rooms. There have to be because those rooms lead into the matrices of other planets, and beyond those there are rooms that lead into the matrix of a galaxy, the matrices of star systems ...and so the angelic host exists and experiences. The nature of God is never just to exist – **it is to exist and experience; to exist and grow.** So there is a constant, fantastic moving around of fragments of the angelic host into other rooms in order to experience other matrices and in order to bring back other experiences to the Whole. Then the planets themselves are withdrawn from physicality and new ones are created – always within the sphere, always within the dot within the circle. Does that make sense?

David: Yes, thank you.

Joseph: So it is an infinite and infinitely exciting, rewarding and challenging celebration of consciousness, of being, of existing, of changing and of bringing new individuals and new experiences to the Whole, because remember, each of those individuals that comes back to the parent or angelic fragment is different to the angelic fragment. The angelic fragment is enhanced by the experience that its projection has had on Earth but the projection itself is coloured to a greater degree by the experience it has had first-hand and so has a different outlook on Creation and brings a unique viewpoint to that Whole. All those viewpoints are coming back to Creation all the time to allow Creation to draw on its established viewpoints and its new viewpoints to create different avenues, different aspects, different planetary experiences and different universal experiences.

I hope I can transmit, through the very flat, written word, some of the joy and bliss of the continuous creative act and what lies ahead for you once you remember who you are – which I hope we have gone some way to explain to this point. Is that a sufficient answer?

David: Yes, thank you.

Tony: Joseph, my mind is spinning now.

Joseph [*smiling*]: My mind is also spinning!

Tony: I could do with some verbal clarity. What I am hearing is that actually people on Earth who acknowledge themselves as spiritual beings and who are working with that in mind should spend less time worrying about past lives and future lives as we consider it because it isn't as we understand it because we, as spiritual beings, rejoin our angelic host and keep our individuality and we actually *create*.

Joseph: Yes, the popular view in so-called spiritual circles is that you are a sum of your lives and that reincarnation is brought into play, and I hope that this book will go some way to expand the spiritual minds and spiritual hearts of people on Earth. I have always said to you that you are angelic beings and I am delighted to have reached *this point* in our journey of communications where you now see that you are indeed angelic beings and why I have said it to you. There is no difference between you and the angels that come to visit you except in *confinement* – and it is *self-confinement*. We are moving very close to that part of the book that then explains how, what should have been a single experience for you, became a repeating pattern, and how the landscape that should have brought you joy was turned to bring you misery.

So, yes, you should concentrate always on your *limitless* potential and 'limitless' means that you do not indulge too much in who you feel you were and who you feel you are going to be. Your point of power is *now*, your connection with God is now and the bliss that I have tried to get across to you this morning (again in the flat, written word) is accessible to you *now*. As you accept who you are, you break the crystalline bonds that are around you that have restricted you for millennia and you begin to shatter the pattern that you believe in to such an extent that you think that there is nothing else. That is a very important aspect of our work together – to convince souls that what they feel is so solid, so immutable and so familiar is really just an energy pattern that has become solidified and confined. They should in their meditations and approach to God allow God to lift their expectations, to remove their shackles and to immerse them in that feeling that will transmute them and allow them to bring Light to the planet to change it and to free the prisoners. Does that make sense?

Tony: Yes, thank you.

Joseph: I must just finally before I leave talk about spiritual logic and how important it is that the people who read these books try to maintain a spiritual perspective and use spiritual logic. By that I mean that many of the so-called spiritual theories that are promoted around the Earth are nothing more than attempts by the Field to re-immerse its prisoners in itself. This book must be tested, my other books must be tested, and any approach to spirituality must be tested by taking the concepts *within* – not into the head because the head will produce more complexity, more prison cells and more confinement – but to take the concept into the *heart* and ask: 'Does my heart *sing* when contemplating this concept?' In other words, does my heart resonate with this concept? Does it feel logical – not through the mind but through the heart?

Those things that *feel* logical truly through the heart are the ones you should follow, but those that come up short through the heart are the ones that are really influences and illusions brought up by the Field and they should be set aside and moved on from. Clarity of thought and spiritual truth comes from the heart and not from the mind.

Chapter Seven
DARKNESS – What Went Wrong

Joseph [smiling]: I wish to begin this meeting with the quote: 'The reports of my death have been greatly exaggerated' [*a humorous reference to the September, 2011 public trance demonstration at which there had been a severe psychic attack from one member of the audience with the express intention of disrupting it, and which had left us all, Joseph included, in a depleted state. This was our first contact with Joseph since that occurrence*] and I wish you to know that there were no lasting ill-effects from the demonstration other than a loss of energy and a great depletion, and disappointment that our purpose was diverted on this one occasion. I think it gives you some indication of the severity and difficulty of our task, and of the locked-in attitudes of humankind that we are trying to unlock and disperse, which leads very nicely into the theme of today's chapter, which is *darkness* and how on earth (literally 'on Earth') could darkness descend into a sphere that was originated in Light; a sphere whose intentions were to further the experience of the angelic children ... a sphere that is *still* a sphere of Light beneath its crust of darkness.

In the beginning, when the Earth was a vehicle for angelic children, there was no society as you would understand society but there was a *brethren* ('brethren' is the closest word I can get to the experience), and a *knowing* – there was always a connection with God and a connection with one another, so individual potential was linked to global and to Divine potential. The planet was a sphere of experience with various landscapes and opportunities, and was almost a... *cradle* (if I can liken the Earth to a cradle), or an area of warmth and comfort within which new aspects of God could grow and 'find their feet' by moving through a series of vibrational bands of challenge.

There was originally a series of vibrational bands, nested, one next to the other, through which the angelic children passed in order to grow and understand their potential and then to create *new* potential that was transmitted back to the angelic host, and was also taken back to the angelic host when the angelic children left the planet after the term of experience was over – once they had come to a point where the sphere had nothing more to offer them. These vibrational bands of challenge were set in place by that proportion of the angelic host that created the sphere in the first place, with God-intention flowing through them and they 'giving birth' to the sphere and also to their 'children' or individualised thoughts. That is how the set-up was originally supposed to run, and in the beginning there was harmony between all of God's angelic children on the Earth.

You have to understand that, as the individual moved through the vibrational bands of challenge and experience, it became quite competent. We are not talking in terms of earthly children or in terms of the cradle evolving a child of four or five that then returns to its parents. At the end of a term of experience across the earthly sphere the angelic individual had the knowledge of its parents, had a certain knowledge of the Godhead and had, particularly and importantly, **the knowledge of how to manipulate vibrations, energy fields and the resultant heavier-matter atoms to create the vistas they wanted to experience.** So, originally, after a period of 'time' (but not time as you would measure it) or experience, the cradle of the Earth presented individuals that were fully formed enough angelically to be able to carry on the business of creation and to work together to eventually create their own further sphere and, therefore, to expand the Godhead through other individualisations and other facets of Himself.

I think if you look at what I have just said, you will see the reason why the universe is expanding and you will understand why the universe branches out from that original central point, because always, in the normal course of things, you have spheres where there are angelic intentions that coalesce into angelic children, and those angelic children move through a series of experiences and then 'give birth', as it were, to their own ideals and concepts in the form of other spheres and other angelic children – so the universe expands outwards from the God-point. I must not get away from the subject but I wanted to touch on that because I want to impress on you that your scientists talk about the expansion of the universe and they don't understand why it is happening. It did come from a central point but it continues to expand because, in other areas of this particular physical universe, there are other parts of the angelic host who are projecting energy into spheres or planets that they are creating, and they are creating angelic children of their own who, on a spiritual level, are then going through a series of activities and experiences to the point where they can project and can create further spheres – and the process goes on ...and on ...and *on*, but let us concentrate on the Earth sphere.

Certain of the angelic children, having gone through a series of experiences on the Earth plane, looked into the plan for the evolution of the Earth sphere and felt that experience wasn't coming to them as quickly as they wanted it to. And, before they were ready to create in conjunction with God's plan and in harmony of the rest of the creative universe, **they felt that they could instigate** *a different way of doing things*. Now, this is fine, and is what happens in many instances; God is always looking for new ways of experiencing Himself and always welcomes individual feedback that brings to Him new ideas, new vistas and new opportunities to express. However, there is a process – not in terms of an earthly process – but a process that must be observed in order to create *correctly*. You would not here, on

Earth, give a child some delicate and destructive machinery before it was ready to handle it because that machinery has to be used in the right way in order for it to function as it is supposed to. There is a 'due process' to creation and that due process involves the manipulation of positive and negative forces in order to create *balanced* atoms that can put around you an illusion of whatever you want to create, and then just as quickly can be de-materialised by extracting the equal positive and negative forces within them; by taking those forces back into proto-matter and deconstructing the illusion of reality that you have created.

Certain of the children (for they were *children*) felt that there was a different way of doing things and that, by speeding up the positive aspect and by withdrawing the negative aspect, they could move through a series of illusions more quickly than had been done at this point in other spheres and in the Earth sphere itself. And, because all God's children have free will, there was no opposition to this, but it was pointed out that this would create an *imbalance* in the way that creation was formed and would be a little like using a new 'cement' that was difficult to degrade, so you would be putting 'bricks' together with a cement that would be almost impossible to remove and, therefore, it would be fine to construct your new illusions ...**but you would have difficulty in breaking them down afterwards.**

Unfortunately, this advice from the angelic 'parents' involved at that time was listened to, but it was felt that here was a revolutionary, new way of creation that would *enhance* God. Always at the beginning there was the intention of enhancing God and of bringing back to the angelic host and to the Godhead 'pearls' or a new aspect of God that would be beneficial to God and would enable creation to run more quickly than it did at that time. There was, I suppose you could call it, 'the impatience of youth' – the impatience of youth coupled with an ability to create at a point in youth's existence where they were not ready to create effectively – or, to use another term: **a little knowledge is a dangerous thing.**

You have to understand that this process went on over what would seem to you to be millions of years (if you were measuring it from an earthly time point-of-view) and there was, if you like, a kindly and loving 'debate' between the angelic host and the angelic children, with the suggestion from the angelic host that this was *not* the way to do things ...and the suggestion coming back from the angelic children that this *was* the way to do things and would enhance the Godhead and the whole of Creation.

Whilst this debate was continuing **the angelic children did not come home.** So invested were they in their quest to bring to the Godhead a unique way of creating that, at the end of their term of learning, they did not return to the angelic host because, from their point-of-view, they were still part of an ongoing discussion about what should be done next. So, again, through not undergoing 'due process' they began to remove themselves from the way that things *should* have happened and to remove themselves from that 'refresher time' when, under normal circumstances, they would have returned to the angelic host; they would have brought the angelic host their experiences; they would have examined those experiences in silence, in love and in harmony; and they would have come to conclusions about those experiences that would then allow them to move on into other fields of creation. So, through *intent* – and the intent was *to help God* at this stage – they divorced themselves from that natural process of returning to the angelic host and regarding the Earth's sphere as simply somewhere that was to be visited with a view to growing in experience and ability.

As the debate – I don't want to say 'raged on' because it was a very peaceful affair – as the debate both ways came to a withdrawal because neither side could agree on what the other side was saying, there came a time when, again in love, the angelic children decided that they would go ahead with their (to them) wonderful, new way of approaching creation *anyway* – and again, 'anyway' is perhaps a volatile word. They decided that they would go ahead with it **for the good of God** – not despite what had been said to them but, having observed and evaluated what had been said to them, they were going to, in effect, show the rest of the angelic host that they had a valid argument; that their way would create a series of experiences for the world that could be put into operation quite quickly and would bring differing experiences back to the Godhead in a far shorter sequence of events than is used in the rest of the universes throughout physical reality.

And so there came a point where the angelic children joined together as an angelic host and began to *create*, having altered, with the tools at their disposal, the positive side of creation and the negative energies of creation, causing both to become out of balance. And at that point the world began to become heavier; began to become more condensed, and its original crystalline formation – which was part of the original plan of creation and, therefore, in harmony with the rest of the physical universe – became encapsulated and encrusted in heavier physical matter than is created elsewhere in order to sustain the illusion of reality.

Having given all their will to this experiment and having invested all their consciousness into it, at the point where they drew the energies together in an imbalanced way, they, too, became entrapped within physical matter and their being became solidified. We will talk later about the 'niceties' of how that happened but, in terms of examining the plan, they became entrapped and the planet became entrapped. Also at that point, because they were entrapped in physical matter, the effect of altering the positive and negative on a global scale and in the surrounding area of space robbed them of their conscious memory of who they were and their connection to the angelic host and to the Godhead. So they *voluntarily* stepped into the illusion that they had created – one second they were angel children and then, in the next split second, they were encased in physical matter, and from that point onwards found themselves adrift and alone, from their point-of-view, because their point-of-view was, and still is, within the illusion that they had created that is out of balance.

On other worlds, where matter is created as a balanced commodity, the landscape and the life forms you see on a physical level are far lighter than you experience here. Also, because of the balance, there is an ability to see *through* the illusion back to the angelic host and the Godhead in consciousness, whereas here, because of the solidity of matter that was caused by the experiment, you have to *punch* a way through that physical matter in order to restore your angelic and Divine memories.

A little about the positive and the negative: drawing on the positive to create meant that from that time onwards on *this level of consciousness* **there was only the negative energy to draw on.** The positive, because it was not infused with the correct amount of the negative, could not be deconstructed. It would decompose because the positive needs the negative in balance in order to hold itself in form correctly, so there would be decomposition of the positive, which was then replaced by other projections of the positive, but the energy that was drawn on by the angelic children was actually *negative* because they could not punch their way through to the angelic host and the Godhead. And here you see – not the beginning of the Field as such, because, prior to the Field there was a matrix of consciousness that could be described as the beginnings of the Field – but certainly the beginnings of the *physical Field*. So, the beginnings of the *physical Field* go right back to that time when the projection of matter into physical form was altered.

[*Pause*]

I have to rest because there are so many different concepts that we have to cover at this point. This is the crucial point (although you will see, when we examine physical society and physical life, how the pattern repeats itself) but this morning I wanted to get to the nub of what went wrong.

...It was simply a matter of mistaken belief in potential. It wasn't an arrogance as such; it was simply a firm belief, and beliefs – such as the creation of physical matter – should be flexible enough to be changed. So the original mistake was to invest too much energy in a belief that was to the detriment of creation rather than to its evolution, and to hold that belief as the *absolute* way forwards and mistakenly believe that that was what God wanted. God wants His children to create endlessly, yes; God gives them ultimate free will, yes, but God is a structure as well. God flows through the structure of the universe and there are specific ways of creating – not as law or as a 'thou shalt', but simply as the way that things work. And it was that *way that things work* that was corrupted originally that led to a consolidation of matter in a loop that could not be swept away and could not be converted – certainly not from *within* the confines and horizons of the venture – that resulted in things as they are at present.

So the angelic children became immersed in their own venture and they could not get out of that venture because they believed in it wholesale (each of them and as a whole) at the point where they immersed themselves in it, and they still do. So, built into the surface structure (not the spiritual structure) of the planet is a belief – and that belief is that **the world is right as it is because it is a shared venture that is right for God.** Do you see the levels of corruption – not earthly corruption but twists of thinking – that have led to this separation from God? Built into the physical form of yourselves and of the planet is an underlying subconscious belief that things are right as they are, and **it is only through the *conscience* that each angelic child is able to discover that things are *not* right as they are.**

So there is a subconscious belief (particularly now, at this point in your 're-evolution' as physical beings) that things should be maintained as they are and that you can change things from within this structure *as it is* …**when it is the *actual structure* that needs to be deconstructed before things can be changed.**

These are difficult concepts because we are dealing in abstracts from your point-of-view (but only from your *physical* point-of-view and not spiritually). To sum things up in a few sentences: the world was a paradise; the angelic children believed that they could construct further paradises of their own using a new wielding of creative matter of positive and negative energies. Those findings were brought back to the angelic host – not directly and not by the spiritual 'physical' presence, as it were, of the angelic children – but by their thoughts, as there was a communication with the angelic host at that time in thought that said: 'We are proposing *this*.' There was then a debate, which you could liken to the legends of a war in Heaven; the 'war' being a very gentle one of *the word versus the new word*, if you like, and argument (although it was not argument with violence in it) or proposals on either side were put forwards until the point where the angelic children felt that they had to *demonstrate* that they had a way that was of value to God and of value to Creation. So, en masse, they joined together to create ...and at that moment they changed the molecular structure of their constructs and they plunged the Earth into a heaviness, a darkness and a stickiness that separated them physically, mentally and spiritually from their prior access to the angelic host and to the Divine.

I want to rest this information at this point because I will have to venture back into it next time to carry it forwards as there is a lot, I think you will agree, to look at in this section, but before I rest Michael (and, I have to say, myself) I will invite questions to clarify anything that has been said this morning.

Jane: Joseph, could you just clarify about the positive and the negative? I can understand how putting in more positive made matter heavier and more solid, but then I don't understand where the negative fits in and why we can now only draw on negative energy.

Joseph: They invested a predominance of positive energy into the illusion and into their ability to create. At the point where they solidified, as it were, their illusion, they were drawing on a limited supply of creative energy because they could not reach beyond their experiment as the vibrational rate of matter was different and also the creative equation was different. First of all they were separated in consciousness from what they had formerly been, and, secondly, they were separated from the normal way of doing things. It is like connecting the terminals of a power supply where the two sources of power are different – you can't connect them. And so they were left with their own creative abilities encapsulated and a predominance of positive energy that they had given into form so that they could only draw on a skewed blend of the positive and negative that was also coupled with their subconscious belief that is still here (and this is extremely important) – **that they were right and that this is the way that you create.** Do you see? They created an imbalance and, at the point that they created the imbalance, they believed in the imbalance *totally*, which is what you have to do in order to create anything. So when you attempt to create you are still drawing on that imbalance. Much of the positive is invested in matter and in form, which leaves the negative energy. Does that make sense?

Jane: Yes, I understand that now.

Joseph: I know that this is a complex series of events to put into physical words but we have to try and point out at some level (as we have done with the other books that inform *beyond* the words) and we have to penetrate that memory. This is what we hope to do with this book – to strike a chord; to strike that chord that happened at that moment of switching over to the venture and, on a soul level, to resonate with people so they say: 'Yes, I don't totally understand *but I do remember* – there is something in this.' And at that point they begin to release themselves from physical matter *as it is* – not physical matter as something that is wrong because physical matter universally is not wrong, but physical matter *here* is wrong because of the mixture and the blend. Does that make sense?

Jane: Yes, it does. I also wondered why, if matter is so solid with the positive, it shouldn't really decay but it does decay?

Joseph: You need a blend of positive and negative in *equal* amounts to allow the illusions that you place in front of you to be easily created and deconstructed. The positive needs the negative and the negative needs the positive, and you cannot extract one from the other or you end up with illusion that seems to be permanent but decays because it does not have the other half of itself in the mix. You need further insight into creation and this will be addressed because we have to redress the balance and need to make those, who are capable of understanding, draw on God-energy once again and understand the mechanics of God-energy when putting an illusion into the world that replaces the one that you have at present. It is something that needs to be set out in a chapter and not as a brief answer to a question, but do you understand the basis of what I have said?

Jane: Yes, thank you.

Joseph: Another question, please!

Tony: Joseph, I have a hundred questions going through my mind at the moment. This is amazing information and, if I did anger, I would be angry to think that we are the product of some naughty kids who did a science experiment, which we are now part of and are held in that position by a group belief that we are doing this as a way to expand God. My question is that, if the universal rules by which everything operates allows this to happen, surely this will have occurred in other places as well as on Earth, or are we unique in being caught in a double-bind where we find it very difficult to extricate ourselves from that situation?

Joseph: In answer to your question perhaps I can throw some *light* on the subject (if you will forgive the pun) by saying that the 'naughty children' were us! *We* were the naughty children; *you* were the naughty children; I was one of the naughty children; Michael was one of the naughty children. At that point we were angelic beings (and still are) and with what we have said in previous talks about the reasons for the spiritual cleansing realms, I think we have also mentioned that we are escaping *ourselves* and that we are opening the 'hatches' (or the way back to the angelic host) to open communication with the angelic host and with the Divine. Therefore, our focus is very much on the Earth plane and the area of surrounding space but we are visited (as I have said) at the highest level by those who have escaped and by those from other worlds, and from what we can see of this particular physical universe there are patterns that repeat but there is nothing at present that is as dire and... (I don't want to say 'irreversible' because that is not the right word – it *is reversible*) ...as 'set in stone' as the venture that caused the present state of affairs on Earth.

Until we escape into Infinity through choice (and we choose at the moment to stay in the tunnel, as it were, between the two points because we wish to help humankind and to extricate those angel children back into the fold) we do not have access to the progress of the universes. We also have to complete what we started – we began the process and we have to end the process before we can move on. That, too, is one of God's – not laws – but *the way that things work*: you work through a situation that can bring you new experience from beginning to end and then you set it aside. But, in this case, we are working on an experience that we haven't set aside so we do not have access to full knowledge as to whether this is happening anywhere else until we escape, through choice, into Infinity. Then, once we have escaped into Infinity, we are back as part of the original angel host from whence we came. That creative angelic host is (as we said at the beginning of the book) part of a greater angelic host and so there are steps always and, at each step in our spiritual progress, a set of blinkers falls away. So the first step, whilst the angel child is on Earth, is to take away the first set of blinkers and then, as we have said in the book *Your Life After Death*, each experience through the spiritual spheres is in order to remove a further set of blinkers ...and, as each set of blinkers comes off, the vista widens.

Am *I* still wearing blinkers? Yes, but I am aware of them and I am aware that once I have successfully seen through the experience that I have decided to invest in – which is to convince as many souls during this present incarnation of which you are a part – once I have done that to the best of my ability then I wish to move on. And I have to tell you that the immersion in physical matter of our last experience together [*reference to the attack at the public trance demonstration*] was extremely beneficial to me in giving me the impetus to make me want to move on totally. I mean that in all seriousness in that it was a little like being trapped in a nightmare (as, of course, each of you is trapped in a nightmare constantly) and, at the point when I returned to my sphere of illusion, I have to admit there was a yearning to move past that and **never to experience it again** – such was the pull of the Earth and the effects of the Earth at that point.

So, I cannot say in all truth, hand on heart, that this has not occurred elsewhere, either in this particular expression of reality you call the universe or in other expressions of reality in other universes. However, I do *feel* (because we have a feeling for physical existence, the higher we climb) that there are at least two points where there have been similar points-of-view, but they have not resulted in the lock-out that you experience on Earth. It is my feeling (although I have not investigated it fully – there is only so much that even we can give our attention to) that the debate and the ensuing to-ing and fro-ing of information has already succeeded in one of the cases in convincing the angelic children that it would not be to their advantage to go that route. The other vibration is still in debate and I would like to say: 'I will keep you posted' but I feel that, by the time the debate has been concluded, you will be well on your way to remembering this experience that you are a part of as simply a glitch in your infinite existence.

Is there another question please?

Tony: Joseph, we do appreciate and are extremely grateful for everything you are doing for us; it is just on such an enormous scale.

Joseph: It is an enormous scale and it is a microscopic scale, because the answer to everything that I tell you in this book is *within* and the switch that stops you producing the imbalance is within. It is a re-discovery of knowledge and so the concepts that we are looking at seem to be so complex and vast but the solution to returning to that blissful co-creation with God is simple, and is not *out* in the illusion of an infinite universe but is *within* the soul.

At this point, David do you have a question?

David: Just a very brief one about the imbalance between negative and positive forces – is that what has brought about our inability to draw on God-energy fully; in other words nothing is being cycled and slowly things are being drained down?

Joseph: It was an instant encapsulation – instant as you would measure time. Imagine that you find yourself sitting in this room now, and then, in the next second, you are totally encased and have no knowledge of the room. It was a matter of the entire host of angelic children on Earth deciding at one point, in conjunction with each other, to set off on the course that they had considered to be valid and, at that point, it encapsulated their creative ability because it cut off their creative source consciously – and subconsciously, to a great extent. So it is a finite amount of matter that you are dealing with on Earth, and I hope this illuminates what we have said in the other books. And, yes, it is an inability – there is not enough ability to maintain form and there is not enough ability to completely destroy form, so you live in a constantly shifting collapse and decay of the beautiful forms that you should be bringing through, and we will talk about it because we have to speak about aspects of the Fall.

And I hope now you understand why we call it the 'Fall', because you tumbled into your own creation; you fell away from the rest of God and the rest of the angelic host – not totally, and you were never disconnected really (and are not disconnected now), but you fell away in aspect and in belief. You fell into what you perceive around you but you can also walk out of it.

You fell in …but you can walk out.

So, yes, the imbalance of matter means that the structures that you create are not stable; nothing you create is stable when you draw on the energies that you encapsulated with you at the time of the Fall. What *is* stable and what *does* last forever – until you decide to deconstruct it – is what you bring through from *beyond* the encapsulation …**and that is the Light** that you reach beyond the encapsulation to bring from the angelic host and from God. Those concepts that change the world are permanent as long as you wish them to be because they are God-energy, which is in balance. Does that make sense?

David: Yes, thank you.

Chapter Eight
Consolidation

Joseph: The word that is most relevant to open this next chapter with is *consolidation,* as part of the phrase: 'consolidation of premise' because, as I explained last time, there was an argument or an opposing set of views that was discussed at length for many, many years. Then there was a point where the advice from outside of the group that fell into heavy physical matter was ignored. *Instantly*, at that point, there was change from perception of the Godhead to perception *only of the illusion*, but by then so much belief had been invested in the premise of the Earth, as it now was, that the belief continued to consolidate and solidify. So, not only was there a moment at which there was a cut-off from the Godhead in consciousness, but there was a continuing process, which took rarefied matter and applied **further substance and solidification to it.**

Prior to the losing of the conscious ability, in this area, to communicate with the Godhead, there had been (as we have discussed earlier) physical forms that allowed the travellers through the sphere of the Earth plane to experience, but those physical forms were *very etheric* compared to what you have now. Following the divorce from the Godhead in physical consciousness, the physical form became... 'corrupted' is the wrong word ...became *dependent* on the energy and the belief within the 'encapsulated illusion' or Earth sphere that was now locked off through the volition of the angelic forms that had become trapped within the exercise of the Fall.

As a result of that, the etheric form of vehicle that the angelic forms had previously put on as a 'mantel', and then discarded when they returned to the Godhead and to the angelic host became more permanent and became dependent on earthly Field-power. I suppose what I should also mention is that, at this point in time, there was the birth of the Field as we know it today – the Field that I have talked about in the other books. The birth of a conscious *Field* that permeated and controlled as a...

[*Pause due to a break in communications because of noise from outside. Joseph then resumes with a slight regrouping of his thoughts and words...*]

...The human form originally was permeable and did not need an internal structure – it was simply an area that allowed others to identify the soul within it travelling through the Earth plane. As a result of the cut-off of consciousness from the Godhead and the dependency, thereafter, on the creative ideas of the angelic children that were locked into the Fall, the human form took on internal organs and a structure because it was expected, through the eyes of those seeing others trapped within the Fall-experience, that the human structure needed to have an underlying skeleton in order for it to operate, to remain rigid and to move – and so there was a solidification internally of structure.

There was also a need to ingest and exhale the power that was available from the Field. The internal organs needed energy, according to the beliefs within the illusion, and at that point it became necessary to ingest power – to eat and to expel waste matter. This is a delicate subject, I know, but if you were to ask me: 'Did the human form have a digestive system and one for expelling matter prior to the Fall?' – then the answer is *no*. The form before the Fall was far more angelic and did not depend on 'internal' energy (that is, energy from within the bubble of the Earth sphere or Field). Therefore, prior to the Fall, energy was taken from the Godhead and there was no need for an internal structure to the human form.

From the point of the Fall onwards there was also a fear and anxiety created, because *subconsciously* the souls within the Fall-experience knew that they had cut themselves off from their source of energy, from their source of immortality, from their source of being ...**from God.** This was a subconscious 'river' that ran through each soul, and, as a result of this subconscious fear, the *conscious response* was to seek energy; to seek power, and whereas, prior to the Fall, violence was unheard of, after the Fall the sense of *me needing things more than you* spread like a disease through the Earth plane and resulted in the first acts of violence in order **to take.**

At that time it was in order to take food, or in order to take shelter, or in order to take clothing, because, along with the solidification of the human form, came a reaction to the climate around that human form – whereas before that had not existed and had not been necessary because climate was not a thing to be considered. Prior to the Fall the climate on Earth was idyllic, the surroundings were idyllic and there was very little reaction between the 'physical' form and the outer circumstances. Following the Fall, because of the perception of self as *being the physical form*, the physical form found itself sensing, reacting and adjusting to its surroundings, and those surroundings became more chaotic.

The paradise was indeed lost because the energy on Earth was now the Field energy and not Godhead energy or angelic energy (with regard to the angelic host that created the Earth), but was the energy produced by those souls trapped within the Fall. So, the Earth *itself* began to change and, as souls looked at and reacted to the Earth through the solidified human frame, their belief that the Earth was a hostile place *increased*. And, because they were (and still are) angelic beings, they *created* the environment that they believed to be around themselves. So, they changed; the human frame changed and solidified; the climate around the human frame also changed ...and changed for *the worse* because it changed according to a belief in a lack of power that was created by the subconscious need to be reconnected to the Godhead. So, over a period that, for the souls within it, appeared to be a mist or a murkiness and lasted thousands of years, the illusion arose triumphant and the original intent was buried and locked away within.

There then came a point where organisation was based on *a need to survive* rather than on a desire to experience in order to enhance oneself, the angels that were one's 'parents' and the Godhead that was one's *ultimate* Parent. So, there came a need to organise into groups to depend on each other, to depend on a 'society', if you like, and to depend on those who appeared to be stronger than others. Those who appeared to be stronger than others were simply those who had a more creative mind *originally* – simply that – and had a greater ability to believe and a greater ability to create ...but what they chose to create **was a need for power and a need for *personal* power.** And, by manipulating that personal need for power, they drew around themselves those that they felt could give them that power. So, there arose societies that would vie for power with each other – with those who were best at creating at the centre of those societies.

Unfortunately, they created more of the sense of lack and more of the sense of power needing to be taken from others around them *at any cost.* And, again you had violence, with one subset of society attacking another subset of society in order to take *perceived power* from it. Simplistically put – **this is the origin of all violence on Earth** because you are still repeating the same pattern. After millennia and after civilisations have come and gone (which we will talk about at a later date), you still believe that there is lack and you still have *those same souls* that gather around them others in order to feed their perceived lack of power, which is an irony, because those are the souls who are *best equipped* to create the future. They are best equipped to change the illusion and are, if you like, the 'masterpiece creators' of the angelic artists, but they are trapped in the illusion and, because of that, they create scenes of devastation for themselves and for others.

I must, at this point, talk about nature because originally, along with the angelic children that manifested themselves as human in form, there were also... (how to describe this?) ... *trends*, or waves of consciousness, that were also angelic, which you would describe as 'devas' who were experiencing the journey as you experienced the journey. They are also angelic but manifest themselves through natural forms – through the creation of landscape and environment, and that is their mission and role within the creation of worlds via groups of the angelic host. So, wherever a group of the angelic host gathers to create a world, there will also be amongst them other angels that you would identify as devas or nature spirits that give texture and detail to the environments that are created by those angelic hosts. Because their nature is to be 'natural', the devas did not engage themselves in the original argument or debate as to whether the world and creation should be altered according to wishes of the angelic children that became trapped within the Fall. But, because you cannot extricate the deva from the natural form (they are one and the same thing) and because their constructs were available as an environment for the angelic children to enjoy, **at the time that the decision was made to alter matter** ...the devas *became trapped within that experiment.*

As a result of the desire for energy, the angelic children trapped within the Fall began to seek power through the environment and began to *call to mind* aspects of the environment that they could use to consume or 'own' (as they saw it) in order to survive. As a result of this, and because the devas always act in harmony with an angelic host in order to bring through that which the host desires and helps to create, there were called forth manifestations of deva-energy, which you would identify as *animals*. So, I want you to consider that when you are consuming or observing an animal, the reason that the animal appears to be different from you is that that animal is, in fact, a solidified manifestation of the creative abilities of the deva, called forth by the angelic children within the Fall in order to satisfy their perceived need for energy. Animals are parts of a deva and are the manifestation of great, shining angelic beings whose consciousness is... not divided ... but *brought forth*...

[*Long pause*]

...I am sorry. I have over-stimulated Michael's throat muscles, which is why we are pausing...

Animals are deva-consciousness given form, and I hope that explains their innocence in all this. The devas are enmeshed and tied up with the souls that are fallen. However, the devas are in no way responsible for the Fall – they were simply 'along for the journey' as an integral part of that journey in creating the illusion that was the Earth originally.

I hope I have given a very *basic* description of what happened immediately after the Fall. I say 'immediately', but this took quite a long time (as you would measure time from an earthly point-of-view). Those first days following the Fall are sketchy and were a time of being in a dream, a time of emerging from a mist and a time of consolidating the Earth into what you see today.

That is why, for each life that is manifest on the Earth plane now, there is that 'murkiness' when that soul tries to look back. For each soul there is that emergence from childlike wonder into adulthood and into a consolidation of belief, from the individual's point of view – a consolidation and acceptance of what appears to be true and real on the Earth plane. It is a repeat of the pattern ...repeat ...repeat ...repeat ...*repeat* ...**repeat**. There is that separation from God and the angelic host, which is the initial incarnation, then there follows a short time when the spirit or angelic consciousness within the physical structure is still strong, but then that angelic awareness becomes swamped and moulded by the effects of the Field **...and re-enters the effects of the Fall.**

And that is how it was at the beginning of the Fall. There was a murkiness and, from the point-of-view of human incarnated-consciousness, at the end of that mist there was an Earth that had certain climates and certain characteristics. There was a society that one could take part in, but it was a society based on fear of loss of power and, in order to survive (as it understood survival), a society that preyed on other societies and on animal life that was manifest thought from the devas.

Have I explained that sufficiently? If I haven't, please ask relevant questions and I will try and fill in the blanks.

Jane: Joseph, when we needed an internal structure to our body – who designed it, because it is very intricate? Who is the designer behind it?

Joseph: *You* are the designers and architects of *everything* that you see. **The designers and architects of everything that you see!**

I would add that the delicate internal structure is a reflection of the workings of the power-points within an angelic being. But the fact that the internal structure is *delicate* is as a result of a belief that the human being is delicate, that the human being needs protection and has to have this hard, outer shell protecting the delicate mechanism that is within it. It is also consolidation of the need to 'demystify' – from the point of view of a fallen angel – how the body works.

Originally the body worked by the angelic individual permeating that very loose, yet still physical, form. It was a shell but it was also primarily a point-of-view. What happened after the Fall is that there was a desire to justify the way that you look... 'There must be an internal structure to this; there must be something controlling it; there must be something that motivates it; there must be something that powers it.' ...And over the aeons the structure was formed by *belief*.

Remember that you are creative beings – that you are angels capable of creating worlds! If you are capable of creating worlds, then creating a structure to justify an external view of yourself is quite a small task. It is not that the angelic beings on Earth today *consciously* create an internal structure – it is that the angelic beings consciously re-enter an area where the belief is *already in place*. So your physical vehicle is, to some extent, dictated by the Field as you grow into it as an angelic being reincarnating to experience the Earth plane again. You are incarnating into a belief, but it is not a Godhead belief. Your solidified, incarnated form is a result of a belief, a result of God-energy having been perverted and channelled wrongly.

There are manifestations of life throughout the universe that are not based on a structure as you understand it at all. I would have you consider, for a moment, how you are when you return to the spirit worlds that nest this Earth in order to help you escape from the effects of the Fall. Do you have bones? Do you have veins? You have form because you are used to looking at and relating to that form, but that form can be dispensed with whenever you want to dispense with it, and brought back again whenever you want to bring it back. What maintains you on the spiritual levels as a physical being? If you consider that seemingly still-physical form… what maintains you? Do you have bones? Do you have a heart? Do you have a brain? If you do, then what happens to those things if you decide that you will become a ball of Light or a vibration for a time, or if you decide you will become a pair of eyes looking from that vibration, but not existing as that vibration at all? You are an angelic being, and the refinement that takes place that gradually takes you away from the effects of the Fall, also takes place with how you perceive yourself, and that flawed perception has to be taken away from you gradually. Or, rather, *you* take it away from yourself as you re-realise the malleability of form and that you are not an outer shell or inner workings – you are a spirit; an angel.

I also have to add that the physical controlling factors within your brain, your heart, your lungs and your circulatory system relate to the creative centres of the angelic being that you really are. In other words, there is a crystallisation and consolidation around your chakras or energy-centres of vital organs and that is why the chakras relate to the vital organs. This is a reversal of traditional thinking, in that the chakras *came first* and the vital organs solidified around them as an expression of the purpose of those chakras. Do you see that?

Jane: Yes. Thank you.

Joseph: Is there something else? Can I expand on this *vast* theme?

David: Joseph, you mentioned that the Field, as we know it, was 'birthed' and took on a sort of life of its own – could you explain a little more about that, please?

Joseph: Yes. Whilst the debate was taking place, there was a 'prospect' and a series of discussions countering that prospect, so the prospect was not *yet* in place. At the time of the Fall, the prospect instantly became *a thing* because, at that point, the angelic children concerned with the Earth plane said: **'This is what we are doing!'** ...And they immediately immersed themselves in it, not knowing that they would divorce themselves from the rest of creative purpose and how that creative purpose manifests itself throughout this particular physical universe.

They took with them the belief and the belief was made 'word', the belief was made 'flesh' ...**the belief became the Field.** The belief was: *we believe that we are right in the name of God; we believe that we can create in this way and we believe that we can advance the way that creation takes place.* Having invested in that belief for millennia whilst the debate took place, at the point that the belief was 'birthed' – with it were created *the effects* of that belief ...and the effects of that belief were a divorce from the normal, nourishing progress of creation around the angelic children that sank into the Fall experiment.

That perception of lack of power that is subconscious (because, remember, those angels knew *subconsciously*, at that point, that they had cut themselves off from God) manifested through the belief that created the world as you see it now. The creative power running through the belief is strong, and the belief was that there was lack and a need for each individual to absorb a certain amount of power in order to survive. That belief, channelled through the millions of minds of the fallen angelic children created (because minds together create together) the Field ...**and you are still believing in the belief**. This is the problem and this is what we are trying to guide you away from – the belief that continues your dependence on the Field on a subconscious level, continues your dependence on a physical form as you see it and continues your dependence on power *at all costs* at the expense of everyone around you so that you can *survive*.

So, the angelic children – *YOU* – created, not only the Fall, but also the Field. Does that explain it to a greater extent?

David: Yes, thank you.

Tony: Can I ask a question in relation to what David just asked? Are you saying that the angelic children that created the Earth are as equally tied up in the Fall as we are?

Joseph: You *are* the angelic children that created the Earth. If we go back to what we said originally, – we touched on creation and the way that creation works, and that certain segments of the universal angelic hosts (the angelic hosts that exist in different universes and on different planes) decide that they want an experience. As a result of that, they then create a world and pass through the opportunities that that world presents to them in order to have that experience, and to take that experience back to the angelic host that they came from. Do you see that?

Tony: Yes.

Joseph: The angelic host created the world and we have talked about how the children are then created from the angelic host. It was those inhabitants of the Earth sphere at the time of the Fall

116

that divorced themselves – as a result of their volition to do things differently and to experiment with the rate at which creation happens (i.e. the rate at which molecules and atoms are created and destroyed) – and those angelic children that inhabited the Earth sphere at that time that were encapsulated and trapped.

The whole point of this book is to explain why you are as you are now, why you come back here and why the Earth is a hostile and violent place of seeming lack, and to give you that knowledge (that should resonate with your soul from a time *before* the Fall) so that you can, through your heart-centre, reason your way out of reincarnation and out of the effects of the Fall. Then the planet can be restored to its former purpose and you can be restored to your former heritage. Does that make sense?

Tony: It does. Thank you, Joseph, it does make sense.

Joseph: I am tiring Michael, but is there anything else regarding today's proceedings that needs clarifying?

Jane: Did we influence the devas so that the animals and other things they created perceived lack, were violent and fed off each other?

Joseph: The deva-consciousness is a single consciousness that then becomes… 'watered down' would be a good term. You can 'move' your consciousness into your fingers, but your fingers are a dim reflection of your central consciousness (which for you appears to be seated here within your head). Imagine that the animals brought forth from the devas are their 'fingers' – there is a spark of consciousness in them but it is not the central and controlling consciousness.

You also have to understand that, because it is a weaker consciousness than the *entire* deva, the animal consciousness is then affected by the dominant beliefs of the Field – and the dominant beliefs of the Field are that you need power at all costs in order to survive; you need to consume that power and, as you cannot ingest it as a vibration, you have to consume it as heavy matter. Much instinct goes back to the time of the Fall, and that belief or instinct is impressed on the animal minds and they simply respond to it because they do not have the strength of individual consciousness to do anything else.

I hope this shows you how guilty we are in affecting our animals' minds and the innocent aspects of deva-consciousness in this way because we do, indeed, impress upon our animals the need to consume each other. It is not that we do this as individuals – we do this as a 'host' manifesting the Field, which gives the instruction to the animal forms (a stronger consciousness upon a weaker consciousness) that that consciousness needs to kill and to consume in order to have the power to survive. Does that make sense?

Jane: Yes, thank you.

Chapter Nine
The Absence of Light

Joseph: The title of today's communication is: 'The Absence of Light', and I wish to put into your minds a concept that you have probably not considered before.

I want you to consider *darkness* – an absence of light – and to consider that the world was not always a dark place, and that what you consider to be night and to be shadowy places did not, in fact, exist *prior* to the Fall. You have to understand that, at the point that the debate ended and the decision was made, the Light was shut out of the equation. And by 'Light' I mean God-consciousness; I mean the ability of souls to tune-in from within and to realise, understand, accept and work upon **the fact that they are part of God.**

So, at the point that the debate came to an end and the decision had been made, humankind was plunged into darkness – a darkness *initially* of the heart-mind. It was as though curtains were drawn around the heart-mind, obscuring the direct vision or direct point of connection between man and God. As a result of this darkness and absence of creative Light, the seat of consciousness or seat of negotiation with the outside world **was moved from the heart to the head.** As there was a coalescing of perception of form into a solidification that included internal organs, the seat of intelligence and of perception was drawn slowly, slowly away from the heart (the *true* seat of perception) into the nerve centre or the commander of the nerves – known as **the brain.**

There was a shift in perception because there was no point, at that early stage ('early' still meaning that thousands of years had already passed since the point of the Fall), in trying to perceive the newly-created type of world that followed the Fall from the point-of-view of the heart. There wasn't enough Light to communicate with the outside world via the heart. Therefore, the seat of interaction, or the interface between the outside world and the inner being, the angelic being, was, of necessity, slowly transferred from the heart into the mind, brain or head, where the necessary sensory organs were nested, in order for interaction between the angelic being and the outside world to take place. Naturally, as this happened, there also occurred a further moving away from any communication, which would enlighten the being – *the now* **human** *being* – and would enlighten the world via the drawing in and giving out of Light via the heart-centre, which had become darkened and imprisoned.

So, initially, there was a rebellious need to draw away from the heart and there was an investment in a belief-system that had been constructed over thousands of years as time is measured now. There was a refusal to accept that the consequence of the 'science experiment' that had gone wrong was the creation of a dark place. There was a turning away from God – almost to say: 'We told you so and it is going to be alright!' There was a distancing from the ethereal and a steeping in the material, so initially the head-mind was a sought-after location! It was a further investment in the belief that the actions of the Fall (another word for the experiment that went wrong) were correct; that it would be alright *eventually*; that the darkness would dissipate and there would be a positive consequence of having taken the decision that plunged the souls into the Fall in the first place.

Over the millennia, as form solidified, there was a drawing away from the heart-centre further ...and further ...and further into the head-centre. The head-centre perceives light and dark, does it not? But the light that it perceives is a small, tiny percentage of the Light that it used to perceive through the heart-mind. The light that you perceive here is a tiny fraction of the spiritual spectrum. It is as though someone has lit a candle in a distant barn, has then put an encasing gauze around that candle and you are standing miles away from the barn at night and you perceive it *dimly*. That is the amount of light that you are, in fact, experiencing at this time in a human body. And you feel that this amount of light is sufficient for you, that you are illuminated by the sun on bright mornings and that you have sufficient power from electricity to illuminate your homes on dark nights.

What you do not have is sufficient power to illuminate *from the heart*. If you were to accept yourself as an angelic being once more, the amount of Light that the heart is capable of giving out is **phenomenal,** is blinding to physical eyes and is enough to illuminate outwards like a burst of energy encompassing *thousands of souls*. This is why I have urged you to get in touch with your heart-centre once again [Joseph referencing his other books] and to send out from your heart-centre, because the amount of Light, each of you is capable of, far exceeds the small spectrum of light and darkness that you originally created as agents of the Fall.

Do you now see how difficult it is for you to realise your spiritual potential when viewing it from the point-of-view of the head-mind? You are viewing your spiritual potential under a dim light-bulb that has been smothered by gauze and darkened by belief. In order to realise your potential, you have to get back to the heart because the heart is where you began, and the heart is what needs to be triggered again to restore you to what you are and to restore the world to what it is.

There is an effect of God-Light upon this world: God-Light vibrates at a particular rate; God-Light has entrenched, enmeshed and woven into it a *harmony*, and it is that harmony that *restores* and is capable of restoring your world; that restores your angelic vision with regard to how you perceive others and how you perceive yourself. **It is vital, therefore, that God-Light is brought back into this world –** it is the restorer of harmony, the restorer of angelic memory, the restorer of the original matrix of the Earth and the original matrix of your angelic bodies. And I hope that also relates to passages I have given you in the past regarding the potency and the effectiveness of Light.

When you are ill, for example, and when you perceive yourself as having some disease, it is because you are perceiving and treating that disease through a small spectrum of light. What we are inviting you to do is to, once again, fling the 'door' open wide so that the original amount of Light available to you, *which has never been taken away from you*, is made available to you again ...and Light heals because Light is harmony.

Whilst we talk about a lack of Light, I also want to bring to your attention the fact that many, many souls carry with them an angelic memory of the Fall and, to this very day, *refuse* to let go of the notion that they were right – despite the view of the world that you have through this dim amount of light, despite the destruction, the carnage, the inability to cope, the inability to heal and the inability to find happiness and harmony. ... Despite all those things there is a rigid, stubborn and inflexible angelic memory within many souls that says: **'We are right and we will prove it!'**

...And you have at your feet a history of how you have proven it – you have proven it with war; you have proven it with torture; you have proven it with illness; you have proven it with poverty; you have proven it with lack; you have proven it with an inability to control physical matter. Oh dear! And it is to those souls that the most amount of Light needs to be given. They need to be bathed in God-Light so that those *stubborn* memories eventually break-down in Light (and they will), but during the span of this current civilisation they have never been given enough God-Light and enough harmony to break down those memories.

You see, originally, there were 'leaders' (to use earthly terms) and there were 'followers' – or *instigators* and *supporters*. Those leaders, not only *still* believe that they were and *are right* and are, therefore, seeking to maintain this world as it is …but they have *buzzing around them* acolytes, supporters and people who reincarnate in order to be with them because, at a subconscious-level (or level of Fall-consciousness), they still believe those leaders to be right and wish to be with them, believing *this time they will succeed* **and this time they will show the others that they were right all along!**

Now, I hope that makes sense of the previous information you have been given regarding souls who were the instigators in the Fall and who rise up, in terms of your world, to perpetrate terrible crimes against humanity, who seek to overturn current world order and to replace it with their order at the cost of thousands and millions of lives. It is simply a memory that is propelling them forwards – a hunger for power and a memory that says: 'I was right and still am and, therefore, all I need to do is imprint on this world my vision of how things should be and harmony, *harmony according to my terms*, will then exist again.' You repeat yourselves …and repeat yourselves …and invest in the same patterns because you have not, either as a leader or as a follower, thought your way *from heart* out of the transgression that you committed yourself in order to instigate the effects of the Fall.

What you call 'darkness' and what you call 'night' is only perceived by you as night because you cannot perceive the Light that is in it. True, one object casts a shadow on another but, with spiritual eyes, within the shadow you can see such beauty and such delicacy of colour – not the black that you perceive now. Black, as a spiritual colour, is invested with other colours; it is not the absence of Light that it appears to be. So, during your daylight hours you see through a limited spectrum and during your night time hours you see through an *even more limited* spectrum and perceive everything to be dark and black, which it isn't. The heavens are alive with colour, are alive with vibration, are alive with prana and energy, but you cannot perceive them because your view has been limited due to the effects of the Fall.

I would invite the readers of this book, intellectually at first, to begin to *imagine* a world where there is no darkness. I invite them to look at the darkness and say: 'Well, *Joseph* says there is Light in this. I must therefore investigate it and must, in my imagination, see Light in the darkness.' And that is your mission in trying to change this world through Light – to always perceive Light through the darkness. You need to be metaphysical about this – not just to see light in the darkness each night, but to see Light in the darkness of a situation, to see Light in the darkness of an illness, to see Light in the darkness of circumstances that appear to be dark, encasing, stifling and inflexible …because they are not. When you begin to see Light in the darkness of any situation you *lighten it*, you make it less heavy, you put more Light into it and it can work out the purpose that it is supposed to work out in elevating your spiritual senses.

Light in the darkness!

Also consider, metaphysically, the darkness that you place around yourself so often – the dark ways that you look at your life and yourself in your personal situations… I suggest to you that you see Light in the darkness of those as well.

So many souls who commit suicide have come to the point where they can see only the darkness. If only they would perceive the Light in that darkness their situation would change! This is not a smug comment – it is a comment designed *to help* and to say, 'Nothing is so black because the black doesn't exist', and to say, 'You are a spiritual being.' You are angelic and you can refocus your vision from the heart rather than from the head-mind into any situation and lighten it. You can see its worth and its part in the 'great machine' that is running constantly to bring you back to a time of God-consciousness, back to the start-point and back to the point where you can say: 'I wasn't wrong – *I was mistaken*. It was a point of view, which I have held for millennia, that resulted in me perceiving this world, myself and others in a certain way. Now I realise that I have an alternative. I have a choice and, in choosing Light, I can throw Light into my own circumstances and understand them better. I can also throw Light into the circumstances of others so that they can begin their long journey back *inwards* to realise who they once were.'

And if you are one of those people who finds comfort in darkness, I would suggest that it is not the darkness but the *no-thing* that you find comforting. It is the fact that darkness takes away much of the materialism that you can see during the daylight hours, and that that materialism is heavy, is a burden, and has attached to it all kinds of demands that in the night time you cannot see and, therefore, are less connected to. If you feel comfortable in darkness, it is not the darkness that you crave, it is the no-thing; it is the distancing from the constant material visions that are placed in front of and around you that limit the amount of Light that you can see.

I wish to talk about the steps that were taken, by those outside of the Fall, to rescue souls who had invested themselves totally in the effects of the Fall, but this will be at a later date. So, the next logical thing for me to talk about is the need for the spiritual realms (as you would call them) and how those spiritual realms function in illuminating the souls who were part of the Fall. That is all the spirit realms exist to do – to illuminate those souls. But, before that could happen and before those spiritual realms could be constructed, there was a time of darkness.

The initial time of darkness was a time when souls outside of the Fall – the angelic host – prayed and delivered their Light *constantly* to the Earth plane and to those who were suffering within the encapsulation of the Fall, in order to bring some perception of Light to the souls within that encapsulation, for whom this was a very chaotic time. It was not that they were in total darkness from a visual point of view, but they were plunged into total darkness from an angelic point of view. That initial burst of an absence of Light led to the desire to *find* Light, the desire to survive and the desire to absorb power, because power, in its purest form, is Light. We will talk about that on another

125

occasion but it is something that pertains to the way that things were initially **...and initially things were extremely dark.**

Unfortunately, things are becoming extremely dark again, because the perception of most of humankind is geared towards materialism and towards a total absorption in the physical universe that is seen through the physical senses and a turning away again from anything other than that perceived physical universe. There is also a worship of that physical universe, so you are worshipping chaos. If you worship chaos, the problem is that chaos becomes your 'God' and chaos serves you as a God because that is what you expect it to do on a subconscious level.

Each night before you sleep, I would like you to see a candle by your bedside that illuminates, not only your room and your soul, but the *whole of the world* – a candle of intense spiritual Light that is capable of transforming. Know that that candle burns actively whilst you are asleep to illuminate your thoughts so that you communicate correctly (as you should do in the times when you escape from this world at night) with those who care for you and can lead you out of this illusion. It burns brightly whilst you are asleep so that it is constantly feeding the other souls who are not so illuminated, to show them a path down from the mind into the heart once again so that they can begin their journey of self illumination (or **re-illumination, because the amount of Light that you had,** *you still have).*

You are your own jailers! You are your own prisoners! You have placed yourself within the jail and you are serving a term of imprisonment that *you do not need to serve* – **and I am offering each of you a key.** Only you – *only you reading this book* – can free yourself from the prison you have placed yourself in. **Only you!** Not me and not any other soul. We can advise, we can teach, we can show the way, but *you* have to take the steps. We have given you the key – this glorious key – to take, to turn and to unlock your spiritual memories, to unlock your history *spiritually,* to unlock your potential and to unlock **your ability** to love your way out of your current situation. But I stress again, as I close this section, that only *you* can do it.

ONLY YOU!

I will not, I cannot and I am not allowed to do it for you, nor is anyone around you ...spouse, father, mother, friend, advisor, teacher... they are not there to do it for you. Please listen! *You* have the power to unlock what you once were and to become that angelic being again. You *still are* that angelic being – you just don't realise it, and you have the power to change you and to change the world around you.

NO ONE ELSE!

...YOU!

Questions, please!

Jane: Joseph, could I ask a question about the repeating patterns and the different progressions of souls? Presumably we all started off as the angelic children who made the decision that led to the Fall, but since then some people have actually progressed through the spirit realms and escaped into Infinity. Others are still in the spirit realms and a lot of people haven't progressed at all, and, as you say, still think that the experiment was right. Why have people progressed at different rates? Why can some people evolve spiritually but a lot of people can't?

Joseph: There is a hierarchy to the effects of the Fall. All of God's children are equal but all of God's children have been given different areas of expertise. In the beginning (and by 'beginning' I mean of life *here* after the effects of the Fall) there were certain elements or groups of souls who were responsible for creating what you see now. It is as though, if you want to build a house, you need a plumber, a carpenter, a painter, a bricklayer, someone to put the roof on, someone to wire up the lights, and someone to put in the carpet... each has a different skill but there will also be a *project manager*. There were, if you like, 'project managers', and it was to those that the other souls looked in agreement with regard to the proposition of changing the rate of manifestation of matter that is at the core of the twist that resulted in what you see today.

Those 'project managers' were involved in the original debate for thousands and millions of years, and their belief was that the project would be beneficial to God and to every form of Creation. So, that belief was carried through into the Fall by them to a greater extent than it was with the 'other workers' or followers of those project managers. In fact, all that they had, once the Fall effects began, was **the belief**. Therefore, it takes longer, in the case of the project managers, to shake off that belief because they are more deeply devoted to it than many other souls. At the periphery you have souls who are able to shake free more easily because they are more susceptible to inspiration, and the belief that they carried with them into the Fall world was not as solidified as it was with the project managers. Therefore, it is those on the outside who respond *first* but it is those at the core that need to change *the most*. Do you understand that?

Jane: Yes. So it is sort of the luck of the draw depending on what you originally were.

Joseph: Not as such. There is choice in all things on an angelic level, and there is a 'rota', if you like, that is tailored to the individual so that the individual can, at any time, examine other aspects of itself and decide that it will invest energies in other aspects of Creation.

If you are saying it is unlucky that the project managers happened to be project managers at the time of the Fall, luck had nothing to do with it. You have to remember that those angels, at that time, had examined their perspective, presented that perspective as a viable alternative to the perspective that God had in heart-mind and had *one hundred percent* decided that that perspective was correct. They (in earthly parlance) became stubborn, became inflexible, became so sure that their viewpoint on creation was correct that they would not allow anyone else to influence that viewpoint until it had been thoroughly examined.

It wasn't as though in the debate there was a faction saying, 'Yes, we are right,' and a faction saying, 'No, you are wrong!' In that debate there was a faction saying, 'Yes, we believe ourselves to be right!' and a faction saying, 'Please be careful! We feel that the effects of your actions will lead to chaos and to an encapsulation of your beliefs in heavier matter, which you may not be able to escape from.' It was not a condemnation from the other angelic forces – it was a very sympathetic ear, as always, to the viewpoint being presented by the project managers. It was an attempt to *gently* show them that their way could and *would* result in a downfall for them. Unfortunately, the project managers had become so enmeshed and so totally absorbed in their point-of-view that they perpetually created it as the way forward, and the promptings, warnings and help offered by those outside of this group were not taken. Do you see?

Jane: Yes.

Joseph: Another question, please!

David: I am reminded of the old saying that *every cloud has a silver lining* and I suppose that little point of Light is always there in the heart, isn't it Joseph?

Joseph: An excellent analogy! You are limitless as the angel that you truly are – *limitless* in the amount of Light that you can absorb, channel through yourself and expel into the atmosphere around you to irradiate yourself and others with. Limitless – because God is limitless and you are part of God. That Light has the ability to reinstate harmony in *any* situation. **Any situation** – even the most dire situation as you view it from the point of view of the earthly mind.

Light is a reconnection and an affirmation of the original harmony of the angelic host and is available to you, is the way to go and is **the source of your being**. Once you re-establish that that harmony is the source of your being – anything else becomes a deception and falls away as a trapping that is no longer real. Your harmonious Light, which exists at the core of your energy wavelength, is perfect. God's way is perfect and it is that perfection that you project into situations around you to change them. Let us take the word 'belief' and substitute 'observe' in its place, and take away the words: 'I believe in this Light' and substitute: 'I re-observe this Light. When you re-observe that Light in people and in situations in your world then, from your point of view, you can *only* observe the Light, so you are functioning as you originally functioned in bringing harmony into everything that you see, think about, touch or project into.

So, yes, indeed, within every cloud there is a silver lining, but we have to bring you to the point where you cannot see the cloud. The cloud only exists within the theatre of illusion that you have created as a result of the Fall. And you are being what you were designed to be by God – you are functioning perfectly as an angelic being capable of creating whatever that being believes to be true. Unfortunately, you are functioning perfectly to produce *perfect chaos* because that is what you believe to be true. You produce perfect illnesses; you produce perfect wars; you produce perfect famines; you produce perfect cataclysms because you cannot do otherwise. You cannot half-heartedly create anything – you are an angel. You, therefore, produce whole-heartedly anything that you perceive to be true – that is your nature.

You have only cut yourself off *on the surface* because you are still an angel at heart (the important thing: **at heart**). Therefore, you create perfectly the world that you created so long ago. You perpetuate it and you invest in it because you cannot see anything else as you are working from the distant seat of perception that you call the head-mind – not even, in many cases, acknowledging that there is a second mind or the *original mind*. You have to get back to the original mind to see the silver lining, to project the silver lining and to dispense with the illusion of the cloud. Is that a sufficient answer?

David: Yes, thank you.

Joseph: One more question before I break the connection.

Jane: Could I ask a question that relates to the last chapter about devas? They weren't part of the decision that led to the Fall but we have trapped them in its effects and they are suffering – but doesn't that contravene what I thought was one of God's number one 'laws', which is free will? Here the devas don't have free will and, presumably, the animals that incarnate don't have free will either.

Joseph: The devas were part of the tapestry of creation relating to this world. The devas flow through all Creation and they flow through you at a very… (I don't want to say 'low level' because that is wrong) …at a very loose level of creativity. They are part of the original 'builders of the house'. Their mind is a group mind and does not react as the individual minds react that were involved in 'laying the carpet and putting the roof on' and so, by free will, they permeated the creative matrix of the Earth as it was.

At the point of the Fall their consciousness was imprinted within the angelic children that instigated the Fall so the devas are integrated with you, and it is their *wish* that that part of themselves that is linked to you *be brought out of the Fall*. They, because they are a looser interpretation of individual form than you are, also exist to a certain extent outside of the Fall. So, the greater part of their mind is invested in creation *outside* of the sphere of the illusion, and, because of that, they are able to hold the matrix together at times when, were it not permeated by the devas, it would destroy itself – as it has done in the past.

So, there is a volition for a certain outcome on behalf of the deva minds and connected mind that exists outside of the Fall, but also inside of the Fall. It is a mark of unending love and a shining example of God-Love and the spiritual love of one individual for another that that part of them that is invested in the effects of the Fall seeks to illuminate the creative matrix of the Earth in order to release the angelic children from the effects of the Fall. In other words, yes, part of the devas is trapped ('trapped' is perhaps a bad word – I should have said 'permeates the matrix') but it is an act of volition in that they seek, always, to maintain the structure of the world …until such a time that the angelic children are able to liberate themselves from the effects of the Fall.

You have to remember that the devas are also integrated with the *very fabric* of the planet. They care and nurture for the spiritual qualities of the world that existed before the Fall, and they bring through structure that allows you to operate on this level. You have to look at animals in the context of them being part of a deva and not the individualisations that you feel they are. They are able to *manifest* as those individualisations and, once they have passed from this physical plane, they are fully conscious of being part of the deva and an integrated part of that consciousness. In the way that a snail can push forward a 'foot' and then withdraw it again into itself, so can a deva push forward aspects of itself that can be recognised as animal life. At the end of its term of physical consciousness, that animal life can then be withdrawn back into the deva and can be pushed out again to be recognised and function as what appears to be an individual intelligence but is, in effect, an intelligence that is consciously linked to part of the Whole and operates on two levels – as do you …but that is another story!

Does that make sense to you?

Jane: Yes. It is complicated, but *yes*.

Joseph: It is far more complicated than you realise!

I must let Michael go. I thank you for the opportunity to expand the themes that we have been talking about today, and I also thank you for your response to the urgency with which I have been pressing Michael to complete the task of bringing through the information on the Fall.

[Michael's note: From this point onwards we had decided that, if we possibly could, we would sit once every two weeks for a communication rather than once a month as we had been doing. This, if everything went well, would allow us to shave some seven months off the production time of this volume, something that Joseph felt was necessary considering the present state of the world, as you can see from his comments at the bottom of this chapter.]

This is a very difficult time of year because there is never more belief in matter than you find at Christmas, when there is a belief in matter being 'the Saviour of all things'. But, quite apart from the Christmas festival, there is a belief in matter that is *accelerating*. Your computers are drawing you in – it might seem to be a more etheric type of matter but it is, nevertheless, matter. Your computers are pulling you in and uniting you. They are assembling you on one set of rails as a united front glorifying the matter that is available to you – the matter that, at present, people feel will solve all problems, that technology is the answer and that being connected to one another is the answer.

I want you to consider that being connected to one another on a *physical* level is quite a different thing to being connected to one another on a *spiritual* level. You are being connected more and more, each and every day, so that you can unify according to the Field in thought and purpose ...and that thought and purpose is to contribute more energy to the Field. So, you *are* being unified, but only on a physical level. Can you say, hand on heart, that the world is being unified *spiritually*?

No, you can't!

Unification must come *spiritually* if things are to change – not materially. **Not materially!** It is fine to be able to communicate with each other via computer links and other various pieces of technology, but you have to understand that there is a *motive* behind *all* physical matter …And that motive is to herd you, to control you, to power you and to lead you in a certain direction. Nothing that you see is without agenda – everything has a purpose and an agenda.

There are two agendas that are happening at the moment:

…There is the agenda of the spiritually enlightened, which is to draw people into a realisation, once again, of who they are and who they were.

…And there is the agenda of the Field, which is to control *at all costs* and to be fed *at all costs* by the energies that are produced from a dependence on the Field.

The Field cares not about cataclysm, the Field cares not about the end of the world – **the Field is the ultimate selfishness!** The Field cares only for the Field, only for *now*, only for *today*, and knows that it wants something …it wants power and it wants to control, but the Field is extremely clever because the Field is a conscious result of having millions of minds, millions of capabilities and millions of concepts poured into it.

So, [addressing the members of the circle] there is an increasing urgency to what we are doing, and I ask you to review your lives (not review as in 'look back on' but review as in 'realise again what they are for') from the point-of-view of who you are and why you are here. And you are here behind 'enemy lines' to present this information – nothing more! You have *done* the things that others need to do in order to reconcile heart and mind – you did them before you came here. You are here to be *used* because you volunteered to be used. It sounds harsh but that is your purpose, and that is your purpose when you switch on the physical mind. It still is, otherwise we couldn't use you.

So, we thank you for the ability to use you and we will attempt to bring through much more information in a shorter time next year so that you can finish this most important of books. *This is the most important book!*

The most important book!

Chapter Ten
The Birth of the Spiritual Spheres

Joseph: There is something of *vast importance* that must be discussed at this point because, having examined how the Fall – that break away from the rest of Creation – was created (and it was, of course, 'created' – it was designed in the minds of those that are still living it) the important aspect that must be examined this afternoon is: **what happened to the rest of Creation?**

Of course, the rest of Creation did not go away because the Fall had taken place. The rest of Creation continued as it always had done and always will do ...with the exception of this 'sore point', this area of insensitivity, this portion of itself that was suddenly unreachable, un-helpable and un-healable.

Of course, the angelic host, involved in the debate that went backwards and forwards for millennia before the Fall took place, were *instantly* aware at the point the decision had been made by those angelic children responsible for the Fall that the distancing had taken place. They were instantly aware (as they had been *before* the debate took place and before the decision had been reached) that those fallen souls were **in trouble** and needed to be reconnected with the Whole in full consciousness.

Those souls had plunged themselves into a darkness of their own making and into a belief in heavy matter and solidified illusion – to the exclusion of any conscious realisation of being more than part of that illusion they had created. Therefore, it was necessary to bring *suggestion of change* into their world; 'suggestion' because, of free will, the angelic beings who were involved in the Fall had taken that decision and, if they elected to remain within that illusion, then there was nothing that any being, or God, could do according to His own structure of His universes. If, however, the 'Fallen' decided, by their own volition, that they no longer wanted to be fallen, then slowly they could be extricated from the 'soup of illusion' or 'thick tar of *possibility turned into certainty*' that they had plunged themselves into by their own thoughts and decision.

The first thing that happened was that a self-elected number of the angelic host decided that they would ring this area of the Fall or area of space and pour Light into it to counter the continuing and accelerating effects of the Fall. So, in physical terms (although this is not an *exact* analogy) they surrounded this area of space with Light ...and continue to do so in part of their consciousness. Then, they **unified in purpose,** and that purpose was to bring an atmosphere into the area of the Fall within which advanced beings (i.e. part of the angelic host) could incarnate, by free will, into the centre of the Fall experiment to teach and to *illuminate.*

And so for some time Light was constantly poured, beamed and projected into the area of illusion of the Earth and its surrounding space to 'lighten' (quite literally) to some extent the solidified molecules of thought that had created a permanence within the illusion – a permanence of ideas and a permanence of creation that was accepted by *the Fallen* as the ultimate and *only* reality. Investing those molecules with Light meant that *eventually* certain members of the *Fallen* were elevated in consciousness to the point where they **began to consider their spiritual aspects.** Not only that, but there was enough Light to begin the process of bringing in members of the angelic host who, despite knowing that a great portion of their spiritual memory would be erased and masked by the effects of the Fall, elected to come in time and again, incarnation after incarnation, in order to bring Light to the *Fallen* from within.

Those souls prepared to enter the physical vehicle via the process that kept bringing people back into this area of physicality. They prepared, and formed links with members of the angelic host best suited to maintaining a supply of Light to them during their incarnations in order to allow them to elevate the souls of the *Fallen* in consciousness, and to bring back to the souls of the *Fallen* a multi-dimensionality to their thoughts so that they could begin to consider **spiritual aspects of their lives** – because for a long time they didn't. For a long time it was 'today' and the life they were living *now* on the Earth plane that was *all there was* according to their philosophy. There was the acquisition of power and the maintenance of survival and that was all that they *wished* to consider. **There was no consideration at all of anything beyond what they could experience with their** *physical senses.*

This is where the beginnings of religion can be found. As Light was poured in to affect the molecules of the illusion that had been created by the *Fallen*, certain members of the community of the angelic children, divorced from the rest of Creation because of the effects of the Fall, were able to elevate themselves (always it had to be elevate *themselves*) to a point where they considered *what* was beyond, that there was *something* beyond, and to address that in their own individual ways by inventing someone *beyond* in their own image. You say that *God made man in His own image* – **originally man made God in his own image** because that was the only image he had at that time. And so religions were propagated in various areas of the globe as points where people could consider and *imagine* – because first they had to imagine the *possibility* of there being something other than the heavy matter that they found themselves trapped in.

Invariably and *inevitably*, as time passed by, these religions would become corrupted by the imbalance in the numbers of souls who were considering spirituality and the numbers of souls who were investing continuously in the illusion of the Fall. So, inevitably (and in almost all cases) religions would become corrupted, but as the souls of the *Fallen* considered spirituality increasingly (albeit under conditions that were imposed upon them by their fellow members and which restricted their approach to spirituality) a certain amount of Light was let into the world. As a result of that, other souls were able to complete their mission of presenting spiritual knowledge that had a higher vibration to the members of the *Fallen*. In many cases they were put to death; in many cases they had to exist as reclusive beings and be content to promote Light from within the illusion. Many souls would spend many lifetimes ...incarnating again *and again* ...to simply sit quietly away from the masses and direct Light towards the masses, and to see the atmosphere being lightened, being rarefied and becoming more spiritual.

Then, because of these teachers and because of religion at that time allowing a certain – not *much* – but a certain amount of Light into the mix, there came a point where, upon physical 'death' (which is simply the exhaustion of available power to an individual on this level), rather than an *instant reincarnation* due to the pull of the Fall, that soul was open to an amount of suggestion and counselling before going back into the effects of the Fall.

Areas were constructed that consisted of molecules of Light and molecules of the effects of the Fall, molecules that were not as *dense* as those found within the world that had been created as an effect of the Fall. As souls were able to be counselled by angelic beings once they had left a physical life behind and before they returned to another physical life (drawn in initially by the immense physical pull of the Field), slowly areas were constructed where they could rest, could contemplate and could be taken *outside* of the illusion to view it from the outside and to consider for themselves that it was an illusion **that didn't need to be returned to** *at best* ...or *at worst* that it could be returned to with them carrying the seed of spiritual truth within them so that they could, during a successive lifetime, enlighten themselves and others by their presence ...to the point where, when they next came back to one of the spiritual resting places, they would consider *for longer* that they needn't go back into the Fall effects and could consider what the Fall was about. It is analogous to a primary school and to a number of successive classrooms becoming available to students as they grow in knowledge and self-awareness ('self-awareness' referring to spirituality).

I have just described the beginnings of the spiritual spheres – those spiritual spheres that in so many religions are considered to be 'Heaven' and to be *all that there is* awaiting the angelic soul once it has left physical death behind. Those cleansing spheres, which we have examined to quite an extent in the previous book [reference to *Your Life After Death*], were constructed gradually. First there was an immediate sphere around the Earth, as it were, not quite permeating the Earth but around the Earth and the effects of the Fall. Then, as souls hovering between one physical incarnation and another were illumined by the teachers from the angelic host within that sphere, the molecules of that particular sphere could be further 'enlightened' or helped to create a more etheric sphere around and permeating that one. Gradually, therefore, the souls from within the Fall were able to extricate themselves **sphere by sphere** as they rediscovered their true heritage and their true potential to the point where they could eventually escape from the effects of the Fall.

The angelic hosts involved in the process initially were legion and spent most of their 'time' and invested most of their consciousness *in love* in extricating the souls that were trapped in the Fall. However, as souls were gradually extricated from the Fall, they themselves became teachers in the spirit realms and were able to take over much of the process of maintaining those spirit realms and addressing those souls that remained within the Fall in an attempt to bring them out of their 'spiritual slumbers'.

I hope that this now also explains why there is a need for guides and the *true meaning* of 'spiritual guidance'. Spiritual guidance is not about which road you should travel upon on a particular day *per se* – it is about which decision you should make on a particular day **in order to extricate yourself and others from the effects of the Fall**. Souls for whom escape is possible, via the spiritual spheres, often decide that they will, *through love*, remain in the spiritual spheres in order to influence certain groups of souls on Earth, through suggestion given via the intuition of those souls, during the lifetimes on Earth of those groups of souls in the hope that those groups are at a point where they can elevate themselves above the illusion to the extent where they can choose to either filter through the spiritual spheres and escape back into the angelic-host consciousness – the God-consciousness – or can influence people on Earth in order to raise their vibrations too.

So, what we have been discussing today is **a gigantic and ongoing rescue operation,** and I would like to say to readers of this book that it is time to consider the spiritual spheres for what they truly are – not the encapsulated and finite heavens that are spoken about in many religions (and remember, as we have discussed earlier, most religions have been polluted to some extent *inevitably* by the effects of the Fall) but, rather, staging posts and a series of steps. A series of steps with each one emerging into a more brilliant amount of Light, and the final step being taken to extricate oneself *finally* from the effects of the experiment and regain one's *original* knowledge of who one was as an angelic being ...**and to remove oneself from the experiment altogether.**

Necessary, I think at this point, to have discussed the construction of, the evolution of and the purpose of the spiritual spheres. It is sad, therefore, to consider that so many souls have chosen and *do choose* to reject that point of their consciousness that is made available to them by teachers and by themselves when they leave the physical body behind for a time. This is something that we will discuss and examine in a future chapter – the repeat of the experiment and the repeating investment in cataclysm rather than in illumination – but for now I feel that I have sufficiently given a 'sketch' of the instigation, birth and purpose of the spiritual spheres. So, at this point, I will invite questions, please.

David: Joseph, you have mentioned in the past that there are souls existing on planets within our solar system that escaped the Fall – are they also investing their experience and time in this rescue mission?

Joseph: It is primarily a project of the angelic host (the 'angelic host' not meaning the *entire* angelic host, which is vast and occupies a number of different creative areas) but particularly the angelic host who were originally involved in the attempt to prevent the Fall from happening. It is those angelic beings who feel more sharply the lack of the souls who are now enmeshed in the effects of the Fall. I wish I could communicate to you the amount of love and compassion that exists within those members of the angelic host who are involved in extricating the souls on Earth from the effects of the Fall. You exhibit and experience grief on Earth when a relative or a close friend passes, but that grief is nothing compared to the grief that is *constantly* felt by the members of the angelic host who are involved in the 'rescue mission' to reach members of the Fall.

Primarily it is an angelic mission, and the inhabitants of other spheres and areas of space are not generally involved in it. They are carrying out God's purpose and *their* purpose as beings passing through certain areas of inspiration and possibility. That is an ongoing purpose of Creation and that is happening everywhere ... *except in this area.* Do you see what I am trying to...?

David: Yes!

Joseph: So, their consciousness is concerned with the ongoing *bliss* of creative potential and, on behalf of everyone, the whole of Creation and God, of experiencing new vistas and situations that are in harmony with the creative matrix of God-thought. It is the members of the angelic host that were involved in attempting to prevent a decision they knew would be wrong and harmful that were mostly involved in the creation of the spiritual spheres and, to some extent, are now involved in the continuing attempted rescue of souls within the Fall.

I have to say that I didn't conclude something (there are so many strands of thought that I have to try and shoehorn into a stream of communication) – in that the members of the angelic host have, to a great extent, left the re-evolution of the members of the Fall to those spirits who have escaped into the spiritual spheres that nest the Earth, and are responsible for teaching and enlightening the other souls.

That is not to say that they have abandoned the souls that are trapped within the Fall – they haven't, but there is a lesser amount of their consciousness involved in the process. They are always there and always present but only to *a degree* now as there is only a degree of their consciousness that is involved in that Fall rescue-mission. The reason for that is to give power back to those souls who have discovered what happened in the Fall and have regained their spiritual consciousness because, in giving power back to them, you empower them to the extent that they have a greater ability to empower the souls who are emerging from the Fall. So, it is, again, a free-will concept that eventually – through a greater and greater and greater free will in saying **this was wrong; we have got to get out of here** – everybody is pulled out. So, the person at the top of the 'pile' is constantly reaching down to the bottom of the pile to pull those souls up in consciousness, so that they can regain a sense of who they were and, through free will, decide for themselves that they now need to move on from this *imprisoning state of affairs*. Does that make sense?

David: Yes, it does. Thank you.

Joseph: Is there another question please? The power is going.

Jane: It is just a quick clarification of the term 'angelic host'. Is the angelic host what you originally said was like in a university where they sat in a room and gave birth to the angelic children who became humankind. Is that what you mean?

Joseph: Yes. It is the glory and mystery of God that **God is one and God is many.** On a spiritual level – free from the restrictions of physical matter and the constant need to draw on form in order to experience – God exists as multiples.

God is one but God is also multiples. If I can try to enlighten you further in what I have just said – you are each one of those multiples and a group soul is one of those multiples. Any group that groups together in *unified purpose* is one of those multiples – just as there are multiples in Earth society ...political multiples ...emotional multiples ...religious multiples. You group yourselves together in areas and in numbers of purpose. **You are each individuals but you are each a part of God.**

It is certain multiples that were involved in the 'university' analogy I gave you earlier that decided that they would challenge the then *proposed* experiment, and it is those multiples that most feel the loss of those souls involved in the Fall (however temporary – for, in time, **all souls will escape**). From their point of view (not quite putting it in earthly terms) it is as though they feel a *responsibility* in that they could not ultimately, and in love, make those souls involved aware of the dangers of going through with the change in the speed of matter that resulted in the Fall. It isn't guilt – it is a great responsibility in them, with them feeling (now with only a degree of their consciousness): 'If only we could have made them see! We tried ...and we tried ...and *we tried* ... and we put forward scenarios and showed them, to the best of our ability, what would happen. If only we could have made them see!' There is a great feeling of *we must involve ourselves to some extent until every single soul has escaped from the effects of that mistake.* Do you see?

Jane: Yes.

Joseph: I will attempt one further question.

David: It reminds me of something biblical – the parable of the return of the prodigal son.

144

Joseph: We have poured images, for thousands of years, into the subconscious in this particular societal structure that are relevant to what has happened. Teachers have brought through repeating 'patterns' of spiritual truth which, when heeded and adopted, cause enlightenment, and those stories and allegories can be found, not only throughout the history of this society, but throughout the history of the societies that *preceded* it.

This is how we work and you have mentioned it yourselves this week in that you have stated how science fiction allows spiritual values and circumstances to be examined, because of course we do not only seek to push this information through those who are spiritually-minded. **We will put this information in wherever we can!** It is group information from those souls that are escaping the Field pushed into the matrix to those who are visionaries. And by 'visionaries' I do not just mean leaders, but those who write and those who produce visuals, those who sing and put together lyrics, those who write poetry ...*any visionary soul* who can tap into the greater consciousness or greater multiple and bring through truths from, according to their viewpoint, *beyond*.

...And so, *yes*, it *is* the prodigal son; it is *all* the biblical stories that have not been polluted by the effects of the Fall; it is every illustration that has been brought to man for millennia through religious outpourings, through mystic outpourings, through poetry and dance and music ...anything that illustrates, from beyond, the path that should be taken to reach beyond the illusion of the Earth. Is that sufficient?

David: Yes, thank you.

Joseph: I wish at this time to guard you over the Christmas period and to protect you from what is quite a dangerous time for many people, and because you have volition and have worked with us for so long I wish to tell each of you that around yourself and your families this Christmas there will be those who will protect, those who will attempt to calm you and those (and I say this with a smile on my face) who will prepare you for the work ahead. This only a 'comma', [Joseph is referencing our Christmas 'break' in transmissions here due to the imminent holiday] this is only a short stop along the way at a 'tavern' where you can eat and drink before you move on to do *even more work*. I should say that I am sorry for this but I am not! Why should I be sorry – and why should you be sorry – for work that actually *changes* souls from within and brings illumination to them?

I bless you this afternoon, and I wish you to know that there are many workers that you do not normally see. We have mentioned them, you have seen some of them and you know them by nickname, but there are many, many souls with you. They each wish me at this point (although I am pushing to put more information through instead!) to remember them to you. And 'remember' is the important word – to re-*member* ...to join again with you as your true family, as your limitless family that has never been away from you, that appreciates what you do, and to give you that sense of *belonging* at this time.

God, through each of us, blesses you! God, outside of each of us, blesses you! God within you blesses you!

We bless you and we love you.

Chapter Eleven
'Original Sin'

Joseph: The title of this chapter is 'original sin'. *Original sin* is featured in many of your religions, but, as with everything that has been filtered through the medium of the Field, it is distorted. *Original sin* should be re-titled: 'original *mistake*' or 'original *misconception*' because religion attributes to original sin a reason for humankind *suffering*, and there is truth in that, but the reason that humankind suffers is because of the original **mistake** – the mistake that resulted in the Fall.

The Fall was only one step in the divorcing of the angelic children that invested in the misconception of the Fall from the rest of Creation. There were and *are* continuing ramifications to that mistake in that, at the point at which the Fall took place (when the experiment was agreed to and invested in), there was a *volition* that permeated the angelic children involved in the Fall ...and that was **to *continue* with the experiment** and to seek the effects of that experiment.

So much faith and so much positivity (ironically) had been put into the experiment that, at the point that the Light was 'switched off', as it were, and the angelic children were plunged into the darkness of the Field and the darkness of the Earth, as you see it now, **at that point each member of the angelic children had faith in the experiment.** That faith and volition to see the experiment through was imprinted onto their vision of what the Earth should be. In other words, the angelic children not only carried themselves into the Fall and brought themselves into the illusion, but they brought with them a *continuing volition* to maintain and have faith in the experiment. Therefore, locked into their angelic creative matrix was and *is* **a desire to continue with the experiment** because they believe: *eventually it will all work out as we thought it would in the beginning!*

And, because each soul revisiting the Earth, ...time ...and time again, revisits its previous heavy-matter matrix of beliefs and past experience, each soul new-born to the Earth is invested with the desire to continue the original experiment through in order to see it to fruition. That is the meaning of 'original sin'. *Original sin* **is a pattern for chaos** that, at a subconscious level, is a desire and a projection from the time of the Fall. It exists on a subconscious level, entrapped within the heavy molecules of the physical and mental vehicles, and it exists as a 'stain upon existence' and as an invisible desire to maintain the Earth *as it is*.

This chapter is, in effect, as *important* as the explanation of the Fall itself because, what I have just attempted to explain, is the reason why it is so difficult to change the Earth from its present state.

Inbuilt into every person is, not only a *memory* of the Fall, but **a desire for the Fall to be *right***; a desire that all that debate was for *something*; a desire that the rest of the angelic host were mistaken and *you* – all of you – were correct in manipulating matter and speeding it up for the glory of God. Do you see the twist? Do you see the subtle poisoning of your reasoning *spiritually*?

It is as though a 'veil' is thrown over your superior spiritual knowledge the moment you incarnate on Earth. It is as though you are dropped into a 'poisoned well' and have become saturated with that poison. This is why it is so important to flood the Earth and yourselves with Light because, in doing so, you eliminate and chase out of the dark corners of your soul the *original pattern* that pulls you back into a belief that this Earth is as it should be – particularly as you grow older and your resistance to the Field on all levels diminishes and it becomes easier for the Field to control your physical and mental matrices within the matrix of the illusion. **The Field draws you deeper into itself as you grow older.**

The point of this book, from this chapter onwards, is to *remind you* that **there is a way to change the effects of the Fall.** We have always said in the previous books, 'Go within!' ...And we say *go within* because you first have to rid yourself of the echoes of the Fall that are encoded into your physical body. You have to realise that there is a God *within* ...and a God *without* – i.e. **without the Earth plane that you have invested so heavily in!** Within you – within the chamber of your heart – exists your angelic memory, and it is the angelic memory that streams Light into every thought and it is the angelic memory that allows you to create.

At the moment you create, but through a filter – through the filter of a memory of the Fall – and, as a result of that, *everything* that you create is tainted and tinged by a desire to maintain the status quo on Earth *as it is*. You have to resurrect the angelic mechanism for creation within you, and you do that by becoming still, by visiting the heart chamber, by pondering on what has been said in this and previous books ...and by entering that state of creative bliss that allows you to change *first* yourself. **First you must change *yourself*** so that you become a 'beacon' for an advanced form of Light, for a 'remembered' form of Light that goes back to a time *before* the Fall, and a beacon for Light that illuminates the atoms of the physical and mental matrices on Earth to revive in them, within their molecules, the memory of how things were before the Fall.

Original sin or 'original mistake' (mistake in thinking and mistake in purpose) exists, but it exists, not as a point in the past, **but within each person as a *potential* for the present and the future.** It exists within each being as a means of repeating the pattern, of progressing the investment in the Fall through a period of degradation of matter to a time where everything is levelled; to a point where the Fall *starts again* and the beings involved in it – *you* – are re-invested into another, similar illusion. To prevent that happening you have to get rid of that original sin, or shall we call it 'original belief' – a belief that you were right.

[Smiling] **Is there anything more stubborn, then, than a fallen angel ?**

...Is there anything more stubborn than a fallen angel in believing for millennia and millennia (as you measure time from the point of the *original* Fall) that they are *still right* and that is still the right choice?

In truth they are – and *you* are – to be forgiven for that thinking, because the original intention was to **glorify God** by showing Him that He had invested in His children to the extent that they could go forth and present to Him a new means of glory – brought about by their own actions in re-ordering the way in which matter is created. So, the original intent was noble but, unfortunately, the original intent was *flawed* ...and as a result of that flaw the Fall took place.

I would say to you reading this book, that by this time, because of all we have said, **you now know that you are an angelic being.** Look at angels in your religions and religious imagery ...at these *great shining beings* that are to be looked-up to ...these great shining beings that bring rays of Light to those who will observe them and listen to them.

...At your core, from *before* the time of the Fall, *you* are such a being!

You are a being capable of wielding those magnificent, superior rays of God-Light in order to create. There is a term, is there not, that runs through religion and through fable, myth and fiction, of the 'fallen angel'. You are not only that being of Light, that angelic being capable of such wonderful, blissful, superior creation ...**you are also a *fallen* angel.** How did you fall? You fell by choosing a darker path *for the noblest of intentions – a darker path*. As a result of that you have suffered for millennia, placing your feet back on that path, time after time, because you believe it (at your core, from the time of the Fall), to be the right choice in order to *vindicate* yourselves and to *glorify* God in greater ways.

What this book asks you to do in your meditations is to look beyond, behind and before the time of the Fall to rediscover, not only who you are, but what you once were *capable* of. As part of the angelic host, as part of God's family and as part of God's children, you, *each of you*, were the creator of worlds and realities – wonderful worlds, splendid realities, beautiful vistas, beautiful scenes ...And you are capable *now* – you still create, but you apply creation through the dark filter of the Field to invest in a world that is far less than perfect.

You switched a 'light' off millennia ago.

It is now time to *personally* and *globally* switch the Light back on.

That is how simple it is – to irradiate yourself with Light in your meditations; to sit and to see yourself enveloped in the Light from your heart-centre to the extent that all else ceases to exist for the time of your meditation ...**and you are placed in *perfect brilliance*.** Do that and you switch the 'light' back on for you personally and enable Light to be streamed into the rest of this illusion in order to help others to see beyond the original mistake. You give them enough Light for them to grow – to grow beyond that mistake and to realise that it was just one action that plunged them into darkness and a similar *single action* can take them out of the darkness again.

Original sin is a cycle. The original mistake is a repeating cycle. Why? ...Because everything that you create in God's name is a part of repeating cycle. Everything you create as an angelic being is part of a repeating creative cycle; therefore, everything you create as part of the Fall (although it is a mistaken part of creation) has to repeat itself until such time as you say, 'No', and until such time as you come full-circle. You can either choose, in the coming years, to come full-circle around the edge of the Fall experiment to repeat it again …**or you can choose to come full circle back into the Light.**

The choice is yours!

…I have given you the tools and means to think your way out of the illusion you find yourselves in, to rip through it, to bring Light into it, to rediscover yourself and help others to rediscover themselves and to break the cycle, to bring it to a conclusion and say: 'That is one thing we tried that doesn't work! Now let us re-invest in our true heritage and try the things that *do* work according to the way that God orders this universe.'

I also want to speak (if I can pull enough power through to clarify this) about the people that you would describe as 'leaders' of the Fall, and to talk briefly about those who had the most creative power invested in this illusion.

Those leaders are the ones that believe most *strongly* in the continuance of the world *as it is*. Those beings are the ones who fight most strongly *to order* the world and, inevitably, they do it through treading on others and by seeking power. I would like to suggest to you something that you may not have considered: those leaders (the ones that always come to power and manipulate and destroy others) are working, at heart and at core, from a desire to maintain the Fall in order to glorify God.

So, their *initial* motive in doing what they do is not rooted in evil; it is rooted in a desire to bring back to God something that *is now right*, to bring back to God *order* (according to their subconscious) that says to God: 'Here I am Father ('Father' in the true sense) – look what I have done for You. **Look what I**

have done for You!' And that strong desire, rooted in their heritage as one of the main instigators of the Fall, propels them, through the negative effects of the Field, to commit atrocities and distortions in the treatment of people in order to satisfy that need within them that they cannot understand *consciously*. It is power at any cost! It is order at any cost! It is **my way and my views** at any cost! Do you see?

They are expressing their involvement in the Fall at a highly creative level. It is an echo from their past and they are expressing it in the only way they know how, by obliterating anything that is *not of their vision* in order to satisfy that subconscious need to please God by saying, 'I *was* right, Father', rather than realising that there is no judgement from God. There is no punishment; there is no perception from God of the 'child' as being a *naughty child* or a child that is out of line. There is simply a desire from the Godhead to express ever greater bliss and love through that child and the relationship to be one of mutual... *'super-affection'* is the closest word I can get to it. What I mean by that is a love that you cannot feel on this level because, as with everything else, it is filtered by the effects of the Field and, therefore, it is watered down and distorted.

So, look to your leaders – look to the people who have caused the greatest amount of destruction, upset, pain and control across the Earth – look to them with an eye that says: 'Here is a leader! Here is an angel who is drawing on a memory that they cannot understand.' ...**And pour *more* Light in their direction.** Address those who seem to create mayhem with as much Light as you can will towards them and as much Light as you can surround them with because they are the ones (more than others, perhaps, to a certain way of thinking) who need that Light to remember who they are and to let go of the things that they are doing.

Around leaders you have followers, and around leaders you will find those who originally lent support to those leaders in vocalising to the angelic host that the way of the Fall was the right way. So, the subordinates or followers are locked into a repeating cycle with those who originally led, and who still try to lead through coming to positions of power time and time again. In other words, clusters of souls reincarnate together by the original magnetic effect of the urge to justify and continue the origins and effects of the Fall. What I am saying is that the people who are around those people in power that cause such mayhem **have been around them before as followers** because their *subconscious* desire brings them to a conscious *magnetic attraction* towards those that they follow. Often they do not know why they have such devotion and dedication to those they follow – they simply know that they *have to follow them*. Again, they are following a course that has been set up within them via that original sin or original mistake.

So, next in your prayers, meditations and your wielding of the Light you must encompass the followers of those who cause destruction and atrocity. You must see that Light approaching their hearts, invading their hearts, illuminating their hearts and *changing* their hearts – reminding them that it is alright to let go, reminding them that they are creative beings and that to invest millennia in the constant creation and recreation of *a mistake* is a tremendous waste of effort and a confining of creative ability.

The leaders and the factions that you see causing such mayhem and havoc today have done so in the past …time …and time … and time again. The Christ said, 'Forgive! Forgive – turn the other cheek. Love those who do harm to you!' …and that is precisely why he said it, understanding, as he did, that those who would seek to do harm to you are those who are most deeply invested in the mechanics of the Fall.

I hope that, in concluding this chapter, I have given you *food for thought*. I hope that I have given you the opportunity to examine what has been said, in the quietness of your own meditations and to discover that, within you, there is that memory that *locks* you into this illusion. It not only locks you into it, but seeks for you to *maintain* it, seeks for you to keep feeding the Field and maintain things as they are. This is a chapter about *deconstruction*. You have to address what is wrong in *the world*, but you also have to deconstruct what is wrong *within yourselves* and within the hearts of others. In doing *that* you then change yourselves and you change the world ... **and change is what is needed to be pushed into the illusion.**

The illusion is in a state of stasis.

We have talked at length about stasis being the end result of a Fall cycle until such time as the Earth and a physical vehicle can again maintain the souls who are in stasis ...so that they can, unfortunately, go through the *same* actions again. You are not only in stasis when you are **outside** of the cycle of physical incarnation, however, you are also in stasis when you are **within** the Field. Yes, your lives progress and, yes, there is change, but only *limited* change, and the societies that are on the Earth do not, in fact, change; they remain fairly static within the confines of the illusion that was set up so long ago. So, there has to be change, **and when you introduce change, through Light, into the Fall in sufficient strength ...there is no Fall!** You eliminate the original discussion and original construction and you replace it with the constant, changing creative capabilities of the angelic children that you really are.

You see things from the viewpoint of the Fall down such a narrow corridor and through such a narrow spectrum. You hear things on so few frequencies and you cling on to those because subconsciously you feel that they are right and this is what you must invest in. Your *true* creative spectrum, your true area of being and area of sensation is *infinite*; is so much brighter, wider and joy-filled than the one you find yourself in at the moment.

Work towards it!

It is pointless me telling you what went wrong unless you ... and I ...*we*... can put it right. It would be pointless to give you all the information on the Fall – every viewpoint, every instance, every happening of the Fall – if you could only remain the same.

What I am saying to you is that you can *change*.

You can change – this world can change – *now*!

I am afraid I have debilitated Michael to a great extent. I will attempt questions but I will limit them to two, please.

Jane: Joseph, in the debate before the Fall and before we made the mistake of re-ordering matter and speeding it up to make it more positive, what was the *perceived* advantage of that to the angelic children? What did we think we would achieve by doing it?

Joseph: In terms of the physical world you felt you would achieve construction in a far shorter time without the mechanics of considering the effects of that construction. In effect, **the Fall was about a shortcut to construction.** It was a group of you (of us) saying: 'There is a different way to do this. It is better, it is faster and it takes out some of the steps. We are young children and we have a viewpoint that you others have not examined and appreciated before. It is there in front of you! It is *apparent* to us and *should be* apparent to you, but it is not. We feel that if we try this and succeed with this, you will be able to enhance your ability to create, and to create in far less 'time' than it takes now. We feel that you spend too much 'time' in contemplation of creation and not enough 'time' in creation itself.'

It is an example that you find, again within the illusion and confines of the Earth, of *the new order seeking to overthrow the old order*, looking for new ways and throwing out, as newly-created aspects of God, that which the older (in your terms) aspects of God had considered, given weight to, examined and found to be the *correct way* to create and to set up scenarios through which the angelic children could travel to enhance their abilities and their understanding of the Divine Creator. If you wish an analogy, it was youth kicking against age and wisdom. A faster and more streamlined way of creating evolution and of creating worlds on a physical level was what was hoped would be achieved.

...fortunately that attitude was tested just on one world.

Fortunately, it did not apply to a *greater* area of physical creation or we would be addressing a far greater number of souls, and there would be a far more rigorous effort by the millions and millions of souls needed in order to get a greater portion of fallen souls out of the illusion they had placed themselves in. Fortunately, it was suggested that this experiment be applied *only* to the Earth ...but, for you (and us) suffering the effects of that one small area that has been affected, it is hardly a comfort. Do you see?

Jane: Yes. Thank you.

Joseph: David?

David: Of the original leaders, have any of them managed to pull themselves out of the illusion?

Joseph: When there is an awakening in one of the leading believers in and instigators of the Fall, when one of those souls is elevated to the point where they remember who they are, unfortunately – because there is such a deal of grief, remorse and self-hatred for what they have 'accomplished' whilst within the illusion of the Fall – there is a danger that often they will seek, *against advice,* to reincarnate **to put right what they feel they have done wrong.**

...And the problem with that is that, not having contemplated for *long enough* who they originally were and washed away the origins of the Fall from their consciousness and volition, once they get back **they very often repeat again that which they have such great remorse about.** Do you see what I am trying to say? Everything is a cycle, and we have to be extremely diligent, when one of the leaders is at a point where they consciously, *spiritually* realise who they are and what they have done, that they do not plunge themselves into the start of the repeat of the pattern simply by wishing to put it right on Earth. Far better for them to put it right by *avoiding* the Earth and by removing themselves from the angelic children on Earth and, therefore, removing a power-point for followers to gather around and for the Field to feed on and amplify.

In answer to your question, several of those leading souls *have* successfully made the transition, but that's not enough. When we describe 'leaders' we are describing a *lot* of souls – not just the ones that you see coming to prominence in your news programmes. There are lots and lots of souls that work at various levels in society who were originally leaders. Many of the criminal element are such leaders, and organised crime is a way for the Field to be fed. Organised crime is also, at its heart, a projection of leading spirits involved in the Fall answering a call from within them that is an echo back to the time of the Fall that says: 'I need to seek power and overthrow society as it is and rebuild it in my own image.'

What I must say, and what I have tried to express within the chapter, is the need for Light to be sent to **everyone** – *particularly* to those who seem to be the instigators of such cruelty, destruction, perversion and distortion. **Particularly to those** because, in sending Light to them, you give them enough illumination to examine, of their own free will, what they are doing, who they are and to change. **Without the Light there is no change!** That is the point and is something we have addressed in the other books. Without the Light there is no change because there is not enough power to make change; there is only enough power to contribute to and be fed by the Field.

So, yes, several have escaped but there are many more who repeat the pattern and have repeated that pattern not just in society and in history as you see it, but have repeated that pattern in other societies from *before* the period of stasis, where you would not recognise society as you see it today, but you would recognise the trends of it. It is a case of: *old wine, new bottles*, and if you were looking at the Akashic Records you would see that the same instigators of chaos in those times are the instigators of chaos now.

I must applaud your desire to continue with this project and, as you can see today, we are channelling as much Light as we possibly can in order to bring this information through and put it in public hands *as quickly as possible*.

...*Thank you.*

Chapter Twelve
Perspective

Joseph: I am instantly ready to speak, and I acknowledge and understand the difficulties that you have in putting aside time for these communications, but the fact that you *do* allow this communication to come through is, as ever, very much appreciated. I would like to talk to you today about *perspective* and about the way that you view the world, the way that you listen to the world, the way that you project vibration into the world on a *physical* level, and the way that you react to other people.

If I take a candle and then place a clear glass around it – the light from outside of the candle can pass through the glass to the candle, and the light from the candle can be transmitted through the glass to the surrounding area. If I then take a vessel of smoked-glass and place it over the candle, having removed the clear glass, the amount of light that can reach the candle is *far less* and the amount of light that can shine out from the candle into the surrounding area is also far less. When you react on a physical level to your surroundings, it is as though the *spirit within* is masked by 'smoked-glass' and your spiritual perspective is tinged by the equivalent of smoked-glass.

I had better explain! If you react to someone via their surface vibration and via their 'vehicle' (which is more deeply entrenched in the effects of the Fall than the spirit within) then there is a signal of irritation from that person, no matter how sweetly you believe that you love them or react to them on a God-level. If you are reacting only *surface to surface* your perspective is tinged by the effects of the Fall, or the effects of that 'smoked glass' that has been put around your true angelic perception. As a result of that, on a spiritual level, you pick up that *something is wrong* because, as the angel you really are, you *know* at your core that the vibrations of this planet and the vibrations of every construct on this planet are difficult, twisted, skewed and are not harmonious with the *you-within*.

So, reacting surface to surface and *outer person to outer person*, you receive back a signal that says at some level deep within your core that *here is frustration; here is anger; here is antagonism*. That is why it is so difficult, person to person and surface to surface, to actually sustain and maintain harmonic relationships one to the other because, if you choose to emanate from the surface only, you are emanating the effects of the Fall that the other person picks up as being skewed and you are receiving back *identical signals*. Now these signals strengthen the effects of the Field, and they also make it next to impossible for you to view the person as they really are, to react to them harmoniously and to provide around them the Light that they need in order to rise above the effects of the Fall.

Similarly, and *particularly* at this time, there is disturbance that you receive via your physical ears, as the vibration of matter necessary in order for speech to be projected and received is a skewed vibration because of the effects of the Fall. So, every word, no matter how sweet and *seemingly* harmonious, has encoded within it the slightly skewed, off-kilter vibrations of the Fall. This should explain why so many of your negotiations fail because, once again, you are projecting towards others via your speech (no matter how well-meant) an intention that says one thing but *feels* like another to the angelic being receiving that pattern of speech. Similarly, their intentions, transmitted via speech, carry with them a disharmony that is picked up by your physical ears so that you have on the one hand the *true* meaning from the person and on the other *the carrier-wave of distortion* that is a result of the effects of the Fall.

If you touch something with your physical hands and with your finger tips, you are feeling, *yes*, perhaps the intended perfection of the piece of furniture, the building, the fabric or whatever it may be, but encoded within that piece of furniture, that building or that fabric is also the skewed vibration of the Fall. The piece of furniture, the aspect of the building or the piece of cloth is, in effect, on a physical level, *at odds with itself* because it cannot decompose itself and it cannot restructure itself according to God's law and angelic law. It cannot, therefore, be in harmony with itself (as we have explained in other conversations) and it cannot degrade totally as it is intended to (dependent on the will of those who have created it) because of the effects of the Fall that have trapped matter between creation and destruction. Therefore, the signals that come back to your fingertips, via whatever it is you touch, are *mixed*. They contain a signal of beauty and perfection but also, intermingled with that, they contain a signal of frustration and of agitation of matter because agitation of physical matter is what happened at the time of the Fall. So...

What you *see* comes back to you with a distorted message beneath it and through it.

What you *feel* comes back to you with a distorted message beneath it and through it.

What you *hear* comes back to you with a distorted message beneath it and through it.

Also the air that you breathe has, within its molecules, that same agitation, and so it nourishes the body to a *certain extent*, but it also invades the body with that slight distortion that you read as aggravation, as frustration, and as a need for speed. Do you see how you are victims of the Fall on a physical level and to what extent the Fall influences and infiltrates you?

You cannot, on a physical level, remove yourself from the effects of the Fall.

...On an angelic level you *can*.

And the message that we have tried to give you over the four books is one of projection and recognition of Light because, in projecting Light, you reach into the core of the person you are projecting the Light to. You receive Light from a similar vibration because Light attracts Light and harmony attracts harmony. In all your dealings with people – in all your speech aimed at people, in the things you listen to and in the things you want to see manifest – you have to react from *within* ...or whatever you send to that person or that situation *eventually* degrades according to the effects of the Fall. It degrades to the point where it becomes part of the Field's 'armoury' or energy and part of that distortion.

You have to wield God-Light in order to change things *permanently* – and I use the word 'permanence' with regard to God-power rather than to your vision of permanence on Earth. When you love someone, the only way to love them *totally* is from the God-heart, otherwise you will find irritation, aggravation and frustration in them. When you love yourself you have to love yourself from the heart or you will find aggravation, frustration and a feeling of inadequacy with yourself. You have to love *unconditionally* to reach beyond the effects of the Fall. When you love unconditionally you become a channel for God-Light that reaches beyond the bubble of Fall-energy and beyond the bubble of Field-energy. ...**You bring in God-permanence.**

That is not to say things will not change – things have to change according to God's nature, but **God Is**, and it is the *God Is* that *isn't* on Earth at the moment. You need to bring the *God Is* into all your dealings with your brothers and sisters; you need to bring the *God Is* – the Light that is – into every word; you need to bring the *God Is* into every constructive thought; you need to bring the *God Is* into play within the people you wish to influence away from the Fall. So, you have to visualise the *God Is* within the people in positions of so-called power. You have to visualise the *God Is* within the people who antagonise you – in fact, within the people who antagonise you the most, because they have the worst effect on you and they are the ones who are capable of strengthening the barrier of physicality between you and your ability to wield the Light outwards.

Everything that you perceive on a physical level has been *tainted* – has been tainted by yourself and the other angelic children who caused the Fall. When you begin to realise this, you react to life in a different way. You react to life as though you were beaming out Light through your words, through your vision, through your touch and through every aspect of you to others and to the Earth. Beaming out that Light allows you to become a 'searchlight' and the Light from within acts as a searchlight to illuminate, in any situation that looks grim, *the truth* of that situation; to illuminate, in any person, *the true angelic core* of that person; to illuminate, in any aggression, violence, fear or frustration, *the true angelic immortal aspect* of that situation, and to bring it out and 'charge' it (as though you are charging a battery) within the situation and within the person …**and that is how you will *escape* from the effects of the Fall.**

Realise, reading this book, that if you react from the physical mind and from the physical surface *only*, then you will receive only frustration, only confusion, and only a 'maze' where there is, in reality, a straight path. **You have to think past *physical* thought.** I would say this to scientists and to the most logical of you because the scientific and logical mind, for the most part, is more deeply steeped in the effects of the Fall than any other type of mind. It self-congratulates itself and says: 'I have got it! I understand it! I understand this world and I *know* how it works. I will not see anything beyond the physical senses because I have reasoned out that *there is nothing beyond the physical senses.*' What a trap, what a confined space and what a 'locked room' is such a mind!

The heart-mind needs to rule again! The heart-mind infuses everything with Light, infuses yourself with Light, infuses your surroundings with Light and infuses the people that you connect to with Light.

The heart-mind brings reality. I say to the scientific and to the logical mind, 'You are measuring the Fall via *vibrations of the Fall* and you feel that is all there is. You have sectioned yourself off from your immortal creative ability. You have sectioned yourself off from what you once were *and still are*, and you have fallen into a 'steel prison' or a 'windowless room' with no escape *until* you embrace the Light. **Until you embrace the Light!** You think you are measuring reality, but I say to you that you are measuring an illusion. Reality is waiting for you but you need to reconnect to it, and to do that you need to open the physical mind to Light and open the physical *heart* to Light. Open the door to your full consciousness – not partial consciousness but your *full* consciousness – and you will begin to perceive things differently.'

I hope today's chapter goes some way to explaining why there is so much violence in the world. We have talked about the lust for power, which, of course, comes from the physical mind and the physical body, but you are living in a vibration or wavelength that also promotes and seeks violence. The most logical and scientific mind might say: 'I am *beyond* violence. I am not a violent man. I am not a violent woman', but the agitation, the frustration, the depression, the pain, the misery and the fear that you feel at times are *there* because you are picking them up on a surface-level from the effects of the Fall and from the illusion around you. You live *literally* in a violent society, a frustrated society, and in a state of matter that cannot exist and *yet does* (to your physical perception) and that cannot be changed when approached from a *physical* level.

It has to go! It has to change! *You* have to extricate yourself from it, but you can only do that by looking *within* to the well of Light that is available to you, by infusing yourself and everything that emanates from you with that Light and by perceiving that Light ...*and nothing other than that Light* ...in those around you.

A simple theme today, but perhaps the most difficult for the Fallen to appreciate and to understand. Please enlighten *me* further by asking your questions.

David: Joseph, you discuss this 'smoked glass' – are our senses what you are talking about in that case and part of that 'smoked glass', which is a filter through which we see, hear and feel everything?

Joseph: It is as though you have sunglasses for the eyes but also for the ears, touch, taste and smell, so you are viewing the illusion or 'film show' from a distorted point of view. Everyone else is viewing it from a distorted point of view too, and those distortions determine how you react to this world and how you react to each other. Many cannot *help* the violence that they put out and the violence they sense because they have *no idea* that there is anything beyond the 'smoked' reality that they are sensing, seeing, hearing, touching and feeling.

The intention of this book is to promote the blossoming, once again, of Light into the world, into society and into individuals so that the smokiness: the Field ...the *distortion* disappears. It will not disappear if *one* person wields the Light (although personally that person will be able to see through a glass *clearly*), but for every person that decides to wield the Light, the Light becomes a stronger force within the 'smoked glass 'of the illusion until such point as the illusion *has to* change because there is not enough of that vibration feeding itself any longer and the vibration disappears. The vibration disappears, harmony is restored, spiritual memory is restored and the Fall, as quickly as it was 'switched on', is *switched off.*

Because the Fall was the decision of the Fallen through *free will*, the end of the Fall has to be a decision of the Fallen through *free will*.

This is why we cannot manifest amongst you wielding Light into dark corners to change the Fall *ourselves. You* have to realise that you are looking through a glass darkly, *you* have to realise that you can wield the Light and change things and, lastly and *most importantly, you have to do it*

...today...

...or in a million years...

...or in a hundred million years...

YOU HAVE TO DO IT!

You have to decide, Reader, at some stage in your infinite existence, that you want things different to the way they are now, you want harmony restored and you want to get out – out of the illusion and out of the density of the physical senses that you have at the moment. And at that point you change things ...but only *you* can do it! Only *you* can lift off that smoked-glass shade ...and you do it by wielding Light and putting Light into *everything* that you do. Does that answer the question?

David: Yes. I presume that it is a two-way effect, isn't it? Not only do we give the wrong information out but we can't receive the right information in the opposite direction, can we?

Joseph: It is always a two-way effect in that through... (I was going to say 'no fault of your own' but that is *totally* the wrong phrase) ...because you are ignorant of what has happened, if you react through ignorance on a surface-level *only* (however well-intentioned you are) as part of your emanation of vibration into the Whole, you send out, via your surface and densest vibrations, *a code* that harmonises with the vibration that exists as a result of the Fall.

So, unless you are totally immersing the messages, impressions and intentions that you give out in Light you are *maintaining* to some extent (maybe only to a very small degree) the effects of the Fall because you are harmonising with them. Not only that, but the other person has a subconscious choice of what they choose to pick up from you. If they are also ignorant of the Light, then they are picking up *what they expect from you* on the surface and from your physical mind, so those are the vibrations they pluck out of the messages you are emanating; those are the dominant vibrations. They, therefore, help to maintain the distortion of this illusion as a result of the effects of the Fall by strengthening, feeding and perpetuating the skewed vibrations that allow this illusion to exist as it is.

I hope that I have shown you the difficulty, but also the *ease* of changing things on your level of consciousness. There is a great difficulty because you are enmeshed in complexity (which we have spoken about earlier) and part of this complexity is that you expect and you almost... (I don't want to say 'desire') ... you *anticipate* difficulty rather than ease. You anticipate aggression rather than harmony; you anticipate fear rather than comfort and, therefore, you attract to yourself, promote, nurture and allow to blossom, *similar vibrations* from the *conscious* whole of the illusion that you are immersed in. I say 'ease' because you can change this now, – initially on a personal level and then on a Global level, by infusing your intentions with Light.

And you might say, 'Joseph, how do I do this?'

In a morning you simply align yourself with the *God-within* and with the *angelic without* (i.e. the angelic host that are not part of the Fall) and you pray that your intentions, your emanations, your projections, your prayers and your imaginations throughout the day are infused with God-Light and that, if they are not so, you will be advised of this, through your intuition, so that you can redress the balance and, to the best of your abilities, wield the Light throughout that day. Similarly, before you sleep at night you ask that you be taken to an area of replenishment as a spirit and as an angel – an area of pure Light and harmony – so that, when you are pulled back into this illusion in the morning, you have recharged yourself with a high vibration that will infuse all your actions and make a difference to yourself and others during the day. Is that a sufficient answer?

David: Yes, thank you.

Jane: Joseph, could I ask something that relates to devas and the channelling of Light-energy? We were told in a previous chapter that the devas were angels that prepared an area for us and weren't part of the Fall or part of humankind but simply created the physical structure. I wondered why the devas couldn't channel in sufficient God-Light to sustain the planet and, thereby, prevent the need for the Earth to eventually to go into cataclysm through lack of sufficient energy. Why isn't it possible for the devas to channel it directly?

Joseph: If there was not a backdrop of mountains, and skies, and rivers, and streams, and continents, and oceans, and contours, and light, and shade, and the flora and fauna of this level, the Fallen would find themselves in *complete* darkness with nothing to react against. There has to be a 'stage' in order for a 'play' to play itself out and there have to be 'props' and 'costumes'. There has to be a matrix against which experience can be measured and appreciated.

The deva-mind is here *through free will* as a backdrop against which the free will of the Fallen can work itself out until such time as it resurrects itself into the Light. Were they not to be here, there would be *vibration without form*. You contribute to the maintenance of form as you see it by recognising it as form. You see a mountain and you accept it is a 'mountain' and, therefore, the mountain continues to exist. If you had no backdrop against which to act out your play of discovery and *rediscovery* of who you are, where you are going and how to change things, you would find yourself (because of your weak *surface* ability to create) in an area that was, not a no-thing area, but an area that was *insufficient* for your requirements …insufficient to allow you to recognise yourself and others and to examine the vibrations that you find yourself in. So, the deva-mind and the mind of humankind are inextricably linked in the normal order of angelic creative expression so that **one creates the backdrop against which the other experiences.**

There is a great kindness in the deva-mind in the providing of this backdrop of Earth against which you can react, recognise yourselves and recognise each other ...and, eventually *please, God*, recognise your origins. There is a great compassion and a great love but the deva-mind does not consider itself to be 'trapped' as you understand it. The deva-mind sees this as necessary in order for you to experience, and would not expect your praise or any recognition of what the deva-mind is doing. The deva-mind is simply harmonising *at core* with who you are in order that *eventually* you escape the illusion. The angelic forces outside of the sphere of the Fallen are doing exactly the same. They are pressing against the illusion to allow communication to take place, to allow recognition of who you are to take place, but they do not consider this to be a 'noble' act. They consider this to be the *normal* rather than the *noble* act in order to reconnect with those brothers and sisters who seem, for a time, to have immersed themselves in a play that has no end.

You must stop thinking, if you can, in physical terms of *what a pity and how terrible*. You must concentrate instead in terms of *there is a situation, that situation needs to be remedied and this is how we do it*. You must also understand that the deva-mind is more easily connected with its Source than you are as an angel of the Fallen. So, although the deva-mind needs to stay here *partially* to create and recreate the backdrop against which you live and move and have your being, there is a portion of that deva-mind that is connected to the greater angelic host that *indeed* brings through that harmony in order to maintain the backdrop that you see, because behind, through and within the texture of the mountain, or the stream, or the river, or the tree there is the *purity* of deva-creation. Without that purity the illusion would collapse into a soup of half-realised projects and half-formed, half-destroyed realities. The deva-mind exists to create the backdrop in the normal course of universal angelic creativity so the deva-mind is maintained and guarded, *honouring* the planet. It is only the surface of everything you see, in relative terms, that is polluted by the effects of the Fall. Do you see that?

Jane: Yes. In the past you said that the Earth was running out of energy because it wasn't pulling in God-Light energy.

Joseph: And so it is.

Jane: And I just wondered why the devas' input of God-Light energy doesn't sufficiently keep sustaining the planet and why the balance is eventually tipped.

Joseph: The devas maintain the backdrop, not the collective mind and not the collective illusion. **The devas maintain the stage-set and not the adventure.** Do you see the difference?

Jane: Yes.

Joseph: And they are not allowed to sustain the adventure – *you* are sustaining the adventure.

The complexity of this particular question is an example of what is happening in millions of minds around the world now – the seeking of *complexity*. **Seek simplicity!** Seek the source and, in seeking the source, you change that energy, which is the very energy I have been speaking about today – that aggravated energy that says, *Why this? Why that? Why is it like this? Why can't it be like that?*

It is what it is until you change it – individually and globally. **It is what it is until you change it!** ...And you change it through accessing the Light, not through complexity. Do you see?

Jane: Yes, thank you.

Joseph: Is there a final question?

David: When someone wields Light is there a chance that other people (for want of a better phrase) have a 'cloudy vision' in that they reject it, or does it always get through to some core-part of a person?

Joseph: The important thing to remember about Light or *any projection* from a human being is that it seeks out, harmonises with, locks onto and engages in a two-way conversation with a vibration of *similar* intensity. If you project Light towards someone that Light emanates out and reaches in towards the core of that person and harmonises with the Light at the core of that person. **The *head* may reject the Light but the *core* responds to the Light.**

What is needed is a projection of many points of Light into those people who seem most enmeshed in the effects of the Fall so that their core is receiving Light …and Light …and Light … and *Light* to the extent that that core of Light becomes the *dominant* vibration that the person is able to perceive in their *conscious* mind. At that point they change, but until that point that Light is never wasted. You are feeding a 'battery' and you must also think to yourself: 'I am preventing that person from sinking any *deeper* into the mire of the illusion.'

The message of this communication and the whole point of the books is to ask *each* human being to consider that they are mighty 'warriors' for the Light and part of a mighty 'army' for Light, and that in wielding Light, even if they cannot see immediately the effects of having sent out that Light, **they eventually change things.** At best they keep the people and situations that they are sending Light to from sinking further into violence, into anger, into frustration and into confusion.

The best case scenario is that *enough* of you remember who you are and then *everyone else* will remember who they are because the amount of Light that you broadcast cannot be ignored, at that point, by the core of each person bringing in vibrations from this illusion. At that point each person cannot ignore the Light that exists, the reason it exists and the choices in life that exist that they will not have considered up until that point.

Light is never wasted.

You can reject it on a *physical* level, but that doesn't mean you send it back to the person wielding it. You may reject it but it gets through because that is *what you are*. You are only rejecting it with this thin 'persona of physicality' that you believe to be you because of the effects of the Fall. You do not, and never would, reject it, at core-level because you rely on that to perceive your angelic universe and you know, as an angel, that that Light is what you are. You know that you are connected to it. You know that you *are* it. You know that you breathe it in and give it out as a natural part of your angelic existence. The head may say, 'No, I don't want Light! I will not have Light!' but the core says, **'Feed me!'** The core says, **'Thank you!'** The core says, **'Bless you! I need that vibration, I grow through that vibration and, ultimately, I remember through that vibration.'** Is that a sufficient answer?

David: That is excellent. Thank you.

Joseph: Before I finally let Michael go, I wish to underline the *urgency* with which these communications need to come through. I am not without sympathy for the amount of energy that it takes out of you all, particularly out of Michael ...**but the time is at hand!** The time for *change* is at hand! The time to *tip the balance* (if it *can* be tipped) is at hand! Certainly the time to *illuminate* as many souls as possible is at hand ...**before the *great change* comes that we have talked about for so long.**

The worst case scenario is that you will elevate a great many souls. The best case scenario is that you will elevate *everyone*, but my urgency, and the urgency of the brothers and sisters who work with you, which I hope you can feel (not just Michael in the vibration of my voice and of my being, should indicate that there is not an infinite amount of time left in which to deliver this *hope* and this means of salvation.

Therefore, I am grateful for and will try to organise further opportunities for communication so that you can then, with our inspiration and help, address the serious business of making people aware of this information *worldwide*. It will roll forwards and will expand but it is not yet complete. **Each book has been a section of the complete message.** It is almost there but there will be a leap forwards once this book is completed because it will be sensed by those who can sense such things as **A COMPLETE MEANS OF ESCAPE.**

Chapter Thirteen
Civilisation

Joseph: I wish to talk this afternoon about *civilisation*. The word 'civilisation' when applied to the Earth plane always amuses me because it infers that there is something *civilised* about the organisation of society. We have spoken in past chapters about patterns and about the ripples of the Fall that continuously manifest themselves in the endeavours of humankind. They manifest themselves in the endeavours of the individual, but they also manifest themselves in the endeavours of society *as a whole*. Society builds itself on dreams and has its foundation in a dream of *organisation*, in a dream of order, in a dream of harmony between its members, and in a dream of expansion of consciousness and capability.

Unfortunately, because humankind residing on the Earth plane draws its source of energy from the Field, civilisation has built within it the *seeds of its own destruction* as the dreams of civilisation and of advanced and expanding society are fuelled by the Field and not by the greater consciousness. In other words, if society is built from an angelic standpoint then it can expand and evolve, and can bring itself to a point where it becomes an opportunity for others to travel through as a means of expanding *their* consciousness. If civilisation is built, from the standpoint of the Earth, from humanity dreaming, those dreams come not from the heart-mind but from the head-mind. And, because of that, the construction of society is from the first *flawed* and contains within that dream of expansion and construction **only**

the vibrations of the Fall – vibrations which are negative, vibrations which hover between creation and destruction (being neither one nor the other) – and eventually into the dream of civilisation come the individual dreams and lusts for power, which in themselves hark back to the effects of the Fall.

It may surprise readers to learn (although I *have* mentioned it in an earlier book) that civilisation, through the repeating pattern of destruction as an 'echo' of the Fall, **has brought itself to an end at least *twice* on Earth.**

You might ask me why I cannot access information from *before* those first two civilisations fell, and I have to explain that the reason I cannot do that is because, the further I go back in records, the *murkier* things become from the point of view of having to disseminate the vibrations of the time. You see, our records are not like yours – they are not words printed on paper. They are a vibrational record of *that which has been*, but the vibrations are still very much alive – as are, indeed, the circumstances within those vibrations. The consciousness of the individuals involved has moved on, *yes*, but when you revisit the records you revisit the actual *time*, the actual *premise* and the actual *desire* held and suspended within the vibrations that allowed those circumstances to manifest themselves. As we therefore visit, in a 'library' as it were, the vibrations or circumstances of the past, it becomes more difficult the further back we go into the history of civilisation within the circumstances since the Fall. So it is *comparatively* simple for me to access details of the civilisation that existed before this one. It is slightly *less* easy for me to access vibrations of the civilisation before that one. But when going further back, the information is there but is *extremely* difficult to read (and certainly for me is next to impossible) because of the heaviness and depth of the vibration that surrounded that civilisation at the time of its Fall or its 'topple', because civilisations *topple* again and again here due to the effects of the Fall.

I can, however, with my hand on my heart, tell you that yours is not the first *advanced* civilisation on Earth – and by 'advanced' I mean *technologically* advanced (I wish I could say *spiritually* advanced!). At the time of the first civilisation that *I* am able to access, going back twice from yours, there was a great deal more spirituality about everyday life because, although the civilisation drew, as its foundation stone, from the effects of the Fall and, therefore, from the Field of human energy, that civilisation was closer in connection to the time before the Fall. It was closer in connection to a time when, as we have seen in this book, each inhabitant of the Earth plane knew it was an angelic being and so there was a greater *subconscious* memory of the state of affairs that existed before the Fall took place than there is now.

Let us take one civilisation step forwards so that we are now talking about the civilisation that existed before *this one*. There we have an incredibly technologically-minded and capable civilisation, but with not as much spiritual-seeking, awareness or investigation as the civilisation before it. The reason for this is that that civilisation is further away in terms of time on Earth from the Fall than the one before it and, therefore, there is less of a memory of the spiritual time and spiritual capability that preceded the Fall.

We now step forwards to the present civilisation and we have, from my point of view, a very *brittle* construct – something that could shatter at any moment (as we have investigated throughout this series of books). This civilisation, for all its *supposed* religious advancements and for all its groups that so earnestly (*or so they say*) seek God …**is the civilisation with the least spiritual mindedness, outlook and outreach *of all* to date.**

So far are you away from the beginning of the time of the Fall that (and this is a theme that has also run through my previous books) **you *cannot* remember who you are or why you are here.** The state of affairs that brought you here you have forgotten, and who you are and who you *were* before that state of affairs occurred you have forgotten *completely*.

This civilisation is built of 'wet clay standing on sand' and it will take only the slightest nudge, only the slightest power-play from one quarter, or only the slightest further imbalance in the input of a cohesive society for this society to topple.

...And topple it will unless the right thoughts are put into it, unless that 'sand' is turned into 'concrete' and unless that 'clay' is fired and becomes immutable. And the way to compact and strengthen that foundation stone and to fire that clay into something that is tough and lasting is through, as we have said all along, **the transmission of Light from the heart-minds of every man, woman and child around the globe** into the current society to 'de-pollute' it and to resurrect it in God's image, in the angelic image, and to resurrect it in the form that it was meant to be in and *was in* before the Fall took place.

Timelines are not important to me. You will have questions regarding dinosaurs; you will have questions regarding pyramids, and ancient civilisation and its form and function, but I am not concerned with those things. I tell you *simply* that this is the third time in *spiritual living memory* – in other words, from the viewpoint of my group soul – **this is the third time that civilisation has reached this peak and this crisis point.**

And you *do* stand at a crisis point...

...If things don't change then society will change by toppling down, and it will be as though a feather lands on a boulder and shatters that boulder. It is a cumulative effect – negativity here, there and everywhere pouring into society reaches a crisis point at which things vibrationally shatter and then have to lie dormant for millennia whilst the Earth recovers from the effect of having been attacked, abused and insulted by humankind.

There are others above me and beyond our frame of reference, who can and do look back further than the civilisations that I am able to view from *my* vantage point. Their purpose is not historical exploration but to assess what happened and to look at ways of ensuring that it does not happen again. From them we receive inspiration and instruction as how best to pinpoint the trouble spots around the Earth and generate Light into them.

History repeats itself!

You say that as a phrase on Earth, 'History repeats itself.' History, I say to you, is about to repeat itself again *unless* you put energy into the matrix of society from the right source – from the source that is able to transmute that which is now so brittle.

If civilisation is once again brought to its knees and you are brought to a point where the Earth cannot sustain you and society cannot exist as it exists now then, at that point, (if you have not realised who you are and why you are here) you will enter a non-world ...not a non-existence... but a non-sentience where you will not be able to relate to the 'physical' stimuli around you. You will be placed in a 'holding area' of the spiritual spheres and you will sleep... and you will *sleep* ...until such time as the Earth has repaired itself and the devas have evolved a suitable physical form to house you once again so that you can re-experience physicality on the Earth and work out, *hopefully*, the effects of the Fall individually and as a group in order to escape the binding vibrations that surround you now.

If your children are caught up in the end of society then each of them has a *choice*. Each of them, on return to spiritual consciousness, can either move onwards or can be placed in the holding area we are talking about. If they have not sufficiently educated themselves to the point where they can recognise the spiritual spheres ...**that inclusion in the holding area or stasis will be *automatic*** as there is nowhere else for them to go! If, however, they have enlightened themselves to the extent that they recognise who they are, recognise why they have been on Earth and recognise that there is an enlightening, beautiful and expansive journey ahead of them as an option – a journey through the spiritual spheres towards escape – then they can *choose* to opt out of that return to stasis and move onwards.

Our mission at the moment is two-fold:

Society hangs in the balance and we urge you to bring Light into the world as *we* do, to bring Light into your *own* heart-centres, to bring Light into the heart-centres of *others* and to join together to negate the effects of the Fall on society that have happened at least twice before.

We also come to urge you to discover your spiritual heritage; to dig it out, examine it and to become harmonic with it; to decide what you feel is correct with regards to what happens to you following physical death; to seek it out, to examine it, to ask the questions that you are at present not asking.

So, we are 'hedging our bets' as you say. On the one hand we are attempting to flood society with Light before it is too late for this *current* matrix. But we are also urging each of you (*you owe it to yourselves*) to examine and rediscover your spiritual heritage; to seek out through the heart-centre what *feels* right for you; to ask us the questions that we would be delighted to answer regarding your spiritual, angelic origins ...so that **whatever happens** you are one of those who will have tried to change this world and will have tried *successfully* to change yourself and to peel away the centuries, not just this lifetime, but centuries of solidification of physical matter around your soul so that you can rediscover your angelic beginnings, your immortality and your amazing potential as creative aspects of God.

IS IT TOO LATE?

Is it too late for this society?

As I have said before if all of you joined together today and...

[Long pause due to interruption of the postman putting mail though the letterbox.]

...sought actively to illuminate this world then it would change now; it would reunite itself with the rest of Creation and society would transmute. The negative aspects of society would disappear *now*. Despair, and fear, and grief, and violence, and famine and torture would all disappear *overnight*. Isn't that what you want? Isn't that what you talk about, 'If only this world were a better place'? **You have to make it a better place.** So, if you join together now *en masse* the world will change.

...I promise it!

...I guarantee it!

If you don't then society will *end*.

It is *your* choice – as it was your choice to enter into the state of affairs we call the Fall. **Your choice!** It is *always* your choice. Do you want things to change? Then you have to do something, and there is pressure on you to do something *now* before it is too late for this particular set of circumstances.

If it is too late for this particular set of circumstances what happens to those who eventually reincarnate?

What happens to them is that, *likely as not*, they repeat the pattern, we accompany them on their new journey *spiritually* through their intuition, we surround them with love, we infuse them with Light and we pray that *this time things will be different*. But remember, they bring back into that new civilisation they will form *the 'echoes' of the past civilisation* that they were a part of. They bring into that equation a memory of physical things from their previous incarnations and so, if they invested *strongly* in politics, or power-play, or commerciality, or physicality, or materiality ...then those are the dominant traits in their new physical mind and they have to struggle from the heart-mind to overcome those traits *or history will repeat itself.*

If you were hoping in this chapter for details of the civilisations that have gone before I am sorry to disappoint you. I am not here to entertain! I am here to point out the current state of affairs, to explain why the current state of affairs is so *grave* and to give you (...all of us, here, seek in our millions to give you...) **a way out** ...a glorious way out, an illumined way out, both here on Earth and in the spiritual realms that surround and interpenetrate the Earth.

The way to reconstruct society and civilisation is to be, at once ...and *at last, civilised* – civilised from a *spiritual* perspective; civilised in the way that you treat each other; civilised in the way that you treat each of your daily tasks; civilised in the way that you dream your future dreams; to honour and respect each other; to honour and respect the God within and to love endlessly and totally every person on Earth despite their reaction to you in the short-term.

If you act as a Light-bringer in a *civilised* way you will bring 'civility' to civilisation and the world will change.

Are there any questions, please?

David: It sounds simple, but all it needs to start the ball rolling is to make a decision, isn't it?

Joseph: This is the single most difficult concept for someone, immersed in the ways of the Earth since the Fall, to grasp. Increasingly your society pushes the burden that should be on your *own* backs onto *someone else's* back. It is, from our point of view (having lived here for quite some time) a very strange state of affairs to not want to be responsible for your own actions, to not want to be responsible for your own world and to always push away from yourself that which is yours by right and by design. It is the simplest of concepts, as you say, but it is the most difficult of concepts from the point of view of someone steeped in the ways of the Earth to the exclusion of *any* spiritual possibilities ...**but it is the only, only, *only* way to change things.**

The change that has to come – whether it comes now or in millennia when civilisation has reinvented itself *yet again* – the change comes from **you** ...from you thinking, acting, loving in a different way.

From *you*, Reader! From YOU!

...And now, please! *Now* please! NOW!

I am already *away* from the Earth sphere – *away from it*, although I weep for it. I think not of myself but of *you*. It is you who will suffer, not because of any judgmental God, but because of a re-investment in a mistake – not a 'sin' but a mistake. Eventually you have to be mature enough to realise that you *make* mistakes and you *made* a mistake. And if you realise that you made a mistake you then have the ability to say: 'Well, that was a mistake – how do I *rectify* that mistake within myself and within society?'

...And you do that by absorbing and emanating Light, which is what you *are*.

Does that answer the question?

David: Yes.

Jane: Joseph, if we all *en masse* sent out love and Light so violence and fear and all those things disappeared, would we also change the physical molecules of the Earth?

Joseph: Yes, you would. You would transmute the matrix of the Field. Rather like cleaning a room that is full of dust or fog, you would take out that 'dust' and 'fog' and fill the 'room' (which is the Earth) instead with Light so the room is a completely different place.

Also you would find that your bodies, which are now so susceptible to disease and decay, would become lighter and you

183

would become more elegant in form as you became closer to your angelic form as a physical manifestation. You would transmute the molecules of your body so that disease would no longer be able to take hold of you because you would not be holding on to those thoughts that cause the disease any longer – thoughts that are fuelled by the Field in a vicious cycle.

You would transmute the Earth itself, by eliminating, as it were, the top layers of structure, heaviness and compactedness, and you would allow the creations and constructs of the devas to shine as you would shine. In doing so, you would not only eliminate violence from your own human-to-human interactions, but you would also eliminate violence from the animal realms, because what presses on the aspects of the deva-mind that exists to serve you is the violence and corruption from the Fall from humankind. So, your animals are influenced, at their base level and their most physical level, by the *supposed need* to exist through absorbing the energy of other animals. With you transmuting yourself and the world you also *release them* from those layers of violence and complexity that compel them to destroy other physical lives in the mistaken supposition that they need to absorb power through those means.

So, yes, you transmute the Earth but first you transmute *yourselves* and, in an ideal scenario, as Light pours into this world you will find a decrease in the number of cancers and in the number of people who suffer from hardened arteries and problems with the heart. And, indeed, one of the signs that you are being successful in changing things will be a decrease in illness. That will be one of the *first* signs because your bodies will become steadily healthier and you will remain younger for longer as Light begins to be effective in transmuting those bodies.

I fear I must, at this point, end the communication. I thank you for your patience in circumnavigating the adverse vibrations that sought to cut the communication earlier, and I am *delighted* to tell you that the bulk of the book will be completed within six chapters.

Chapter Fourteen
The Separation of Male and Female

Joseph: The theme of this afternoon's chapter is *separation*. As a result of the experiment that, as we have seen, went so badly wrong with such devastating consequences, the immediate effect on humankind – on the souls that were trapped within the effects of the Fall – was a *severe feeling of separation*. I want to elaborate on this, and I want to say to every man, woman and child reading this book that every time you feel alone, every time you feel that there is a missing piece within your life and every time you feel that there is a need *unfulfilled* – **that sense of loneliness and incompletion is due to your sensing separation from God.**

The experiment was originated by the angelic children that created the Earth, but that experiment went *against* the natural flow of creative energy that comes from the Godhead. Therefore, by its very nature, being of a different vibration than the vibration of the Godhead, it has set itself apart from, blocked out and pulled down a 'curtain' over God-consciousness. God-consciousness remains within you because *it is you*, but it is masked, hidden and imprisoned rather than being the open and conscious experience that it should be.

There is a *greater* consequence to the effects of the Fall too. The effects of the experiment separated, on *this* level of earthly consciousness, the male and the female. It separated the two elements that work in harmony to create, destroy and rebuild ...

and, as a consequence of the Fall, you – *each of you* – was split in two. Each of you, as an angelic being, is a delicious and wonderful blend of male and female. However, because of the Fall experiment you can only exist *on a conscious level* as opposing poles rather than a harmonious integration of the two creative energies. So, each of you manifesting as a physical being has only half of yourself reflected in that physical being.

Now is it, therefore, possible that you exist as two people at any one time?

Yes, it is!

…And those two people are a male and a female and are not always the same sex in each successive incarnation. You will not always be male and your other half will not always be female, but always there will be a male or female counterpart of yourself that, when re-integrated, will lead you to becoming the angelic being that you once were. At times one of the two halves will be in the spirit realms, at times both halves will be on the Earth plane, and at times both halves will be in the spirit realms making the decision as to whether they should travel forwards or return to the Earth plane. Let me then expand on this last concept to give you another view of the effects of the Fall and of getting out of the effects of the Fall:

Not until both halves of the angelic being agree that they must move onwards *do* both parts of the soul *escape* the pull of the Earth.

In other words, there are now, at this present time, souls that exist within our realms who are waiting for their counterparts on Earth to agree to move on into the spiritual spheres and away from the effects of the Fall, and until they do so that other half – the soul that remains in the spiritual realms – *must remain* in the spiritual realms waiting for the other half of itself to agree to take the journey. Only in completeness can the soul move onwards into Infinity.

I said that this would be a book of revelations, and the revelation I have just given you gives you some idea of the *difficulty* in extracting, from the effects of the Fall, those angelic beings that were a part of it. It is as though, quite literally, you can be in 'two minds' with regard to whether you wish to revisit the Earth plane or journey onwards back into Infinity and back into your total spiritual heritage.

How can this be possible? How can you be two people at the same time?

Well, to make this easier for you to understand, we have examined the fact that you are all part of the same thing, that you are all part of God, that each of you exists as a facet or viewpoint of God with the illusion of individuality and yet is an integrated part of the Whole of the Godhead. This is what is happening on a smaller scale with those angelic beings, who are trapped as a result of the effects of the Fall. The two halves of each angelic being exist as two individual viewpoints and yet that angelic being embraces both soul-fragments. The next inevitable question, therefore, is:

Is there a re-integration of the two halves as both decide that they will journey onwards into Infinity?

In the spiritual realms, *initially*, there is a growing together in harmony and purpose (as you see in the actions of group souls), but, as those two souls grow closer together and closer to Infinity, there comes a point where they *re-integrate*. This must seem like a scary prospect to some of you reading this book, as though you are going to lose half your mind or lose your personality, but, as we have always said when discussing the fact that you are part of the Whole yet individual at the same time …**this is not going to be so.** Your angelic heritage and consciousness is *vastly* different from the *shoehorned-into-a-physical-body* consciousness that you find yourself experiencing as you read this book. Your angelic consciousness is able to function as both halves of the equation *at the same time* or as an integration of

187

the whole equation *at the same time*. It is also able to function as *part* of the rest of the angelic host as an *individual* and also as the *whole* angelic host at the same time.

It is a concept that is difficult for you because you have distanced yourself from it. You could say it would be like you having a *playful* version of yourself ...and an *angry* version of yourself ...and a *thoughtful* version of yourself ...and a *sleeping* version of yourself ...and an *active* version of yourself ...all these things are aspects or facets of you as an individual on Earth – and yet they are not individual beings. They are all parts – aspects – of you, and you visit them at certain times during your experience of consciousness as a linear journey.

It is the same with you as an angelic being: there is the female half of yourself and there is the male half of yourself, and the angelic being is the integration of the two. The two function as individuals and also as a complete unit. They are both parts of the same thing; it is just a matter of you switching your viewpoint from one to another or choosing to experience *both* at the same time.

The effects of the experiment were *far-reaching* and that experiment, which is *still* in progress, does not allow matter to be completely and purely created or completely and purely destroyed. It exists in a kind of stasis or semi-creative state, but as a result of that semi-creative state any body or physical being that exists within that sphere of being is polarised and has to exist as either a male or a female form. Before the Fall there was no need for physical reproduction and before the Fall you would take on the form of a physical body from the ether around you and then discard that physical body when the time came to end the adventure and return to the Whole – to the angelic host and to the Godhead – for a time.

Now on a physical level the creative act is *necessary* to polarise the next body that will be put forwards into the sphere. The creative act is necessary to give either a male or female 'spin' to the body that comes next so that it can house either the male or female side of an angelic being. It was not always so. It is because, when you exist on this level, you have to react within the confines of the experiment and have to behave and exist within the matrix of the experiment that causes matter to be expressed in a certain way.

This splitting of being and purpose is a reflection of matter not being stable. It is as though each angelic being, spilt into two, is warring against itself and that the female form is only *partially* effective and the male form is only *partially* effective. It is in re-integrating those halves that you get the creative ability you had *originally*.

If only it were that easy!

If only you would look on the other half of yourself with open arms! But the effects of the Field have served to push those halves *further apart* over the ages. There has always been the barrier between men and women and always been the *seeming* inequality in the abilities of men and women whereas, if male and female were to come together harmoniously, you would re-create your original ability **...which is an ability to create perfectly and purely.**

Am I then saying that if you take on board the information within the books that we have made available there will come a point where you re-integrate as male and female into one cohesive whole? Well, *yes*, I am saying that, but that would be a point in the *far* future as you would judge time from a physical viewpoint.

First of all there has to be the creation of harmony and Light upon the Earth plane to restructure the atoms of the Earth and the atoms of physical bodies and, therefore, at a certain point, bring back the elevated thinking and creative ability that you had as angelic forms. **It is a slow process!** It is, hopefully, a *rapid* process to bring the *Earth* to a stable position, but after it has been brought to that stable position there has to be a period of adjustment during which the physical mind remembers and recovers its original capabilities. At that point you would see a gradual re-introduction into a physical level of beings that were whole, that were neither male nor female but *both* and had that wonderful harmony of mental capability that comes from drawing on both aspects of yourself *equally*.

Of course, we are talking about great changes in physicality when ...*and if* ... that happens, but happen it would as you are not (and I stress this) **you are not naturally only male or only female but are a combination of both** and your abilities have been divided. 'Divide and conquer,' you say on Earth, and that is a very apt expression because there is no better state of affairs for the Field to prey on than the fact that you are split into 'two minds' quite literally. The Field says to women that men are less than perfect ...and the Field says to men that women are less than perfect, and it emphasises the divisions and differences between the two sexes when, in effect, the two creative energies *need* each other to become united **to progress, sanctify and** *change* **the Earth.**

There is a great deal of talk at the moment about elevation and 'ascension'. *Ascension* **is not a physical thing.** You cannot take a physical body and lift it to planes that it was not designed for, but you can 'ascend' in the sense that there is a re-integration of creative capability. If all goes according to plan and Light is poured into the Earth, this will be seen in unities and harmonies that have not been witnessed before. When the male and female forces are present in any organisation or group and are working in tandem and harmony then you see great growth and positive effects as the outcome of that group's endeavours.

This will be your signal – things are slowly returning to how they were if you see groups emerging that are successful in a kind, harmonic and ecologically-sound way, and eventually those groups will join together – just as group souls in the spiritual realms 'join together' (in a manner of speaking). You will see that grouping together of purpose around the Earth and then *at that point* you will see a transformation in the physical body, you will see a transformation in the physical Earth and you will reach the point where angelic beings can once again 'walk' amongst you and 'inhabit' the Earth, as it were, in order to undergo an adventure and gain experience that they can take back to the Godhead.

I would ask you to bless both the male and female aspects of physicality. I would ask you to accept that one needs the other, that both are part of a greater purpose and greater capability of mind and creativity and I would ask you to consider, in your quiet moments, that your feelings of separation from life, from an energy that you feel you have not found yet, from a state of mind you feel you have not found yet, from a peace, harmony and happiness you have not found yet **...stem from the fact that you are only half the being that you once were** – at least on a physical level. On a level of elevated consciousness you are still united (and on a physical level you are still united but cannot sense it). I ask you to consider that, at one point in your infinite spiritual existence, you will re-integrate with the other aspect of yourself (be that male or female) and you will from that point move onwards into Infinity as a re-integrated being. Not only that, but, as part of a group soul, you will re-harmonise with, work efficiently with and be totally integrated with other members of that group soul.

I hope you can see that the migration of souls towards Infinity brings you towards greater unity and greater harmony ...re-integration on an *individual* level as you understand it ...then on a *group soul* level ...and then a moving onwards to a level where group souls re-integrate with *other* group souls. You are becoming 'yourselves' again, degree by degree, so that when you *all* emerge into Infinity, away from the effects of the Fall, you will be the whole, angelic creative force that you were before you decided to steep yourselves in the experiment that has resulted in your being of two minds ever since.

Lots to think about, but I would invite questions on what is a complex subject. I hope you can see that in this book we have, little by little, revealed pockets of the truth about your origins and I hope that we have slotted into their correct position within the book, truths about yourselves that reveal more about who you were, what went wrong and what *now* needs to be done.

Jane: Joseph, on the level that you are at, are you now re-integrated with your other half?

Joseph: No. I am aware of my other half and I am able to function for part of my time in the delightful experience of alternating points of view. In other words, I am allowed to spend part of my time either communicating with that other half or *being* that other half. The 'tie that binds' (...*there* is an appropriate phrase) becomes more binding and integrated the higher up the ladder of re-integration, purity and remembrance you go. Also, to illustrate that further, I have to say there is a *special* bond with my 'other half' that is more integrated than the bond I have with the members of my group soul – and yet that bond with members of my group soul is also totally committed. It is a matter of *sensing* and of *feeling*.

I should mention that it is very important to say to the readers of this book that **they should learn to love themselves.** The Field doesn't want them to love themselves; the Field wants them to remain rather ashamed of themselves, as though there is something quite wrong with giving themselves affection. Why I am saying this at this point is that, when I regard my other half, I am loving *myself* – I am loving the other aspects of myself that are missing to some extent and that serve to make me whole.

So, it is important that you should cultivate love for yourself – there is nothing wrong with that. You should immerse yourself in the concept that it is not only *good* to be you ...**it is a wonderful thing to be you,** and, by doing that, you draw to yourself your 'other half' and those aspects of yourself that may seem missing from the Earth matrix at this time. To look at yourself darkly and to say that you are less than capable, less than loving and less than likeable actually *strengthen*s the effect of the Field around your split individuality. It makes it more difficult for you, in sleep state and subconscious state, to reunite with your other half and draw *from* and donate *to* that other half the energies that each of you needs to operate as a more *complete* human being and a more complete member of the angelic children. So, it is extremely important that you allow yourself patience, sympathy and love at steps along your journey. It will also prevent you from attracting illness or disease to yourself **because 'dis-ease' comes from being *ill at ease* with yourself.**

So, *yes*, I am aware of my other half, I am integrated at times with my other half, and that integration increases in conscious time the closer we get to the Infinite or that step out into total re-integration so that we can once again take up our mantle or persona of an angelic being.

I also have to tell you that, at that point when you step out into Infinity, these millennia will appear to you as a 'blink of an eye', as though you put a foot in mud and have now taken that foot out, washed it and are continuing your journey. It will be as though it had *never been*, except that the effects will be there to examine and to bring back to the Godhead, because the Godhead learns not only from creative harmony, but also from the missteps that were taken along the way.

The overwhelming desire from beyond the effects of the Fall is, yes, that the angelic children involved in the Fall escape from that experience, but also there is a desire to *love* those souls – *you* – out of that experience. There is no judgement for you because it was not a 'sin' or crime but *an experiment*. There will be great joy when each soul has escaped the effects of the Fall, and also when the effects of the Fall can be *examined* so that younger 'teardrops from God' or 'rays of experience' can have access to that record of the Fall so they can *hopefully* decide (they have always the right to decide either way) that ...**that is not an experience that needs to be undergone again by *any* creative force.**

Is there another question, please?

David: Joseph, much of what you have said this morning explains why so many sexual taboos have been brought about by religions, and I presume that is the effect of the Field. Currently today it is suggested that women go into things like business and take part in what was once a masculine world, and at the same time men are being given the opportunity to look after children – is that an actual step forward or is that just another trick of the Field?

Joseph: The Field literally plays with people's heads and it ties up its 'denizens'. Put simply, the role of men and women – the two *seemingly* opposing forces – is to love each other and is to have respect, appreciation and understanding of the other. Male and female are not opposites, they are reflections that have within them certain skill-sets that have become divided due to the effects of the Fall on Earth – skill-sets which, when brought together, bring forth a creative whole – a pure and effective creative being.

It is not so much the roles of male and female that have become skewed, but the *perceived* need of the male and the female to adopt the role of the other and the discontent with the vibrational skill-set that is either male or female. It is important that a woman in this particular life loves being a woman (and remember that it can be an alternating process, and in the next life they might be a man) and it is important that the man loves being a man because, in doing so, they then have access to the skill-set that has been given to them as part of their God-capability so they can make the most of that skill-set in any situation to bring forth love and Light to children, to colleagues and to the Earth. At the moment that is not happening so you have a terribly discontented populace and a populace that is not sure what it is *but knows that it does not like what it appears to be.*

We have talked about dispensing Light ceaselessly into this physical plane and it is time for us to also say that **you must treat**

yourself with Light too. In your meditations, prayers and endeavours to change this world, you must also bring the luxury of Light to yourself and envelop yourself in Light because *you*, too, need to be nurtured, nourished, happy and harmonious. In bringing Light to yourself, you can actually begin to see the way and that the attributes you think are not enough **are *actually enough*** for that half of you that you happen to be at this time. In loving them, you draw to yourself the other half of your attributes during subconscious endeavours and sleep-state and the both of you ...that may physically be continents apart... can operate more *effectively* because you have accepted yourself as you are.

That does not mean that you should not strive – please don't get me wrong on this. Of course you should strive, of course you should be creative – being creative is what you are. But you should accept yourself ...accept that you are male ...accept that you are female ...accept that you have certain personality traits and *love* them. Love the things within yourself that you see to be right, and love the things within yourself that you see to be wrong. In doing so, you transform your consciousness and you strengthen your angelic consciousness, which then flows through, not only *you* as a man or a woman, but through *your other half* as a man or a woman too, because **whatever you do, and however you strive, you affect your other half.**

It cannot be otherwise. Just as you affect humankind totally by every thought and every deed, you also affect, on a more immediate level, your other half as an angelic being because you are more closely linked to your other half (from the viewpoint of you being a single angelic being) than you are with other souls. So every choice, every perception of self – whether you love yourself or whether you hate yourself – affects your other half and affects to a lesser extent (but still an effective extent) every other soul on Earth.

So the choices that you make in sending Light out to the world and other souls are extremely, *extremely* important, but equally important is your self-perception and the way you treat yourself. When you treat yourself with Light you are treating yourself with the acceptance and love that God has for you, and you empower yourself to be able to send out Light to a greater degree to your brothers and sisters and to the Earth. Also, by accepting yourself and accepting the role you have with regard to your vibrational skill-set, you empower your other half. Does that make sense?

David: Yes. So, really, when we ask for Light we should first think of ourselves as an individual, then think of ourselves as one of two halves, and then think of ourselves as everyone else as well.

Joseph: That is well said! It is simple multiplication and that is the way you should approach your prayers, and you can then bring back that multiplication, as you come out of your meditation for Light, to the *Point of One*, which is God. In other words, do not withdraw the Light, but withdraw yourself from the image of the continents that you are (for example) bathing with Light …withdraw yourself from the image of the town that you are bathing with Light …withdraw yourself from the image of the friends and relatives that you are bathing with Light … .withdraw yourself into the image of yourself that you are bathing with Light … **and then give up all to God.** In doing so you keep the flow going into every situation and you also replenish yourself with *life-giving* energy, ' life-giving', of course, from the point of view of the physical body. **If you would heal the world – start with healing yourself.** Also, through drawing in Light to yourself you heal yourself of those ills that you suffer from on a physical level because the Light is more powerful than any of those ills. Is that sufficient?

David: Yes, thank you.

Jane: Joseph, just following on from David's question – gay men often seem really kind, gentle and nice, as if they are embodying the feminine and the masculine. Is that so?

Joseph: That is an excellent observation and it is *exactly* right. What you are witnessing is, to *some* extent, a re-integration of the two powers.

Now, doesn't that turn on its head what your religions say *should* be thought about two people of a 'similar vibrational intensity' that come together, for example? You trample on that concept as being 'wrong' because you only view it from a physical point of view. From a spiritual point of view that concept comes about because the people who exhibit that different approach to physicality have actually understood far more about themselves *on a soul level* than most people do, and they are, in fact, experiencing a blending of the two forces or two aspects of self.

Is it not true that many of the people who are regarded as 'different' in that way are *highly creative* and accomplish great things? …So do many other people… but in particular, if you are looking at that aspect of your society, you can say that many have gone into a creative area, they are involved in art, and beauty, and colour, and form, and it is because of their realisation, at a level within themselves, that there is another part of themselves to be embraced.

The barriers between male and female will not come down overnight. It has to be a gradual change, but the barrier that I would take away from you today is one of your perception of being individual and within a 'walled castle' that no one else can tear down and become a part of. That is not the case, and in the integrated and spiritual society that awaits you (if you project Light as we have suggested you do) will come the realisation that you are **each a part of the other**.

We have spoken today about the other half of yourself and that you will attract that other half to yourself, but there is also the fact that you are a part of each and every soul that you meet … or don't meet… whilst you are experiencing physicality. That is a tearing down of barriers, that is a new way of thinking, and

197

that new way of thinking must come if the effects of the Fall are to end and this Earth is to be transformed. That is the *ascension* we are talking about. **It is ascension of physical mind through permeation of spiritual energies – that is ascension.**

There is no escalator *physically* to a higher level of being. I want to make that straight ...and I want to take all the books that talk about ascension in that way and I want to *burn* them.

I want you to consider what has been said: **ascension is to do with integration of spiritual heart and physical mind.** Ascension is not an 'escape' from this Earth – not in the sense that most people think it is when they look at that word. It is to do with the re-integration of spiritual heart and physical mind that brings with it remembrance of who you are, that brings with it a renewed expressing through yourself of your spiritual abilities, and that brings with it a way out of current difficulties.

Ascension is not a state of being that is for some and not for others. It is not as though you can get on that 'escalator' and leave all the other souls behind.

Why would you wish to do that?

Ascension is an acceptance and remembrance of who you are and a sharing of that knowledge with everyone else ...so that *every soul* can, spiritually speaking – not physically speaking – put their foot on that 'escalator' and emerge into a remembrance of their true heritage.

Chapter Fifteen
Karma and Creative Cycles

Joseph: The purpose of the remaining chapters of this book is to give you a means of altering the situation that you find yourself in, and that is what I would like to lead into today by first reminding you (or first telling you, if you haven't read the other books) that **every experience you have as a spirit and as a human being is 'circular'.** You set out from one point on a circle and you guide yourself through a series of circumstances that then return you to the start-point with new wisdom and with the *correct* expenditure of creative and destructive energy – because all you should bring back to you, from whatever experience you go through, is the *knowledge and history* of that experience.

With any situation – be it an emotional one, be it a creative one, be it a business opportunity – whatever that situation is, as you go forwards into it you build whatever you need around you to experience the full potential of that set of circumstances. Then, as you pass the half-way point of the circle, you deconstruct the circumstances around you so that when that energy-wave gets back to you (or you return yourself to your original position) you will have absorbed into your consciousness and wavelength *the effects* of the experience you have gone through but *none of the constructs*. You will have observed and absorbed the implications and results of the experience you have gone through but, at that point, you should not have any surplus energy that has been used either in the construction or destruction of the circumstances around you as you come back to your start-point.

That is the nature of existence throughout the universe.

God is circular in nature.

...And you, as another viewpoint of God, are also circular in nature. Whatever you embark upon is a circle of energy or a pulse of energy that emanates out from you and grows; you immerse yourself in it; it then reaches a midway point and shrinks away in materiality ...and you return to your original start-point having absorbed the opportunities, implications and expansions of consciousness that the journey brings to you. I now have to apply that circular motion to your physical existence as an angelic being living within the effects of the Fall.

The Fall is a circle of energy and you are, in effect, trapped within that circle of energy ...but it is a circle of energy unlike anything else in the universe because *this* circle of energy cannot *complete* itself. It cannot divest itself of the materiality around it that has been used to create it. It is steeped in heavy matter and so, instead of a circle that brings you back to a point of God-consciousness, it is a circle that brings you back to another point on the *same* circle, which then expands again. This is because of the effects of the Fall on creation and destruction – you are sandwiched in an area of reality that will not allow the normal function of creation and destruction to take place.

As an analogy: you have set off from a very quiet area of life – perhaps you are in a beautiful park somewhere – and you head towards a city with the best of intentions, and, from the beautiful countryside around you, you now find yourself surrounded by roads and the odd building. As you go deeper into the city, you find that there are skyscrapers, more densely-packed buildings and all of the furnishings of city life around you, and it becomes denser ... and denser ... and *denser*. That, in the normal course of events *spiritually*, would be perfectly alright, but, as you try to get out of the city, you find that the buildings do not thin as they should do to take you back to the countryside, and that you are dragging along with you some of the rubble of the city. You are surrounded by its grime, bricks, traffic lights, cars and roads and, try as you might to get out of that situation and back to your wonderful start-point in the beautiful park ...you can't because you are physically dragging with you the effects of the journey that you have set out upon.

Originally, before the Fall, when you set out on this circle you completed the circle and came back to a point of total God-consciousness from the viewpoint of an angelic being without any of the material trappings. In the normal course of things, as exists in other spheres of reality on other planets and in other areas of this particular physical universe, you complete the journey and you have within you the 'jewel' of experience of that journey.

Not so on Earth because of the effects of the Fall!

You bring yourself back to the start point and your *only* option, if you are not sufficiently spiritually aware to remove yourself from the cycle of the journey, is to start out again. But you start out again not from a point of view of being totally *released* from the last journey, but from the point of view of having aspects of the last journey bolted to you as though you were wearing a backpack and carrying heavy bags and luggage. You are setting out again with baggage from the previous journey in your hands, already colouring your experience of the next journey that you are undertaking. Now I hope that this explains, very simply and very logically, **why karma exists.**

Rid yourself of the view that karma is something that is piled upon you by a God who wants you to evolve! Rid yourself of the view that karma is something that is piled upon you by the Lords of Karma because they want you to evolve! **God wants you to return to the start-point and return to Him and *nothing more*.** Your karma is caused by *you* embarking upon the same cycle again ...and again ...and again. Your karma is simply detritus from the past journeys you have undertaken heaped upon your back **by you** because you are unable to rid yourself of those historic memory molecules that cling to you whenever you set out on a journey in physicality on the Earth plane because of the effects of the Fall.

When *we* enter this level of reality karma also applies to *us* to a certain extent, and we are *very* reluctant to spend an extended period of 'time', as you would understand it, on a physical level, because the molecules that were attached to us as part of the uncompleted journeys we undertook whilst we were on Earth begin to cluster around us again by magnetic attraction.

All karma is simply the 'dust on your sandals' of previous journeys.

The reason that your journey brings with it so much accumulated rubbish is that you, on a subconscious level (as we have said in previous chapters), *still believe yourself to be right* in having chosen the path that you wandered down in creating the Fall and its effects.

What I want to suggest today is a way of illuminating your path so that you complete the cycle. I want to suggest something that will perhaps seem a little alien to you at this point, but I want you to look at the words and the meaning behind them and try to absorb and appreciate what we (not just me, of course, but millions of souls in the soul group) are trying to impress upon you:

Into *every* situation in your life you should bring Light from beyond this particular realm of existence.

Remember that you are a multi-dimensional being and, as an angelic being, you could enjoy multiple experiences at once and experiences from different planes of 'reality' at the same time. Although you may, as a physical and a mental being, be *trapped* within the confines of the Fall ...**you as an *angelic being* are still able to operate on multiple levels of existence and from multiple** viewpoints. Therefore, you still have access through your heart-centre to your ability as a God-being. You still have access to everything; it is just that you choose, through your physical mind, to have access *solely* to the limiting parameters of the Earth plane.

So, we are suggesting that you inject Light into *every* situation in your life on a *daily basis* and that you start your day by going to your heart-centre. By moving your point of consciousness down from your physical mind into your heart-centre, and by remaining there for a few moments, **you flood yourself with the white Light that *changes* things.**

So, before you set out upon your day, imbue the situations that you find in your life at this time with that Light. If you are experiencing a serious illness ...flood the molecules in the areas of your body affected by that illness with Light.

If you are undergoing mental stress, perhaps it is a work condition or something imposed upon you by family, friends or colleagues ...flood the circumstances of that stress with Light.

If you are suffering from a perception of yourself as being weary, old and lacking in energy ...flood that viewpoint of yourself with Light.

...And, in doing so, you *reconfigure* the patterns of the molecules and atoms on a mental and physical level that are part of that situation; you reconfigure them so that they can carry out the purpose for which they were manufactured, which is to bring you an experience, to take you through that experience, to dissipate so that only the experience is left and to disappear back into the wavelength of energy so that they can be used again to provide new experiences for new souls.

We talk a lot about Light in this book and in the other books in the series, but what we haven't touched upon too much is the fact that you, Reader, need to escape this plane and escape 'reality' as it is at the moment.

In order to escape reality as it is at the moment you have to rediscover your ability as an angelic being.

...That may seem, through the filter of physicality, to be a momentous and unobtainable thing to attempt, but it isn't. It is simply a matter of switching your perception to seeing everything in your life as being a circle ...your emotional experiences ...your material experiences ...your expectations of life ...the way that you are physically ...the way that you are mentally ...**all these things are cycles of energy**. If you immerse those situations in Light on a *daily basis*, not only will they bring you the experience that they are *supposed to* bring you so that you can progress in the understanding of everything, but they will also ease their grip on you if they appear to be negative. They will conclude that much more quickly and you will be completing your circles of experience in the *correct* way, which will liberate you from the effects of the Fall in your thinking and understanding.

In other words, if you practise what we are suggesting you do on a daily basis, you will *lift* yourself out of the effects of the Fall because the heaviness of matter around you, mentally and physically, will begin to fall away. It will allow you to see clearly so that the words in this book and in the other books will make perfect sense to you from *within*. At that point you are liberated from the effects of the Fall, even though you will still be living on Earth, and you will be a soul that has elevated itself beyond the limiting effects of the experiment that went wrong so long ago.

Of course the next stage is to spend time in your daily spiritual approach to God and yourself bringing Light into the other 'circles' that you see around you.

I hope that I have explained sufficiently in this and former chapters *why* the negative effects of the Earth seem to repeat. They *are* repeating. What happens in any situation on the Earth plane is that it does eventually run out of energy because of the effects of the Field and, in running out of energy, the cycle begins again ...but the cycle brings with it the detritus of the past. So, you might have a situation on Earth where there is a great war that takes place and millions of people are returned to the spirit world, millions of people are injured and your buildings, property and possessions are destroyed. Eventually the conflict runs out of energy and, at that point, people say: 'We have had enough of this way of life! We want peace and we want to build a new society. We want to build a new approach to society *and this time it will work!*'

No. It will not!

It will not because it doesn't have Light in it.

...What it has in it, as the means of constructing that new society, are the molecules of the Fall. So, you are drawing on the molecules of the Fall that cannot completely, beautifully and perfectly *construct* and cannot completely, beautifully and perfectly *destruct*. Not only that, but you are starting off with the karmic effects of the cycle of war that you have just left behind, so you are building into your hopes of peace ...*the destructiveness of war*. You see how messed-up your creative abilities are when you are creating only from this level of consciousness? You are drawing up into your aura molecules that are already polluted that you will then send out again ...and so the cycle continues.

The cycle continues in so many different areas and this is why the noblest of intentions on Earth don't work. They work for a while and then they become swamped by the effects of the Field *around* them, but they also become swamped by the effects of the Field *within* them. You are using a finite amount of energy and that energy is polluted.

To give an increasing chance of success to those organisations that are coming from the right place and using the God-within as a basis for their projection of society in the future, you have to immerse them in Light every day. In doing this you transmute the karmic molecules that are around them from past cycles so that what they are creating is imbued with more God-Light than with Fall destructiveness. In doing this you lessen the grip of the Field and the effects of the Fall on the noblest of intentions.

So, your daily projection in all areas of your life has got to be one of *lighting* the way ahead through Light-projection … lighting the way ahead for yourself …lighting the way ahead for those around you …lighting the way ahead for the organisations and individuals on a global level who are trying to make a difference in the right way. They need your help and they need your help *now* if things are to change for the better and not for the worse.

I hope this also explains why so many things in life seemingly repeat in a negative way …the illness goes away and then comes back …the pain of loss goes away and then comes back …the anger goes away and then comes back …the perceived lack of finances and materiality goes away and then the problems return. They return because you are setting out on so many circles that you have set out on countless times before. **Countless times!** You are on 'the treadmill of life' *literally* and you are walking the same paths that you have walked so many times before. Those paths will only change *when you make a move to change them*, when you accept them for what they are and remedy them with *spiritual* medicine **…with Light from your higher self.**

You have to break the cycle …or, rather, you have to bring each aspect of your life to a successful conclusion in that you come to a point with each aspect where you are brought back to the start-point of your journey, but with the added experience of having passed through the set of circumstances …set of circumstances emotionally …set of circumstances mentally…set of circumstances physically. When you return to the start-point and all you have with you is the history and enhancement of having gone through the experience, but without the physicality and materiality, then you liberate yourself from that cycle and you are free to move on into more exciting areas of creation and destruction.

And, should you choose to return to Earth, you will be in a world that makes more sense to you spiritually than it has to this point. Our hope, of course, is that you will choose not to come back, that you will recognise the cycles in your life and will step away from them into the Light. It is as simple as that – to make the move into the Light and say: 'I can see my life for what it was. I can see the missteps that were taken. I can see the cyclic nature of it. I can see why I keep putting myself back into those cycles of existence ...and I decide at this point to move away from them.'

Do you see now, with regard to the life review that we mentioned in an earlier book *[reference to **Your Life After Death**]*, that that review is not a judgement but an *opportunity*? The life review exists to enable you to look at the missteps and to see the patterns and cycles, which are pointed out to you by the people that are around you to advise you in the spirit realms. The life review is there to free you, but some of you are so steeped in the cycle and so used to, quite literally, 'going around in circles' (because that, after all, is your nature as an angelic being) that you look at the life review and see not the things that have been going wrong but an opportunity to put them right from *within them* ...which can never be *unless* you bring with you back into a physical existence the Light that is needed in your body, is needed in your existence, and is needed to illuminate your steps through physicality.

I suggest to you at the end of this chapter that you try to love *all* experiences in your life – whether they appear to be positive or whether they appear to be negative. In a perfect or angelic existence your experiences are neither positive nor negative, but are a mixture of both that exist in order to bring you experience.

You push yourself into certain experiences through the habit of lifetimes and you will find that there will be a *bias* in each experience with regard to which of the molecular rays is prevalent in that experience. You will find that there are certain ones that seem to have too much positivity in them and certain ones that seem to have too much negativity in them. These cycles repeat when, if they were balanced, you would get out of them a supreme amount of satisfaction without the suffering and the things that appear to go wrong because the creative balance is out to either side.

I have spoken for quite a while this afternoon and there is quite a lot for people to digest, but is there something you would ask me, please?

David: Joseph, in the life review where advisors try to point out the pitfalls in a person's life, I can't understand what would draw them back into another life here!

Joseph: It is something we have mentioned in the previous book – our shock, sadness, exasperation and frustration when people decide that they wish to re-inject themselves into physicality. With successive lifetimes it is as though the person develops a 'thick skin' (literally) of base matter and yearning for that base matter around themselves because that is what they have invested in as being the ultimate reality. They look at their physical life and see, within the darkness and difficulty of it, opportunities for *conclusion*. You could say that the recognition of an opportunity for conclusion is recognition on an angelic level of everything having a cyclic nature and, by design, having to come back to that start-point. The end-point and start-point have to meet.

It is a distortion of angelic intent that draws souls back into physicality. It is the recognition within the life review of the opportunities that should have been within the cycles they have been living within. They are so tuned in to that physical and mental vision of life *only* that there is a powerful pull back into that to conclude the circle, but there is not the knowledge that **the circle needs to be *changed*** that comes from having a higher spiritual understanding.

In other words many, many souls have lost their way and have lost their angelic-being viewpoint and, therefore, choose, because of that blinkered view of *what is*, to re-immerse themselves in physicality due to a subconscious desire to complete a journey that they know must be completed. **But that journey needn't be completed in a negative way and needn't be undertaken *here*.** There are ways to complete the cycle, to adjust energies and to bring back experience that are *outside* of physicality, outside of the Earth plane and outside of the effects of the Fall. Unfortunately, no matter how persuasive our arguments, many people choose to come back and many people lose the angelic perception that they have at the point of the life review.

We cannot push them beyond their point of understanding and beyond the point of volition and desire. Do you see that? It is complex, but your statement of frustration at why anyone should come back is magnified a thousand-fold by ours. And remember that we must not start a *cycle of expectation* and so, in 'sitting' with someone (relatively speaking) in a life review, we have to remove from ourselves and dissipate into the Light any expectation that this particular soul or that particular soul is going to choose a return to physicality rather than joining us on the less dense levels of reality that lead to escape from the effects of the Fall.

Jane: Joseph, with karma and the repeating patterns, to what extent do they repeat? Say, for example, if somebody died of starvation or they were really poor in one life would they come back to the same thing? On the other hand, if someone had a positive life and was involved in the arts and creativity, would they come back and do positive things?

Joseph: They will come back into the same *expectation*. They will come back into a set of circumstances that will deliver the same experience, but not always by the same means. Each soul has around it a finely-tuned reservoir of 'karmic detritus', if you will, that is tuned to them. So, in one life the person may starve …in another life the person may be starved of affection …in another life the person may be starved of material success ...in another life the soul may be starved of what it perceives it needs on a mental or emotional level. The same pattern can occur, but bring towards that soul different physical circumstances in order that the same cycle may be gone through.

Remember also that around each soul is an army of souls working to elevate that soul and make that soul aware that it can transmute its karma through Light, whether that Light is *conscious* Light-infusion into their life or whether that Light occurs through a gradual realisation that there is a different way.

With regard to creativity, the lesson in a creative life is more rewarding, perhaps, and that lesson allows souls to see their ability in manipulating physical matter. The *danger* in a life like that is that they become trapped by the need to create *physical* matter and a love of the objects that they have created ...to the extent that the objects become an anchor point in existence for them, and draw them back because they want to create more of the same or expect to be surrounded by exactly the same objects when they reincarnate into physicality.

So, it is balance in all things that we seek. It is the illumination of life in all circumstances that we seek in the souls that are undergoing the life review. It is the ability to give souls the means of freeing themselves from the cycle of partial creation and partial destruction by illuminating all circumstances in Light that is most dear to us, and *ultimately* to get souls to the point where they say: 'I can step away from these cycles. I no longer need them and I collapse them!' It is as simple as that ...*I collapse them* ...but, on a physical level, you invest so much into the circumstances (be they positive or negative) and you invest so much into the illness, you invest so much into the acquisition of money and you invest so much into the *expectation* **that you fuel the cycles.**

You don't realise that the simplest way, on an angelic level, to conclude the circle is to say: 'I have had enough of this! I conclude those circumstances. They are no longer a part of me and I withdraw myself from them.' That doesn't mean you have to withdraw yourself from them *physically*, but you withdraw from them *spiritually* so you no longer fuel them with power and they collapse. They may not collapse today; it might take a week or it might take a month, but they *will* run out of energy because you are not feeding them. So, you bring yourself out of creative cycles by refusing to be a part of them.

What we are expecting you to do on a greater level is to bring yourself out of the effects of the Fall by refusing to be a part of it ...by refusing to invest in it ...by restructuring it ...by giving it a spiritual spin through Light ...by saying: 'This is not what I am! This is not what I expect or want from the world! *This* is what I want from the world,' and putting in your vision of an angelic spirituality that is already yours but has become masked because of the effects of the Fall. Do you see?

Jane: Yes. It is great because it is so simple.

Joseph: It *all* is, children! It is all so simple! The complexity that you experience minute by minute...hour by hour...day by day... month by month...and year by year is of your *own making*. It is something that you immerse yourselves in, but is not the way of the universe, nor is it your way *at heart*.

I have to say 'at heart'...be young at heart ...be peaceful at heart ...be happy at heart ...be abundant at heart ...be spiritual at heart because *at heart* is where you connect to **who you really are** and heart ...to heart ...to heart ...to *heart* changes this world!

Chapter Sixteen
Forgiveness

Joseph: There is a word that has been bandied about in spiritual books and spiritual circles for a long, long time, and it is often looked at with some cynicism, or with trepidation, as though it is a word whose meaning is extremely hard to embrace and put into practice ...and yet this word is perhaps one of the most important words in this book, and I intend to explain why today.

The word is *forgiveness*.

Because of the effects of the Field it is extremely difficult to forgive; because of the effects of the Fall you find yourself operating from a position of physical ego and physical mind, and the physical ego and physical mind work together to *preserve* you as the physical being you appear to be. It is, therefore, very difficult to look past anyone's attack on you – be that verbal, mental or physical – because you seek to survive ...not to *be* ... but to *survive*. As a result of this almost everyone you come across is also seeking to survive, and so any perceived disturbance in the vibration that is sent towards you is looked upon as a threat and as something that needs to be put down, attacked or run away from. This is *extremely* important:

When you forgive you let go of the vibrations around you that are holding you to your idea of physicality and your idea of 'spirituality' on a certain level.

You see, because you are all one, you make connections minute by minute with those around you. Not only that, but you make connections with the present and with the past and, because you are living as a perceived physical being within a bubble of physicality, those molecules that exist and cannot be completely destroyed **still have power**. So, when you perceive something in the past that you consider to have brought you pain and upset, you *re-activate* those molecules that connect you to the event, which still exists within the bubble of the Field, and you reconnect yourself to those people who you consider to have done you harm. In other words, the inability to forgive (which is a cleansing process) actually *maintains* the effectiveness of the Field around you and ties you to those very energy points within the Field and within your consciousness from the present and the past, and those energy fields feed and maintain the Field and keep the status quo against you.

We have come to the point in this book where we are examining what must be done in order to rectify the effects of the Fall and, *above all*, what needs to be done in your personal life (and by 'personal life' I mean you as a point of energy perceiving the rest of your physical universe as an individual)… and what needs to be done *most* is to forgive.

…And you need to forgive on so many levels.

First of all you need to forgive *yourself*, because so many people suffer by measuring themselves as being less than perfect. Now that is a memory; you know you are perfect on a spiritual level, but on a physical level you *sense* that you are operating at less than your full capacity and capability, and so the mind interprets that as a feeling of inadequacy, of being less than perfect and of not measuring up to *you know not what* but you know it is there. You know that sense of lack and sense of less than perfection is there so you attract to yourself, around you and through you, powerful molecules that maintain that illusion of you being less than perfect and less than deserving.

After many years of revisiting these molecules and activating them in your subconscious time and again ...you attack yourself ...you condemn yourself ...you 'crucify' yourself, and this constant subconscious and partially-conscious attack on who you really are begins to degrade the physical body. This (tell your doctors, tell your nurses, tell your patients) is one of the prime causes of illness and of disease ...'*dis*-ease' with yourself ...'*dis-ease*' that you believe on a subconscious level you deserve because you are less than perfect, believing *everyone else to be* perfect and that you have not attained what they have attained.

The first point in rectifying your own position with regard to the Fall and your escape from it is to forgive yourself, is to be easy on yourself and is to let go of those beliefs and tendencies from the past that you have created, constructed, bought into and are maintaining. You have to let go of those molecules, you have to allow them to disperse ...and you *free* yourself from that perception of being less than you should be. **How can you be less than you should be?** The only area in which you are *less than you should be*, in physical terms, is in your perceived separation from God (which we have explained in earlier chapters and books), and your perceived separation from the other parts of You, in that the Fall gives the illusion of you being a self-contained unit – when of course you are not.

So, you have to forgive yourself regularly... perhaps *weekly*. Go into your heart chamber in your meditation and seek out those areas where you perceive yourself as being less than perfect and address those areas by saying: 'How can I be less than perfect? I am part of God. I am an angelic being. I let go of those untruths! I let go of those molecules. I will *never* revisit these areas and again believe that I am less than I should be, less than I can be, less than I am.' ...And in doing that you *nullify* the effects of those constructs you have placed around yourself.

Next you need to look at your opinions of the world. A great example of this is the Second World War, where people still believe that those they feel were instrumental in causing that conflict need to be punished and, following their deaths, say: 'Well, they have gone to meet their Maker now and I hope they are still suffering because they deserve to do so!' You have to turn around that concept of the ringleaders needing to suffer, needing to be judged and needing to be punished, and you have to let go of your concepts of who was right and who was wrong. In a sense, because of the effects of the Fall, any endeavour into which energy is put, which has originated from this level *only*, results in **you** *all* **being 'wrong'!** I am sorry, that sounds a terrible thing to say from your perspective, but I want you to examine that statement. You are all 'wrong' because you all lead to a point where someone who is more receptive to the effects of the Field can raise themselves up and drag you with them into conflict … and it still happens.

It is still happening!

So, what you have to do with regard to your judgement of conflicts from the past and your desire to see the people involved punished **is to** *forgive* **them** …is to forgive the whole conflict … is to forgive the whole struggle …is to let go of your memory of that struggle and deconstruct the molecules that are waiting around you and millions of others to be called back into action at some present or future time. Do you see that, in not forgiving, you keep around you and store in your 'pockets', minds and hearts the potential to repeat the exercise? Because every time you look at this world and say: 'What a terrible conflict! Look at what has happened in the past. Look at what needs addressing and punishing,' you *activate* those molecules, and those molecules vibrate at the same rate as similar molecules around other souls across the globe – and they have *power*.

They have power!

I will tell you something else: **the need for forgiveness on a global scale goes back to the time of the Fall.** It goes back to those memories you had before you became so immersed in matter that you could not remember, and it goes back to the time when you found yourself immersed in a physical plane, unable to get out because of the experiment, and said to yourself and others, 'What have I done? What have we done?' So, you have a conflict at your core, not your angelic core, but your *physical* core, that you have built up over lifetimes because of the effects of the Fall that bring you back into physical matter time and again.

That conflict is, on the one hand, you wanting to support your decision because you cannot believe on a physical level that you were wrong, but, on the other hand, you have this need to forgive yourself and to let yourself out of the effects of the Fall by letting go of those molecules that trap you within it. Do you see that? You created the condition which, on one level, you seek to maintain because you want to see through the experiment (as an echo of that impetus that took millennia to arrive at in the first place), but you also sense, on an angelic level, that you need to let go of those very molecules that you seek to constantly reconstruct and re-energise.

It all goes back to that term 'original sin' – or original *mistake*, – and you set yourself free from that original mistake by letting go of the circumstances that you still carry around you – circumstances that can do so much damage if you continue to energise them.

So, you need to forgive on a 'primal level', or the part of the Fall that still resonates within you. You need to forgive those circumstances from the past that you (and you may not even have been a part of them *physically*) still hold in judgement. You need to forgive yourself for feelings of inadequacy that stem, not from your physical life, but from your realisation on a subconscious level that you are not where you should be, that you have not done what you should have done and that you are capable of *so much more*. It is an echo from the time of the Fall and you need to let go of it. In order to free yourself from it, to rise above it and to be an example of how to bring Light into this world – **you need to forgive yourself.** Let go of those circumstances, realise that you are perfect and cannot be otherwise, realise that you attack, destroy and shackle yourself on a physical level because you are immersed in the physical level that you created, but find difficult to forgive yourself for.

You also then need to change your perspective regarding those around you. When you see people at work attacking you verbally, judging you, judging others or proceeding in a manner that is alien to you and which is harmful to them, you have to perceive in action their inability to stop re-creating around themselves the effects of the Fall. Remember that the core truth of this book is that **you are angels** and, as angels, you have the 'right' to constantly create because that is your nature – **it is what you are!** It matters not whether you think you are creative on a physical level or whether you feel you have a scientific, mathematical or artistic mind **...on the level of angelic being and angelic perfection you create *constantly*** so you have to create in the *right* way.

You have to forgive those who appear to be operating against you and against themselves, and to focus instead on the molecules that *you* are able to create by drawing them in from beyond the barrier of the Field. That barrier is only there because you perceive it as being there. You (as we explained earlier) have a choice that can be made *every* minute of *every* day, and that choice is:

...Do I bring energy to myself and to the situations around me in life that is drawn from the Field that is polluted energy?

Or

...Do I constantly strive to project energy that I have drawn in from beyond the effects of the Field that is God-energy; perfect energy?

If you do this and forgive on a primal level, on a personal level, on the level of the past and the level of your interactions with others **then you *shine*.** You *literally* shine and you draw in Light

217

that transmutes your physical body and your physical mind and transmutes the experiences of others who are drawn into your 'adventure' or physical life. You also increasingly then have the ability to, not only touch the lives of those around you in a positive way, but to shine out that Light into the darkness to begin to transmute the molecular constructs and the physical and mental attitudes of those around the globe.

To be a 'warrior for the Light', and to be one of those who turns the key that opens the door that lets in the Light for others, you have to first be able to forgive yourself, and you have to love yourself as what you are and what you were (which is what you *still* are beneath the surface). Before you entrapped yourself in physical matter there was no consideration of whether you were worthy, and [*laughing*] there was no consideration of *did you measure up against others*, because 'against' was a word that really did not exist ...there was only 'for others', 'by others', 'with others' and 'part of others'. You have to get back to that perception of yourself as simply *being perfect*. But again, at that point, the physical mind will come in and say that that is arrogant. No, it is not arrogance – it is fact! **You cannot be other than perfect because it is what you are.** It is not an attitude, it is not something that you are trying to impose on others ...it is what you are. You are perfect, but, in order to remember that you are perfect, you need to reach outside of the vessel that indicates to you that you are less than perfect ...and the way to do that is to forgive.

Forgiveness is freedom.

It will be difficult because you will say: 'Those around me do not share that vision. Those around me have a vision that is of the Field and, therefore, are violent, are distrusting, are argumentative, are inflexible, are arrogant, and there is no way that *I*, in forgiving *them*, can make a difference to them.' If you have read that sentence and agree with it you are still operating from the effects of the Field and not from the position of having forgiven yourself and drawn Light into your body to flood this physical plane with.

Read that again! Read that previous paragraph again, and if you believe that the people around you will not respond if you send them forgiveness and Light then you are drawing from the effects of the Field. Once you begin to draw from the effects of the greater reality, the *true* reality, the reality that is outside of the bubble that you have created (and permeates you even now), you will see that **every act of forgiveness is a 'blazing sword of Light'** held high for others to observe, to emulate, and to seek to 'hold' themselves to illuminate their brothers and sisters as to the true nature of God-reality.

So, on this day as you read this paragraph in this chapter, I ask you to examine the personal, social and global areas where you feel there is a need for change and where you feel that you hold in judgement either yourself, or your friends, or those around the globe, or those from the past, or those in government and, at that point, you have to examine those particular pockets of energy and seek to collapse, destroy and get rid of them.

There's a paradox, isn't there? Because at this point, due to the effects of the Fall, you cannot fully destroy those molecules ... but you can alter their spin, you can alter their charge and you can infuse them with Light so that around you and through you there exists God-Light. As a result of you being able to forgive *on all levels*, there is a beacon for the Light in this world and a point at which a difference is made, and a point at which there is an 'infection' of the molecules and constructs around you *by your Light* – and not the other way around. The normal course of things within the effects of the Fall and within the physical bubble of the Field is that you are infected by the molecules of the people around you, which you agree and harmonise with, and you re-infect people by what you give out and what you believe to be true about yourself and others.

You have to be the one!

Each of you has to be the one that is the 'One' – the *One* that you came from, the *One* that you are part of (and by the 'One' I mean the angelic children that created the distorted Earth via the effects of the Field). You have to be the one so that eventually you will be the *One* again that is re-infected by Light and is, therefore, elevated out of the bubble of reality we have called 'the Field' and that bubble of reality is deconstructed totally as the effects of the Fall *fall* away and you put away your experiment and say: 'Here I am – back again. I won't try that again!'

And then there will come a time when the word 'forgiveness' is no longer a word that has any power because you will have moved through the point where you forgive yourself, forgive your friends, forgive others and forgive the past to the point where you say: 'There is nothing to forgive!' ...And at that point you are drawing on your angelic heritage and are illuminating yourself and others to the extent that you see through the effects of the Field and rediscover that each person you meet is a facet of an angelic being and not what they appear to be on a physical level. [*Laughing*] We are advising you to move to the point where you join together and remember your *angelic* personality and see the construct personality of the Field fall away so that the very best of what you now exhibit is all that remains.

Not that you discard who you are and who you have been, but you recognise that what you project through the medium of the Field is polluted, is distorted, and is not who you really are or how you would really act. The angelic children who created the globe are polluted and poisoned by the effects of the Field and, therefore, act out of their minds. Each of the people you see who cause so much violence, so much trouble and so much disturbance are 'out of their minds', and by that I mean out of their heart-mind and into the physical mind that seeks (as a reflection of the needs of the Field) only to survive ...only to fight its own corner ...only to be safe ...only to dig its feet in ...only to be here tomorrow *for more of the same.*

Look at it this way:

You can be a reflection of the Field and be, in microcosm, what the Field is and you can reflect that mistaken need to survive.

Or

You can reflect that ability to be *All* – to be without worry … to be without famine …to be without pain …to be without illness – to be without by being *within* what you are.

Are there questions, please?

David: Forgiving is bringing in Light, isn't it? The physical mind, as you said, is a reflection of the Field and forgiving is dismantling it brick by brick.

Joseph: Yes, you are a 'deconstruction crew' taking walls and barriers down; you are thinning the sticky effect of the Field on your ability to *be*. The Field seeks to make you hallucinate and to make you believe that you need physicality and that you **NEED** – full stop. You need warmth …you need food …you need admiration …you need respect and, yes, you *do* need things on a physical level, but all you *really* need in order to manifest what you think you need **is to be who you are.**

It is so simple, but we can't explain it in *that* way to begin with as most people would see that as too complex an equation. We have to get you used to the idea that everything negative around you continues to exist and things don't change because you are accepting the charges that you have put into the Field and the dreams that you have created around you. We have to get you to begin to deconstruct, as you have said, those dreams. It may seem quite difficult at first, but as you practise this on a personal and global level then it becomes easier, and you will see the effects of it …you will feel energised and you will feel that *you* are in control of your *own* destiny and ability and not under the constraints of any other person.

The hardest forgiveness is the forgiveness of self. When you apply what we have suggested in this chapter you will find (if you are used to thinking in terms of physicality only and if you are one of those people who has a negative view of themselves) that the most difficult start-point is forgiving yourself because you have chosen, year in, year out, to construct around and within you a view of yourself as being less than perfect. You are the creator so, before you can apply a change to creation for the rest of humanity, you have to change the charge that is within and around *yourself.* That is for many people the most difficult point. 'I am not worthy,' you will say. Of course you are worthy! What else would you be except worthy? You created this whole world! See what you are capable of through a mistake! Imagine, therefore, what you are capable of if you are harmonising in accordance with the greater laws of Creation.

So, you have to spend time forgiving and reorganising your physical manifestation so you become a vessel for Light, which is what you have always been and still are. All you are doing is peeling away the outer layers and saying, 'I need these no longer!' ...And in doing that you *instantly* energise yourself and the benefits, even on a personal level, are *wonderful.* As an angel you have no illness or pain ...as an angel you have no worry for tomorrow ...as an angel you have no monetary considerations ...as an angel you have no lack ...as an angel you do not worry about death because death cannot occur to you ...**you are an angel.** You always have been and you always will be. *You Are –* you are part of *What Is.*

So, imagine! **Imagine – that is exactly what you need to do!** Imagine what your life will be like the moment you begin to be less demanding of yourself in a negative way. More importantly, imagine what you are then capable of in transmitting that view of reality you have altered back to what it should have been in the first place. Imagine what you are capable of by transmitting that view into the lives of others, not to control or brow-beat them, but to *illuminate* them so that they can then begin to grow themselves and begin to revert to what they were. When you illuminate the constructs around people, when you illuminate their heart and their soul and put into the Field enough Light to influence and alter one of the angelic children they then begin to respond to that Light – as a plant responds to sunlight. They begin to remember who they were and, in the measure that they remember who they were and who they are, they continue to charge the molecules around themselves positively and their life begins to change – as your life has begun to change.

They say *fight fire with fire*, but you cannot fight fire with fire. Fire is agitated molecules – how can you bring the two together and hope that something positive will come out of it? You have to stop running your lives on a physical level *only*, because the physical level is your playground and not your prison. You have to understand who you are – sooner or later you have to understand who you are! You have to strip away the layers of illusion and discover that you are perfection, you are part of God, and you are an angel.

You are an angel!

There is no need to be bowed down with perceived 'sin' and, once you flood your life and the molecules around you with Light ...*then you 'sin' no more*. In other words, you make the mistake no longer. You are incapable of doing that once you realise your angelic heritage because it is logical to you to proceed in a certain manner as, having imbued yourself with Light once again, there is no other path open to you. It is not that you are under the cosh of religion or because people are saying: 'This is the wrong way to act! *This* is the right way to act!' It is because you are infused with Light and, therefore, cannot ...will not ...*do not* want to have anything to do with anything that is less than the creative power of White Light. So, you '*sin*' *no more* ...you make the mistake no more ...you are part of the Fall no more. You have restored yourself and others to what you were before you fell into the mistaken area that we call the Field. Does that make sense?

David: Yes. Thank you.

Jane: Joseph, I don't have any questions, but I just wanted to say that of all the religious groups the Buddhists seem to have got it most right because they place great emphasis on avoiding anger, on being forgiving and on being aware of the pitfalls of ego.

Joseph: Yes, we are trying to enhance that philosophy and there are other areas where that religion is far more open in nature spiritually than many religions. But what I am trying to emphasise is the need to understand and *to feel* your potential and ability. It is so difficult within the confines of the Field not to externalise your outlook on life and so, unfortunately, many religions affected by the Field become a distorted externalisation of what was, at source, perfect spiritual knowledge. In other words, they become doctrines, with you having to adhere to their vision of spirituality *outside* of yourself, and having to obey that doctrine in order to honour an externally dictated version of spiritual 'clarity' rather than honouring what is *within*.

What we are trying to infuse you with is the knowledge that all those truths that some religions get closer to than others are *within*, and once they are visited within then the texts become redundant because they are external. Once you have visited the **Light within**, the Light within illuminates your way without the need to make judgements according to your externalised beliefs second by second. Do you see?

Jane: Yes.

Joseph: And that is the difference. Running through everyone – running through the atheist and running through the fervent religious zealot – is the same truth at core and at source. It is vitally important that we bring you back to the 'religion' of *being* and bring you back to the 'religion' of fulfilling your place in existence by acknowledging your ability and your status …**and your status as an angelic being is no *more* or no *less* than the status of any other angelic being.**

So, in revisiting your core and in letting out the 'genie' within the bottle (and that is why you have legends about letting the genie out of the bottle), in doing that you elevate yourself to your original status, but also discover that your original status is no more nor less than the status of anyone else you will ever meet on this plane. You are all equal and, if your mind says to you: 'I am not – I am better than some and worse than some,' then you are receiving instructions from the molecules and the force that is the energy from the Field within the effects of the Fall.

You are all equal!

But I must expand this, as we draw to the conclusion of this chapter, by saying that *you* are equal **and everything else is equal**. The exquisite artworks of the devas are equal to you, and the beautiful constructs that you find yourselves in are equal to you in that you have to be equal to your creations. So, everything that you encounter on your journey in the name of Light should be treated as your equal ...and it is fine to talk to the walls of your house ...it is fine to address the animal forms that you come across as your equal and to communicate with them, because they *are* your equal.

There is nothing else but your equal on a spiritual level, and respect should be shown for *all* things: for the planet, for the trees, for the animals and for everyone that you meet. Respect should be shown as these things are your equal and, when you treat them as your equal, they will respond with a kindness and sweetness you will not have witnessed before because you will have elevated them, for a moment, out of the effects of the Field that they are suffering from. Do you see?

Jane: Yes, thank you.

Chapter Seventeen
Spiritual Distractions

Joseph: At this stage in the book it is my intention to turn things around within your mind, within the physical world, and within the effects of the Fall. You have to come to terms with the fact that there is a dominance of physical mind in this physical sphere at this time.

A dominance of *physical* mind!

And that physical mind *filters* the information you receive from outside of yourself and within yourself. That physical mind is polluted by the effects of the Fall and by the influence of the Field of human consciousness that pervades every molecule of physicality that you interact with at this time.

In order to release the original energies of the Earth plane and the original energies of your soul you have to understand the dominance of the mind and that the mind is set to negative and is constantly seeking to tie you to the Field that you believe to be the *true* reality. The mind is influenced by the Field, you are influenced by the mind, and you feel that you *are* the physical mind. The reason why I am re-iterating this information, which we have covered in earlier books, is because at this point, having read the information that we have given you so far in this book, **you will *hopefully* want to do something about redressing the balance**, about bringing yourself out of the Fall, and about bringing others and the Earth plane out of the Fall too.

In order to do this you will probably look around and see what calls to you *spiritually*. There is a cornucopia of literature available on spiritual subjects and there are groups here and there that purport to be advancing spirituality and evolving the human soul. There are people you will meet who will try to convince you that *their* way is the correct way, that their approach to spirituality is the correct approach, and that all you need do is invest in a certain set of beliefs and circumstances and you will liberate and elevate yourself ...and, in effect, escape the effects of the Fall.

Much of what you will come across in the early stages of your spiritual seeking is a *distraction* – a distraction constructed by the Field and filtered through your physical mind to your soul **to keep you interested *but not powerful*** ...interested in seeming spiritual subjects, but not powerful in that you will not actually be able to *influence* your own soul, the souls of others or change the face of this world. I want you to consider in each step of your spiritual seeking whether that which you are embracing at this time and at this moment is actually of benefit:

To yourself.

To others.

To the physical world.

So-called spiritual literature is full of diversions and distractions. I want you to consider, for example, that the study of a certain set of beliefs does not necessarily *elevate* your soul. I want you to consider that investment in certain objects ...in certain groups ...in certain sounds ...in certain actions ...or in certain exercises keeps your physical mind active and keeps you physically active and seemingly involved in spiritual pursuits ... **but in reality does not elevate you one jot!**

There is a fervour when setting your feet on the spiritual path; there is a longing to belong and a longing for the peace and the power that you feel when you centralise yourself from within and centralise your being on *what you really are.* But, in order to reach what you really are, you have to strip away many layers of learning with regard to the physical world, physical matter and its many layers of distraction. It is the intent and purpose of the Field always to pull you into your perceived need of *it.* It is in the interests of the Field, which is set to negative, to keep you hooked into it and dependent on it and **to keep your spiritual 'eyes' away from the main goal.**

...And the main goal is to illuminate yourself once again, to illuminate others, and to illuminate the world and *change it* ... change the power of the molecules around you ...change the power of the molecules in your physical body and physical mind ...and revert to that time when you and the Godhead were consciously one and consciously created *perfection* – not distraction – together.

So beware! My request is that you re-read the book if you are not totally happy with what it says. My request is that in all spiritual seeking you first seek from *within.* Take the circumstances that you feel are important and are calling you within. Examine your symbols, examine your pursuits, examine your beliefs *within* – in that secret chamber of the heart. Sit in your 'comfortable armchair' in the sphere of your imagination at your heart-mind centre and consider, without the bias of the ego and the physical mind, whether the attractions that you are currently involved in spiritually are correct.

...Do they resonate with you?

...Do they harmonise with you?

...Or are they just a construct that embellishes your ego, and makes you feel 'special' and satisfied through the physical mind?

I tell you: **you can never be satisfied *spiritually* through the physical mind!** The physical mind is a maze and a minefield, and constantly feeds you misguided information – '*dis*-information' and distraction!

If what you feel at your heart-centre is harmony then by all means embrace those circumstances *spiritually* that you are spending your time on ...until such time as you feel they are wrong for you, or until such time as you elevate above them and enhance them with further knowledge. If you feel that there is a disharmony between your heart-centre and the things that you on the surface, through your physical mind, find attractive, then acknowledge that disharmony and acknowledge that those things are *not* the way.

We worry about the current state of spiritual seeking and about the current state of so-called spiritual truth. We see groups sitting as 'groups', feeling that *they* have the message, *they* have the way and *they* have the means... but that way and those means are physical only. They are satisfying the ego and are bringing limited comfort and supposed security.

Believe me, seeking to change things through Light does not make you secure *physically*! In fact, the further you go into the Light in your ability to draw, wield and project Light, the *less* secure your physical world should feel. If you consider that this is a construct (as we have said throughout the book) and that this construct is set to negative as a result of an experiment that went wrong, and if you, in true spiritual seeking, are uncovering the absolute truth and the absolute reality of your being of the Godhead then, as you approach from within the reality that is right for you (i.e. your connection with the Godhead and the state of matter at a creative level of perfection) does it not make sense that the world that you have invested so much in, in terms of time and physicality, should become *less real* to you as your pursuit of Light and the reinstatement of Light expands?

In other words you should expect (I am afraid) discomfort and dissatisfaction through the physical mind as your quest for spiritual knowledge and Light becomes more stable from within, because you are disintegrating the illusion around you and within you. You are re-establishing your inner truth; you are re-affirming your perfection, and, in doing so, you should find the world around you dissatisfying. You should find that the world *around* you does not measure up to the world *within* you. You should find that the world around you begins to become too loud for you …too fast for you …too aggressive for you …and too empty for you. **You should find the physical world to be a world of lack and the inner world to be a world of fulfilment.** If your spiritual pursuits are, therefore, feeding only your spiritual senses and you feel comfortable with them *on a surface level* then you are hooking yourself deeper into the effects of the Fall.

We wish to strip away and get back to basics with this book. Having explained what went wrong, we wish to now strip away what went wrong from *around* you and from *within* you, and to leave you with *nothing more* (and yet everything) than the Light that is within, because the Light that is within is you and the Light that is within is God …**and the Light within is the creative force that can re-establish you as who you originally were and this world as what it originally was.**

THERE IS NO OTHER WAY!

…There is no way through complexity.

…There is no way through complacency.

…There is no way through constructs that distract you and involve you in certain practices that may seem wholesome and may seem secure, but in the long-run do not advance your ability to free yourself from the entanglements of this world and your ability to teach and free others and to restore the wounded Earth.

Having illustrated and explained how things have gone wrong, the message we bring is that there is only one way to put things right. That message is simple. The way of creation is simple. The creative abilities that you have are simple. For example, if you were truly in touch with your origins as a completed and unified angelic being, creation, or the manifestation of the world that you want, would simply be a matter of bringing that world forth in perfection through instant spiritual thought. That is how simple it is, and yet can you do that now? Can you manifest in front or around you now, as you read this book, *any* thought that you have, any dream that you have, any object that you want?

You cannot!

...And you cannot because the complexity of the Field makes it easy to manifest negativity around yourself but very, very difficult to manifest the creative positive force that you have *as a birthright* as an angel in this sphere of twisted and accelerated matter.

Complexity in spiritual matters is even more dangerous than being purely a distraction for you. Complexity in the pursuit of spiritual truth strengthens the Field. Let me say that again! **Complexity in the pursuit of spiritual truth *strengthens* the Field** because you are investing in and seeking to satisfy the physical mind only and the physical mind is polluted by the Field of human consciousness.

So, you have to be *extremely* careful in the choices you make when addressing yourself spiritually and addressing others spiritually. You have to constantly use your 'compass within' to steer you in the right direction ...and the right direction is *simple*. The right direction is simply a matter of reconnection with your roots and is simply an acceptance that you are an all-powerful being, that you are part of an all-powerful Divinity, and that you, as an all-powerful being, can and will and *want to* change this world.

The fact that you find the Earth attractive is a reflection of your investment in the illusions and distractions of the Field. As you truly wield Light and truly return to your origins and, as you bring out Light to change yourself and this world …**your view of this world should change.**

Your view of this world should be of a place that is bedlam; of a place that is insanity; of a place where you can sense (as *we* can sense) the conflict in matter, where molecules come up against molecules and atoms against atoms, all vying for a position of superiority, a position of power and a position of *dominance* – dominance of the global mind and dominance of your mind also. You should find this world disconcerting and you should see it for what it is. If we could share with you *our* vision of the world, we would bring to your attention and vision a sea of conflict … a sea of disharmony …a sea where dream vies against dream for positions of dominance and supremacy, because that is what you have invested your constructs with since the time of the Fall.

On a conscious level and on a physical level you believe that it is *your* power that has to be held onto and established *at all costs.* You cannot successfully create as you used to create, or destroy and disintegrate as you used to within the effects of the Field, and so you seek to superimpose ideal dream upon ideal dream. You cannot see this on a spiritual level, but you can feel its effects: the wars that you have; the disharmony that you have on personal, friendship, family and global levels; the effects on the Earth that is cracked and misshapen because of the weight of creation that cannot be released and is pressing on it all the time. You can see these things, but you cannot see, as *we* can see, the actual flow and swirl of the polluted imaginings that are given out by millions and millions of angelic beings that have trapped themselves within a never-ending nightmare.

It is time to awaken!

There is much reference to 'awakening', but *awakening* is not a matter of reaching out and 'switching on a light' – if you think it is then you are being influenced by the Field. It is a matter of reaching *in*. It is a matter of finding the switch *within* yourself. It is a matter of bringing out the Light that is always yours (and always has been) to 'infect', pervade and to change the molecules of your body, your mind and your surroundings back to their original state so that you create around yourself and inject into the lives of others a little oasis of calm; a little oasis of God-creativity; a little oasis where the all-pervading dominance is harmony – not conflict, not struggle, not the fight for dominance.

They say *a little knowledge is a dangerous thing* and I would suggest that you are privy to a great deal of knowledge, but I put the word 'knowledge' in parentheses – I would say that you are privy to a great deal of 'information' and much of it is bewildering and is *intended* to be bewildering.

Daily you need the calm of your inner oasis, of your inner self, of your contact with God. Over the weeks and months the Light that you begin to redisplay (it is not coming from anyone except you – the Light that you are drawing upon is coming from your God-heart or God-centre) as you begin to draw that Light into your body **will change you and you will think differently**. And, as you begin to view the world for what it is and wonder why you have never seen it like this before, your first indication that you are on the right path should be your determination to be somewhere else ...to be in an area of reality that is different and more harmonious than the one you find around yourself *physically*. Once you find that unrest, that need and that longing, then you are truly bringing Light into the world, into yourself, into your physical body and into your surroundings.

My message, therefore, today has to be one of seeking unrest – seeking harmony *spiritually* but seeking unrest *physically* ... and one leads to the other. For the time in which you exercise the wielding of Light, the bringing out of Light within you will surround you with a peace and a harmony that you will not have consciously experienced during your lifetime. However, in bringing out that harmony, you will find that when you have to re-address the world you will look at it with loving eyes, yes, but you will also look at it with increasingly critical eyes as to its current state, because you will know increasingly, day by day, week by week, month by month, that this is *not* how things are supposed to be, that you are *not* as you are supposed to be and that the world is *not* as it is supposed to be. That is good! That unrest and that dissatisfaction with the status quo of the physical world is excellent and should be your marker as to whether you are on the correct spiritual path. You will be content with the feeling of Light that you discover in your meditations and your ability to transmit it, but you will be dissatisfied with the Earth and what it has to offer you.

Let that be your yardstick as to whether you are progressing correctly! If you find yourself content with runes, or with sounds, or with exercises, or with group movements in the name of spiritual advancement, and these things give you a view of the world that seems to be harmonious, then I would ask you to question what you have discovered spiritually thus far.

As an angel – as who you *really* are – you can never be content with this world as it is now ...only with how it *was* and how it *will be* and *should be* again. You can never be content with your view of yourself fitting into the world and finding it harmonious. You should be discontent with your connection to the world and yet content with the Light that you are able to bring into it. A complex subject! Not a simple subject, but a simple way of measuring whether you are aware of the effects of the Fall, whether you are correctly approaching your God and spirituality, and whether you are making a difference to this world.

Do not misunderstand me, the love that we have spoken about throughout the books is yours to wield ...love for yourself ...love for others ...and love for the Earth. It is not the original construct that is wrong and it is certainly not love that is wrong – love changes things, love is Light – but it is *the illusion* that will suddenly present itself to you as an illusion if you are truly working for the Light. It will be as though the scales have fallen from your eyes, as though you realise that you are on stage and that the play has been going on for ever such a long time. It will be as though you are looking through a different 'set of eyes' –

which you are. You are looking through your *original* set of eyes, the set of eyes that are still yours, the set of angelic eyes which you have as your birthright as an individual viewpoint of God.

I ask you then, at this late stage in the book, to please work for the Light, to spend time away from the clamour of this world by going within to that secret chamber, and to release your creative energy as an angel by revisiting your vision of who you originally *were* and who you *are*. Decide for yourself, yes, whether these words are true or nonsense, but decide through bathing them in Light. Decide what you feel about this world by bathing it in Light. Decide what is important to you – the aspects of your life, your work, your family, your pursuits – decide how important they are and how they need to be approached by first bathing them in Light. If you want to reveal the truth bathe something in Light, energise it with Light and then you will see what I am taking about with regard to the Earth seeming to be a less than perfect place. You will have bathed it in Light and will have revealed the truth ...and the truth *at this stage* is not pretty.

It is up to you to make it beautiful.

I invite questions.

Jane: Joseph, regarding our discontentment with the world we have to be a bit careful... in being aware that it is imperfect, we can't spend too much time thinking about how awful it is because otherwise we would be feeding the Field with more negativity. It is a bit of a fine line, isn't it?

Joseph: I must not have made myself clear in the distinction that I am making. The Light *within* brings total contentment and wielding the Light brings total contentment, but if you cannot see that something is less than it should be ideally with regard to God-Creation, how are you to put it right? What I am suggesting is that you will become more discerning as you become more spiritually aware, and I am asking you to look at the so-called spiritual options available to you and to be discerning with them too …to be able to see when something is not of God …to be able to see when something is not constructive …to be able to see when something, as I have said, is a distraction. Having seen it as a distraction and less than perfect and having the tools to make it perfect once again, you will surely apply more energy to making it perfect rather than dwelling on seeing it as imperfect. Do you see that?

Jane: Yes, I do.

Joseph: It is a good point and it is important that I have made that distinction for you. It is not a matter of seeing things as being wrong and dwelling on that, but is a matter of being able to see that there is a need for Light; of being able to see that the areas you perhaps previously felt were extremely important to you in life do not completely hold up when viewed through spiritual eyes and need an inflow of Light to rectify them and to re-harmonise them with the Whole, and to turn over the effects of the Fall and the negativity of the Field. Does that make sense?

Jane: Yes, it does. Thank you.

Joseph: Is there another question, please?

David: Just to try and get this right in my own head – what you are saying is that as we progress we realise that the outside world, as it were, is disharmony, but rather than turning our back on it we should feel compelled to put it right by wielding the tools – such as forgiveness that you mentioned in the last chapter. Is that right?

Joseph: It has to be! It is *your* projection – it is everyone's projection. It has been your projection since that point when you decided, en masse and as one spiritual mind, that you would attempt something different. It has been your projection since that point when you encased yourself within the Fall experiment and within the seemingly endless dream that you have repeated for millennia.

As a result of you becoming more spiritually aware you will reawaken your kinship with all men, women, children, animals and all things, because these things are a part of you, these things were summoned by you and these things you have invested part of your momentum in since the time of the Fall and *before*. Therefore, it is not a physical volition, but a spiritual one. It is a spiritual need that you will find as you grow in knowledge of yourself and your ability to wield Light. It will *never* occur to you to turn your back, for example, on your brothers and sisters, or to turn your back on the Earth. It is not a *physical* emotional choice ...**it is a need for completing the program *spiritually*.**

There are two courses to take, of course. There is the course that leads to you releasing yourself from the effects of the Fall once you return to the spiritual cleansing realms following physical death. And there is a need to also involve yourself in the transformation of the physical matrix back to what it was, the nullification of the negativity of the Field and the transformation back to pure God-creativity that was in place before the Fall experiment was decided upon by you and by everyone around you.

So, in your daily approach to the Earth, to others and to all aspects of Creation, as you grow in realisation of who you really are, you will find that it is a *natural* volition to want to change ...**not to turn *your* back but to turn *things* back...** to turn things back to how they were before you invested in that movement that has led you to this point in time.

The souls who go ahead and who 'fast track' (*I think is the modern parlance*) their way through the spiritual cleansing spheres and emerge into Infinity, even though they are restored to the *nth* degree to their original glory, still find there is a small, small percentage of their consciousness that is not complete and is not harmonic. Even though they have escaped the effects of the Earth plane and have successfully negotiated the cleansing spheres and rectified their error of judgement they are still connected to the brethren that are suffering as an effect of the

Fall. They are still connected because all is One, because there was a unit involved in the creation of this sphere and that unit has to rectify itself, cleanse the sphere and return to infinite possibility *en masse*. You cannot, for example, truly march onwards into Infinity if you still have a 'toe' in the door or a 'finger' trapped in the window case – and that is the analogy I would give you. Souls *do* escape, but even at that level they are *concerned* with the elevation and liberation of the rest of the angelic children that were involved in creating the Fall experiment.

So, it is a natural volition here on Earth, in the cleansing spheres and beyond, to want every aspect of the angelic children involved with the Fall to rectify their mistake, to escape from the effects of the Fall and to re-designate the planet in God's name back to its original intention. Do you see that?

David: Yes, I certainly do. Thank you.

Joseph: Is there anything more?

Jane: The most attractive thing on Earth is nature, with all the different creative designs of flowers, plants and animals, but from your point of view can you still see all the discord and disharmony that you were describing before in their molecules?

Joseph: You consider nature to be beautiful, and it is, but you are seeing through a 'glass darkly' and, because of the Fall, inherent within nature are the seeds of its own destruction. Just as you are an angel encased within a physical body – a beautiful seed waiting to expand and become who you were, but are unable to do so because you are trapped in physical matter to a lesser or greater extent – within every aspect of nature, because it is operating in the same sphere, there is trapped within the physical form (beautiful and perfect as it may appear to you) a greater perfection and a greater expression.

Nature is limited in its creative expression of joy and glory as you are. So, for example, you may see an animal, which to all extents and purposes is expressing its purpose, but what you are seeing with the animal (as with yourself) is a case of physical matter imprisoning, for a time, a divine spark that is far more appealing to the senses and far more capable in terms of what it can do than the 'object' that you see.

When *we* see nature, we see both things simultaneously as we see both things with you – we see the angel *within*, simultaneously seeing you as a compressed, restricted and limited physical being. When we see nature, whether it is an animal or a tree or a stream, we see the potential, the perfection and the capability entrapped within the physical shell and physical limitation. The outermost layer of matter is (as I said earlier) a conflict and a fight for power, and all physicality on this level, because it is drawn from the well of the Field and the creative but finite and distorted matrix of the Fall... [*pause*]

(I must apologise. I have reached the end of the transmission, but we must answer the question).

...all physicality is limiting, all physicality is confining, all physicality is only a small expression of what lies within. So, we look at nature and we look at you and we see everything coated and surrounded by the limiting vibrations that you have created. **You are a beautiful butterfly trapped within a hard chrysalis of matter that is vying against itself all the time.** Do you see that?

Jane: Yes.

Joseph: And that is how we view nature and how we view you. What we are trying to bring through to you is the ability for *you* to see that too – not quite in the way that we do but with spiritually-opened eyes, and that is what I have been talking about within this chapter ...the ability to see the imperfection and not to be satisfied with that, but to work to release the 'butterfly'. Not to become bogged down with *isn't this a terrible*

239

place but to become focused on *this is less than it could be* – how do I make it what it *is* again?

Does that make sense?

Jane: Yes. Thank you.

Chapter Eighteen
Remember Who You Are

Joseph: Remember! What a wonderful word: *Remember*. In remembering who you are, you re-ignite your spiritual creative potential. Everything that has been discussed and illuminated in this book is for a purpose **...and that purpose is to allow you to** *remember*.

In a quiet moment reach inside to the heart-mind and, within the heart-mind in silence, in contemplation, and in appreciation of the God-spirit that flows through you, **ask to remember**.

Consider the points that have been raised – from the act of creation, to the act of instigating the Fall, to the point of forgetting who you are – *every* aspect of this book should re-ignite your creative ability. Ask that you remember, and do not expect to remember in the way that you remember your life on Earth. Do not expect to look back to a time when you were younger, for example – do not expect childhood memories. Expect memories that are stronger, more realistic and more energised than any that you have experienced since you incarnated into this present form and present life. Ask to sense who you *really* are; ask to be reunited with who you really are; ask to be shown your potential and to experience the *wonder* of being a creative being freed from the shackles of dogma, freed from the shackles of expectation on an earthly level and freed from the shackles of responsibility within the confines of society.

Ask to experience …and then *feel* the Light well up within you …then feel a sense of total wellbeing …then feel as if you could conquer *anything*, as if you could project and could create anything, as if you could put right all the wrongs you perceive to be in your physical life and all the wrongs you perceive across the Earth plane at this present time.

…Because, in remembering, you *can* put right all the wrongs.

In remembering you reach back *beyond* that time when you fell into a deep sleep, when you became a dreamer of the wrong dream, when you became a prisoner of the illusion that you created. Allow me to repeat that: **you became a prisoner of the illusion that YOU, the reader, helped to create.**

YOU created it!

You created it because you thought it was right. You created it because you thought it would enhance the way that the creative process from the Godhead unfolded, and then you placed yourself within that mistaken area of perception …**and you *forgot* who you were.**

Remember that you have not lost who you are; you have not separated yourself from who you are as an angelic being – not totally. You have not severed each connection. You are not less than you ever were – you just *believe* that you are. Remember that that creative ability, in line with God-creative ability, that you used for aeons before you fell into the trap of the Fall *is still yours*. It is yours because *at core* you have not changed. It is only the outer layers of your vibration that have changed. It is only your perception that has become narrow and a straight-ahead rather than a three-hundred-and-sixty-degree view of things.

You are a fragment of a greater angelic being – that is all you have *ever* been.

That is *all* you have ever been!

That is *all* you will ever be!

At this moment you have entrapped that perception, that acknowledgement of your ability, that release of creative energy that you are capable of in its purest form. You have entrapped it within a confining 'bubble' that is within a greater confining 'bubble' we call the 'Field' that represents the sum total of belief of the angelic children who are operating within this Field of illusion and contributing to it, day by day, as a belief of who they are.

Do you feel, do you think, do you believe that you are the flesh that you see when you look in a mirror? Do you feel, do you think, do you believe that you are nothing more than that point of consciousness that seems to be centred around your head and signify *you* as you?

You are so much more than that, and you are so much more than your earthly memories. Your earthly memories are that part of you which is trapped in the Fall. They are nothing more than that, but you attach such weight and gravity to them, as though they are you and they are all you are. They are only a surrounding shell of polluted experience that confines your *limitless* angelic capability. Your true memory is of who you originally were before the time of the Fall ...and who you still are.

I am trying to put into words the need to dispense with the view of your physical life as being *all there has been of you*. You are so much greater than that; you are so much nobler than that, and the tiny personality that you set such store by is confining and limiting you (according to the desires of the Field) as to the *great task* ahead of you, if you wish to negate the effects of the Fall on yourself and on your brothers and sisters around this world. In other words, in order to be the most effective being you can be in the fight to convert the illusion that you find yourself and your brothers and sisters trapped in, and, in order to be the most potent weapon for good you can be, you have to access your angelic memories and not your physical ones.

I am not saying that you should dispense with your physical memories – your physical memories are part of the cycle that you are going through at the moment. They are important and they link you, in a limiting way, to the *limited* perception of the people who are part of your family, part of your friendship circle and part of the society that you interact with. But there is a greater store of energy, a greater store of memory, and a greater store of being that you have access to *if you wish it*. And the people around you ...your brothers ...your sisters ...your husbands ... your wives ...your mothers ...your fathers ...your children ... *each* of these points of consciousness is really a small portion of angelic consciousness. If you get back to the basic of who you are and you remember (and I mean 're-*member*' in the true sense of the word – i.e. if you reconnect to the whole that you are as part of a greater Whole) you are so much more effective in bringing about the change that is so needed across this world now.

How will you know when you have accessed your angelic memories?

Will you remember running around in an Earthly paradise, perhaps, with 'wings', and being an angel child? No. It is not that type of memory. **You will feel energised in a peaceful, immortal and powerful way that you have not felt before through meditations.**

Remembering is *knowing* that the words that have been put down in this book are correct. At any point when you remember and accept who you are (and you can do it daily or weekly) ... **you can change this world.** You become a beacon for Light; you become a directional focus for Light; you become someone who projects Light, and you will find that you can sweep this Light around, in your knowing of who you truly are, to illuminate various areas of your life, the lives you touch and the lives you ultimately are a part of around the globe.

You will find that you can look at someone's illness and see it for what it is: simply a 'trip in the dark', simply a soul that has become further enmeshed in the illusions of the Field ...and that you can shine your greater belief of perfection into that illness and around that person and *relieve* the illness. You will find that you can project the Light you wield as an angelic being into *any* negative situation. And the whole world is a negative situation, but I am talking specifically about conflict – whether that conflict be in an office or in a war zone. You will, with great conviction that is not hampered by the limiting effects of the physical mind, project the Light (that is yours as your birthright in the Divine) into that area – be it a small conflict close to home or a huge conflict on the other side of the globe. **And you will *know* that you have illuminated and changed that situation,** and your purpose in illuminating that situation is to shine enough Light into the hearts of others that they, too, begin to remember.

In remembering who you are – the greater existence and the greater part of you – you have no choice but to forget the things of the Field, because the things of the Field are but shadows that are chased away when the Light is shone into them.

...And, *if* and *when* enough of you remember and enough of you wield the Light, the darkness will be dissipated for good and forever. You will have restored balance and, at that point, one moment you will be looking with physical eyes and the next you will be regarding the world as a changed place with angelic eyes, and you will regard each person that you come across as a facet of 'yourself', in the greater sense, and as the facet of an angelic being that they really are.

Each of you has tortured yourself for aeons. Each of you has stubbornly pursued a negative choice, and supported and upheld that negative choice believing, at your mistaken core and at the point at which you decided to enter the illusion of the Fall, that you were and *still are* right. Let us look on a personal level:

If there was a way to stop yourself suffering wouldn't you go for it?

If there was a way to stop the suffering of your family members wouldn't you choose that way?

If there was a way to stop the suffering of your friends wouldn't you choose that way?

If there was a way to stop yourself suffering physically, mentally and spiritually wouldn't you choose that way?

If there was a way to no longer have that yearning within you for 'something' that you cannot quite pinpoint but is always a step ahead of you so that you are never totally satisfied today because there is that missing aspect that you *may* find tomorrow ...if you could satisfy that need, wouldn't you take that option?

The need you have is to restore yourself to full knowledge of who you are, and the way to restore yourself to full knowledge of who you are is to remember *within* yourself and to once again *accept* yourself as what you really are. You are not this flesh. You are not this limitation. You are part of the Divine. You are part of a greater angelic being, and it is your role forever ...and ever ...and *ever* to create and to experience, and to enjoy, and to grow, and to evolve.

And you will say, 'Joseph, your way is so simple!' And *there* you have it! The way is so simple. Look at that sentence – 'the way' ...**THE WAY**. Didn't someone once talk of: 'The way, the truth and the Light'?

The way is so simple!

You burden yourselves with: *it must be complicated; it must be more complex than that.* You say, 'Surely *I* cannot change the world.' And because you are an angelic being and because you create what you believe to be true ...*you cannot*. It is time to realise that you *can*! It is time to realise that you *will*. It is time to realise that *You Are* – (capital 'Y', capital 'A') – **You Are part of the Divine.**

You made the decision to put yourself into this illusion; it is *now* time to make the decision to take yourself out of it. It is as simple as that! It is as simple as 'switching on' the Light.

For aeons we have attempted to show you this and we are *excited* that now, because of the point in your societal evolution when communication is universal, finally we may reach –*have to* reach – those who are ready to hear these words.

You have within you a well of angelic experience: you have created worlds; you have created far more beauty than you can ever imagine with your physical mind; you have created patterns, shapes, colours and experiences that are exquisite because they are part of the Divine intention of ever expanding and glorifying Creation. **You have done this!**

Let me raise you up today as you read this book. Are you tired? Are you depressed? Do you feel old? Do you feel confined? Do you feel poor? Raise yourself up – you are a creator of worlds; you are a creator of universes; you are the most glorious, wonderful, everlasting, unchanging, pure, loving being of Light …but you have to remember that.

Remembering is different from believing. Believing is a wall that you have to shore up daily and put buttresses up against, because you know that someone can come along and say: 'This is not the way!' …and the wall will shake. 'Are you sure?' …and the wall will shake again, because you are using belief and you are using the physical mind. The only way to erect a fortification that will not change, that will not crumble, and does not require belief is by remembering. Remember! Be yourself! Do you not say on this level, 'Be yourself'?

Be yourself – your *true* self.

The only difference between us and you at this point in time is a point of view. Your point of view is clouded. Ours (*thank you, Father*), due to the cleansing effects of the spiritual spheres, is lighter, is clearer, is more certain. We have complete belief in who we are because *we know who we are*, but we are linked to you; we are, in the right sense, 'in love' with you and we cannot leave you here in this illusion.

I would speak just for a little time about your lives, because, as you read this book, which re-introduces to you concepts that are universal and beyond the *physical* universe, you will inevitably think (because your head-centre fed by the Field will tell you): 'This is too big for me. My life is nine to five. My life is a certain set of boxes that lead to an 'inevitable box' and I had better enjoy it now using what is on offer even if it is polluted because the inevitability of my life ending is ahead. That is all I can see. I am this particular person (I am a father; I am a mother; I am a brother; I am a sister; I am a work person; I am a scientist; I am a driver – I am one of a million things) and I know what my life is.'

No. You don't!

You only perceive through a glass darkly, slowly, narrowly – you perceive so little of what you are, and you are not (as we have said again and again) who you appear to be on a physical level. It is simply a suit of clothes, a badge of 'honour' because you are working out certain things by the *long* path, but that is all it is. Only when you come to full knowledge again of who you are, can you change and *expand* that view.

The great glories of Creation we have tried to touch upon in a small way in this book are yours **by right** ...without guilt, without restriction, without people saying you cannot possibly be this and without *you* saying, 'I cannot possibly be this!' You are a child of God, and in your own hands and at your own heart-centre lies the way out of the problem that you have at the moment.

We worry because we can see the increase in individualisation and isolation between you. We can see that, ironically, through the same technology that we are using to spread this message, you are becoming more insular and less able to communicate with your brothers and sisters, even on a physical level. The Field at the moment is diminishing you ...and diminishing you ...and diminishing you so that at the basic level of communication you are failing too. You assume that you are communicating; you assume that you are transmitting your beliefs, ideas and wants to others, but it is empty thought. They are empty words, and you do not see that, in contacting *so many* but actually having *physical* contact with *so few*, you are further hardening the shell of illusion and isolation around you.

This is why it is so important that you remember who you are, that you break that shell around you, that you find yourself able to reach out to and care for others, that you see through the web of deceit that the Field has placed around you and you communicate Light, communicate brotherhood, communicate oneness in everything that you do, in everything that you say, and in everything that you *dream*.

You have always *dreamt* as the angel that you really are. In the beginning you dreamt ...you dreamt into reality worlds, you dreamt into reality situations for your benefit and the benefit of others, and also so that you could experience and enjoy every degree of possibility this creative matrix that is yours as a birthright has to offer. You now find yourself using this creative matrix to diminish yourself.

Remember who you are! I will help. **We will help.** For every person who meditates on the meaning of this chapter, we will be there during your meditations to inspire you. Don't look for us. Don't attempt to see us – some of you will, but don't attempt to see us because that, too, is a trap of the physical mind. It is our *intent* transmitted to you, our *love* around you and through you, that you will pick up. It is our *encouragement* to open your angelic eyes that you will feel. It is our *support* in your endeavours to change the physical world that you can expect from us.

Time, as you view it, is growing short. Your lives are growing smaller. The Field is growing stronger, and all it takes to change things back to how they were before the Fall (which has been said again, and again, and again by seers and by the ancient religions) is for you to remember your potential.

Remember who you are!

...Don't forget!

Is there a question, please?

David: Isn't the process made simpler by simply quitting the Earth, Joseph, and remembering in the Higher Spheres?

Joseph: You have to remember too that you have initiated a process, that you have initiated the circular journey we have spoken about in this and other books. You have started certain processes along that journey; you have opened certain wavelengths of energy that need to be concluded whilst you are still in an earthly body. So, it is the balance of knowing that you should not return but also knowing that you can transform the situations you find yourself in. Also remember that those situations you find yourself in are a very strong magnetic pull back to the Earth plane unless you have risen above them in knowledge.

So, the intent of part of your life, once you have remembered who you are, is to *illuminate* those circumstances and see them fall away here. Also remember that, because you are here you do not know whether you have been pulled back here by your own desire to re-experience energies that you found delightful in the past and situations that you want to re-energise. You do not know whether *that* is your purpose in being here or whether you are one of the souls who has elected to come back to spend this particular time in the circle of physical existence **shaking this world out of its belief in the Fall.**

The act of remembering brings you to a 'warrior stance' – a stance for the Light. An opportunity, yes, to illuminate yourself and determine that when your time comes to step out of the physical you *will not come back*, but also to look at the situation around you and leave your mark …leave your mark in Light that has enabled *others* to partially or fully remember who they are.

I am not supporting an opting-out process. I am supporting a process of rediscovery that will quite naturally pull you out of this physical situation once you have left it behind. But I am also asking that, in contacting your angelic memories, you study who you are with regard to you being *here*. And many of you will find that you have a purpose that you have not imagined before; you will find that your purpose is greater than your nine-to-five job, your purpose is greater than what you consider to be your physical life and the track it is on …**and that your *true* purpose is to act as an illumination for others – to help others remember.**

Remember the chain – remember that every soul has to come out of the Fall; every soul has to work to bring itself in *full consciousness* out of the effects of the Fall that it put itself into in *full consciousness*. Like a plant or child there has to be energy put in, in order for that plant or that child to grow. The energy that is put in at the moment is the energy of the Field, and the energy of the Field turns inwards, begins to diminish the physical and eventually pulls apart the physical, and then has such an effect on the individual that the individual wants to revisit the sphere of the Fall.

If you are of a mind, if you are generous enough, if you recognise and remember who you are and that everyone you meet is your brother or your sister and that this planet, too, is under your care and guardianship, you have to be brave enough to spend some of your time (and as much of your time as you can donate whilst being in a physical body) **feeding others …**

feeding the child, feeding the world, feeding the planet, feeding the landscape ...feeding those things with the right vibration, with the Divine vibration that changes and chases away the darkness, that brings in the Light that originally was there before the Fall took place.

So, you in effect escape the moment that you truly remember who you are. You look at the world but you are no longer *of* the world, and you are also able to use *who you are* to change the world because you are still within it physically. Do you see that?

David: Yes.

Jane: Joseph, I am not asking this question from the point of view of trying to justify the mistaken Fall experiment, but when we are all out of it and it is concluded, will we have brought something *very unique* to the Godhead? This situation hasn't happened before in the universe so we are bringing things such as bravery, self-sacrifice and, perhaps, humour and other unique things. It will have some worth at the end, won't it?

Joseph: You are looking at it, unfortunately, from the point of view of it being a *major* event. What I would like to point out is that, yes, it is a major event from the point of view of being within it, but from the point of view of being outside of it, it is but a momentary vibration within the infinite vibrations and possibilities of everything.

What I mean by that is that you are able to look back over the years and centuries and view the world as having been in struggle, and there being noble people and destructive people, and there being a great deal of 'history' because you are immersed in that history. But once you extract yourself from it and are in the spiritual cleansing spheres you regard that history as a rather diminished thing with regard to its effect on everything else. If you have a stopwatch and you stop the hands at a certain point – that is an analogy I could use with the effects of the Fall – the watch was working perfectly and you stopped it by volition. When you restart that watch how much time has passed? When you restart that watch, it starts again from the point at which it had stopped …And *you* start it.

The Fall is a 'bookmark' or a 'page' that has the corner turned down. It is rather less in terms of spiritual everything, in terms of spiritual perception of progress and time, than it appears to be to you with you being in it at this time. You are immersed in a 'time between times' – a time between normal progress and normal progress. You are in a capsule or bubble, and because that is your perception of everything, because all you can see are the effects of the bubble, you believe that the bubble has a great significance. The only significance of the bubble is to get you out of it – that is the only significance of the bubble.

That is not to diminish the noble aspects of humanity, that is not to diminish self-sacrifice, and bravery, and courage, and love, and kindness and selflessness, but I have to explain that all those things are yours by right anyway. **All those things are who you are.** When you exhibit those aspects of humanity you are exhibiting *your true angelic temperament.* It is not as though there is a great reward waiting for those who have exhibited those aspects of the angelic temperament. What is waiting for those souls is an instant transportation through harmonic vibrations to an area where those higher aspects can be fully expressed – that is the reward. The reward of selflessness and self-sacrifice is to rediscover and remember who you are and, therefore, to escape the cycle.

This pulls us out of the book somewhat, but the universe has *infinite* possibilities. The universe has infinite vibrational opportunities to experience bliss and wonder, and instant opportunities to celebrate and worship the Divine that runs through you through what you create. That is, in human terms, a vast and infinite state of being and state of mind. By comparison you find yourself in a tiny state of mind that you put yourself in as though you have become trapped in a revolving door or locked yourself in a lift-shaft and can't get out. It doesn't mean that there aren't wonderful things beyond that revolving door or outside of that lift-shaft, but all you can experience is the revolving door or the inside of the lift.

When you remember who you are, you begin to measure this world differently; you begin to see aspects of your life and other lives differently; you begin to put different values on to aspects of living here. Do you see?

Jane: Yes, I just thought we might have created some very unique things – like food, and books, and athletics, and clothes and architecture that no other angelic host would have done because they don't have the physicality. We have taken something unique back to the Godhead, but I know it hasn't been worth all the suffering.

Joseph: First of all you have not yet taken it back to the Godhead. This is the problem – *you have not yet taken it back to the Godhead.*

Secondly, and this is my view and it is the view of many of the souls that are part of my soul group, [*laughing*] if each experience of being (and I mean to be humorous here) was a 'book' on the shelves of a 'library of possibility' of what has been and what could be and, if the Fall was such a book, when you came to the last page it would be our advice to take this book of the Fall and walk as far as possible into that library, take it into an empty room, put it on a plinth, under a bell jar of glass and back away from it ...and we would hang a notice on the door of that room that said: '**DO NOT TOUCH!**'

The noble thing to do is **to move away from the Fall**, not to discuss what worth it has. Do you see?

Jane: Yes. Would we then perhaps work as advisors to other angelic children in the future who might want to go through this experiment as we could advise them not to do it?

Joseph: We are looking at areas now that are far beyond the encapsulation of the Fall. You are looking at concepts now that are very difficult to put into words. As you eventually and *inevitably* escape from the effects of the Fall, it will be as though you have taken off a dirty vestment and have put on one of Light, and in taking off the dirty vestment you will say: 'Well, that didn't really work, did it?'

What you have experienced will be written into you as part of your experience and will be worn as part of the raiment of Light that you then have, but it is not something you will *consciously* seek to avoid. Our intent is to bring you back into the creative realm; our intent is to resupply you with that feeling that you do not have *now* that will prevent you, for ever and ever, wanting to re-experience the effects of the Fall.

That experience is there as a display within your vibration for others to see, but it will not be a conscious hair-shirt approach to visit other spirits and say: 'Don't do this!' They will be able, should they *wish* to, through the universal factor of free will, to see your experience as part of your vibrations. Do you see?

Jane: Yes, thank you.

Joseph: I must vacate now because I have seriously strained the instrument. God bless, until the final chapter of this book!

Chapter Nineteen
Disconnection, Reconciliation and Ascension

Michael: As stated in this book's introduction, delivery of the final chapter of the Fall was challenged by certain 'thought forms' and discarnate negative forces whose intention was to halt delivery of the vitally important information it contains and delay the printing of this title. These attempts at disruption resulted in me initially being pulled out of trance several times [not a pleasant experience, I can assure you], and us having to regroup and pray hard in order, in tandem with the spiritual team that works around us and around Joseph, to raise the available energy levels so that we could reconnect and allow him to successfully deliver the concluding message of this book. The notes that accompany the text chronicle the sequence of events as we seek to identify and combat the psychic 'attack', these being included as we felt that the delicate nature of trance communication and the very real threat posed by negative spiritual energies could be better illustrated and understood by allowing the reader to 'sit in' not only on the delivery of Joseph's message, but also on the highly unusual happenings of this last session.

Joseph: *Reconciliation...* The aim of this book is to reconcile you with your true self, with your true family, with your true potential and to reconcile, with the rest of the creative universe, this area of distorted matter or vibration we have called 'the Fall' in the preceding chapters.

I would like you to imagine for a moment what it is like to have a member of your family at a distance from you; a member of your family that you love dearly and *completely*, but cannot reach, cannot influence, cannot communicate with and, most of all, cannot welcome back into your home. That is what it is like for us and that is what it is like for the rest of the angelic host who are aware of the shift of being...

[*At this point there is an unexpected pause and a break in the trance connection.*]

Michael: I will have to start again. I am sorry.

[*There follows a two-minute silence whilst Joseph attempts to re-establish the link and take Michael back into a trance state.*]

Joseph: It seems appropriate that the communication today with regard to the last chapter begins with disconnection. *Disconnection* is the problem; disconnection is what you are experiencing on Earth at the moment and have experienced since the time of the Fall. **You are disconnected.** You are disconnected from your true self, you are disconnected from your true family, and you are disconnected from your *essence* and from your ability to create and '*un*-create' correctly. So, there has been a disconnection since you decided to invest in the experiment that you were advised not to invest in.

The disconnection at the moment is becoming worse because each of you, no matter how spiritually-minded or materially-minded you appear to be, is in truth constantly seeking *to reconnect* ...to reconnect to the God-within and to reconnect to the angelic family that surrounds you but which you cannot sense. You are seeking to reconnect the creative potential within you with the rest of Creation, and to re-harmonise and reconcile your vibration with the vibration of the rest of the universe.

Unfortunately, at the moment most of the people on Earth are translating that sense of disconnection into a need for greater materialism and a greater establishment of a personal power-base on Earth, and, as a result of that, you are *strengthening* the disconnection. You are cementing together those distorted molecules into a non-cohesive whole which you are then immersing yourself into, believing that it will bring you happiness, that it will bring you fulfilment, and that it will bring you the missing quotient or missing aspect of yourselves that you yearn for so much.

In the past this need to reconnect and *mistakenly* re-invest your energies into the effects of the Fall has created disaster, resulting in cataclysm and in the expulsion of the spiritual form from the Earth plane until the Earth plane could rest for a sufficient time to re-nurture a physical....

[*Pause*]

...Until the Earth plane and the devas working together could....

[*Long pause*]

...create a suitable physical shell to house the spirit being or the angel that you truly are.

[*A pause of some five minutes follows as the connection is broken and Michael comes out of trance again.*]

Michael: There is something terribly wrong this morning.

Jane: Maybe we should do it another day?

Michael (*communicating with Joseph clairvoyantly*): Joseph wants me to stand up.

[*Michael stands up and is once more taken into a trance state.*]

Joseph: I apologise for the break in transmission and for the difficulties we have had this morning. It is not always possible to create the connection we need in order to communicate. The problem, as always, comes from your side of life and will be made apparent later. Let me recap and let me attempt to lay out the format of this final chapter.

In it I want to talk about disconnection, and I want to ask you, the reader, to consider the fact that millennia ago you were an angelic being living in a blissful society, existing to create, creating bliss, entering into that bliss and, through experiencing that bliss, creating *greater bliss* for the rest of the angelic host and for the Godhead. You then entered into an agreement with a rest of the angelic children to experiment with a different way of creating …believing that that different way was advantageous to yourselves, to the rest of the angelic host and to the Divine. You were advised against that move, but, because of free will, you decided that it was *still* the right thing to do. You moved into that frame of spiritual mind, from one micro-second to the next micro-second, and as a result of that you encased yourself within an area of matter **that does not react as matter reacts within the rest of the physical universes.**

You have been suffering because of that disconnection from God and from the rest of your angelic family ever since. Not only have you been suffering, but you have been working within a pattern that brings itself to a point of destruction. You have done it at least twice that I can see looking back in the Akashic records of this Earth. I know that it has happened **more than twice**, but I am not privy to that information and am not allowed to see back further than that point.

The point of this book is to remind you of who you are, but also to say to you: **you are about to turn the wheel full circle again into that point of destruction.**

YOU ARE ABOUT TO FACE DESTRUCTION ON A PHYSICAL LEVEL AGAIN.

You are about to face the point where your physical vehicle is taken away from you and you enter into **a state of stasis** ...until such time as the devas and the Earth plane, working together, can evolve a form that is of sufficient dexterity and flexibility to allow you to enter into it ...to experience the pattern of seeking personal power and materiality *again* ...until you shake yourself out of it, and return in *full consciousness* to the angelic host that you are a part of.

You are disconnected, and it is as though someone has pulled the plug on your creative abilities, on your creative consciousness and on your true identity. You are a pale shadow, as you exist on Earth, of what you truly are and of what you are capable of, and your society is a pale shadow of society on a spiritual level of angelic society.

You *know* that you are disconnected. As you read these words *feel* them in your heart. You know that you are disconnected. Every person on Earth knows, at his or her spiritual core, that they are disconnected from the Godhead and disconnected from the angelic host. They feel a *need* for 'something more' – a need for something more that they express on Earth as a 'want' ...a want for a better relationship ...a want for a better house ...a want for more finances...

[*Pause*]

...Always an investment in physical matter – *this will solve the problem*. But it won't, because the investment you need is a re-investment into your angelic family.

[*A further pause as the connection is severed and Michael is yet again brought out of trance.*]

Michael: What on Earth is wrong? ...What on Earth is wrong?

Jane: Maybe we should do it on Friday.

Michael: We are never going to get it finished! …Why is this happening? …What the hell is wrong! …What is causing this? …What is blocking it? … I have no idea…

[*Pause*]

Michael: Can I have some water, please?

[*Pause as Michael takes a drink.*]

Michael (praying): What do you want us to do, Father? I can't carry on unless I can get a connection, can I? First of all, P.G. [*reference to the guide we call the 'Persian Gentleman'*], or whoever is there, will you please surround this room with protection? If you want us to do this, please surround this room with protection, and whatever there is in here that shouldn't be in here, **will you take it out?**

[*Pause*]

Joseph: It should be noted at the end of this final chapter of the book that there was an attempt by the dark creative mind, the creative mind of the…

[*Pause. Michael and Joseph's trance connection is broken one last time.*]

Michael (*tiring and frustrated, addressing Joseph clairvoyantly*): It's useless! It can't happen. Sorry, I can't do this if you don't come closer. Sorry, I can't do it! You have to clear things or I can't do it otherwise. (*Addressing the group as we wait for the atmosphere to be purged of its negative elements*) Shall we make a drink?

[*The circle adjourns for a half-hour tea-break, after which Michael enters a trance state, and this time Joseph is able to take him over, maintain control and successfully deliver and conclude the final chapter.*]

Joseph: If I took away your possessions, if I took away your job and if I took away your societal framework – where would you be? What would you be? ...If I took away your physical body – where would you be? What would you be? ...If I took you out of the Earth plane, so far away that you could not *remember* your day-to-day life – where would you be? What would you be?

You would be *who* you were.

You would be *what* you were.

...You would be the angelic being you once were (and still are) before the journey, before the mistake, before the investment in physical matter. You are surrounded at all times on the physical plane by 'interference' ...by the collective head-consciousness of man. That collective head-consciousness is *sentient* (as we have said so many times) and that collective head-consciousness seeks to immerse you constantly in the illusion of the Earth plane that you created so long ago ...in order that you are reliant on *it* and it is reliant on *you*. It is a symbiotic relationship that traps you, imprisons you, stifles you *creatively* and stops you being who you once were and who you *still are* within the shell of physical matter.

At the time of the Fall when you invested your creative abilities in the experiment and when you believed in that experiment to such an extent that you created its distorted view of reality around you, you *disconnected* yourself willingly and consciously from the God-within, from your angelic family and from your true creative abilities ...and you invested *all that you are* in the maintenance of the illusion you find yourself in now.

It is time to let go!

...Not to let go of your earthly life, not to let go of the Earth plane as it truly is, but to let go of your subconscious, *one hundred percent* belief that you were right in investing in the experiment. **That is all that *separates* you from the blissful**

angelic life you once led. It is time to let go, but instead of letting go, the greater percentage of the angelic children on Earth still believe *subconsciously* that the experiment is correct, and that they were and *are* right to invest their creative abilities and consciousness in it.

All creative projections are a cycle. All creative projections start at the point of investing desire of form into them, and then they have to be concluded at some stage and taken back into the 'nothingness' so that you can create further illusions. The trend on the Earth plane, even though it is encased in heavy matter, is exactly the same. It is a creative cycle but, unfortunately, it is a *distorted* creative cycle that cannot break out of itself and cannot conclude itself. It can neither create further nor can it destroy itself and put itself away so that further creative cycles can be put into operation.

As a result of this, the distorted creative cycle that is the 'bubble of the Fall', eventually brings itself round to a point where it attempts to eliminate itself and attempts to put itself back into the no-thing. **Unfortunately, this has the result of collapsing civilisation.**

It has happened at least twice before. It has happened *more than twice* and I do have knowledge here that I am *not allowed* to share with you that goes back beyond the boundary of that first total disruption of civilisation. Suffice it to say that at least twice in *your* cycle (in other words in the cycle that has involved civilisation and physicality as it is at the moment) you have destroyed your physical vehicles twice. You have taken yourselves to the point where civilisation has been wiped off the face of the Earth so that the Earth plane can regenerate itself and the devas that create the natural backdrop of the Earth plane can, through evolution of form over millennia (as you understand time), bring forth a suitable physical shell to house you again so that, once again, you can reinvest yourself into the distorted illusion of the Fall and play out the *same* scenario.

What is the point of that?

Why would that happen?

...It happens because your faith in the initial experiment, on a soul level and on an angelic level, is *so strong* that you pull yourself back into its effects.

In other words, there is a *stubbornness* with the angelic children who were involved in the Fall. At the point of investing in the Fall, there was a hundred percent belief that the effects of the Fall would be beneficial to the whole angelic host and to the Godhead. That belief, at the moment you immersed yourself in distorted physical matter, was the *strongest element* of your soul and of your remaining angelic memory, and that is what you are constantly calling upon as you reinvest yourself into physical matter. In other words, that memory of the point of the Fall, when, with much excitement and enthusiasm, you instigated the change in physical matter that resulted in the illusion you see around you and through you now, is the only memory you are able to draw on angelically unless you consciously, through the heart-mind, seek out the Godhead and your true spiritual inheritance and memory.

So, your initial investment in the Fall is something that you hold onto subconsciously and is something you know is angelic. It is, therefore, at subconscious level your *only* connection, in many cases, with the 'paranormal', with the spiritual and with something that appears to be beyond the Earth plane. So you hang on to it ...and hang on to it ...and hang on to it, not realising that it is only a fraction of what you are and that you are hanging on to a glimmer of your full angelic potential.

You, therefore, reinvest in it ...reinvest in it ...reinvest in it and turn the 'great wheel' of creative cycle to the point where you solidify the matter around yourselves and within yourselves to *such an extent* that it cannot sustain a spiritual form within it and it has to be swept away and re-organised.

If you were operating as part of the angelic host that is *without* the Earth plane (in other words, the angelic host that was not involved in the Fall), you would simply bring forth a dream into a reality; you would step into that reality; you would experience, understand and examine the consequences of the reality you have created; and then you would put away the reality and step back into the consciousness of the angelic host *knowing* full well that the reality you have just created and destroyed was **an illusion for your benefit**.

What has happened *here* on Earth, because of the Fall, is that you do not realise you have created a reality you can step through and disintegrate. The molecules of the reality you have created as a result of the Fall are imprinted with that willpower for the effects of the Fall to succeed on behalf of the Godhead, as an honouring of the Godhead, as a 'treasure' that you are bringing back to the Godhead and as a celebration and a worshipping of the Godhead. So, you retain that soul-memory of this being a project in honour of the Godhead, but you do not retain that *momentary realisation* at the point of investing in the Fall that it was wrong, that matter in the way you have altered it does not harmonise with the rest of Creation, does not harmonise correctly with the Godhead and does not harmonise correctly with the rest of the angelic host.

Therefore, you cannot draw on energies using the head-mind that are beyond the 'bubble' of the Fall. You draw solely on the available energy within the physical matter of the Fall – and that available energy can sustain you in physical form time and again for millennia, but eventually it runs out. If you do not recharge it with spiritual energy and if you do not put it to one side and invest in a more spiritual illusion instead *eventually* that available energy runs out and cannot sustain you physically ...and you reach a point where civilisation collapses.

You are about to reach such a point. You have *few* generations left in which to change your mind (and 'changing your mind' in this case means changing your mind from the head-mind to the heart-mind) **...but the point of this book is that changing your 'mind' is all it takes.**

You don't want the Earth to be as it is at the moment? Then change your view, change your mind, switch from the head-mind to the heart-mind. Invest in the Light that is your heritage and spread that Light into the Earth plane and into the heart-minds of the people you love and the people you *don't* love.

You wish there to be an end to war? Then stop creating wars, stop investing in war ...and the way to stop investing in war, investing in violence, investing in perversion, is to realise that *all these things* disappear at the moment you let go of your belief subconsciously that you were right at the point of the Fall.

And you will say: 'Well, I don't understand. I wasn't there at the point of the Fall.'

Yes, you were! *It is why you are here.*

'I never invested in an experiment that went wrong.'

Yes, you did! *It is why you are here.*

'I am frightened of letting go.'

Let Go!

Let go of your view of this Earth as being something that will be *exactly* the same each morning when you wake up, that will follow the same pattern, that will follow your present expectations, that will be an Earth with some joy in it but quite a good deal of pain, that will have within it upsets in certain areas of the world, that will have within it family pain and personal pain, that will have within it illness because, 'that's the way things are'.

Let go! That's the way things are until *you* decide there is a different way for things to be.

That's all it takes to 'un-invest' your belief in you being right at the point of the Fall – that, and to declare: 'It's time now, I have had enough. I am putting away this illusion. I am creating another one.'

In its simplest form the remedy to your current predicament is *simple*. It is a matter of seeing the world you want and investing that vision of the world you want with Light from the heart. Light that is brought in from beyond the confines of the Field, beyond the confines of the Fall and beyond that expectation that *everything will be alright* because you have invested in a certain set of circumstances, which you are going to present to your God and say: 'Look what I have done, Father!'

Look *what* you have done!

Look what *you* have done! Look what *we all* did! Look what *I* did! Look what *the guides*, who come to you to try to open your spiritual eyes, did! We are all part and parcel of the same experiment. We are all part and parcel of the same plan that went wrong. But if something goes wrong in life – if you are in a laboratory and you heat something up and it explodes, you take a broom and sweep up the pieces, you put the glass in a litter bin and you start a different experiment. You do not try and glue together the broken shards of glass into the receptacle it once was and maintain the same experiment so that it explodes again ...and again ...and again ...and again – but that is what you are doing as a result of the Fall.

You are bringing yourself to extinction because it is your nature as an angelic being to start a cycle of creativity, to bring out of no-thing something, to examine the something and then to put away the something and create something else. Unfortunately, because of the nature of the experiment that went wrong, you cannot truly collapse the something and you have invested so much of yourself in it that you believe you are a part of the something. So you take yourself to destruction time and again with 'the something' that is merely *an illusion* – an illusion you could put away at any point by saying: 'I am greater than this. I can bring through something greater than this. I can change things.'

You can change things.

There is *still* time...

...but not *much* time to re-invest this world with angelic Light, with God-Light. By investing it with angelic Light, you tear apart the thick skin of belief that surrounds the spiritual molecules that form this area of being and of illusion; you break away the heavy thinking that takes you back to the point of the Fall, and instead you re-invest this illusion with the correct values of creation and destruction. In other words, you bring this whole area of experience back into harmony and you reconcile this area of illusion with the rest of Creation. And at that point everything changes forever, your eyes are opened and you are illuminated once again from *within* and *without* because the illusion will be of a spiritual quality rather than a distorted material quality.

You speak very often about ascension and about a sudden change that you expect to come. **That change cannot come unless you change yourselves.** There is no 'hand of God' coming down to scoop you up and take you up to a higher level of consciousness. *You* have to scoop yourself up and take yourself up to a higher level of consciousness. *You* have to relinquish your belief in the experiment that went wrong that we call 'the Fall' ...and until such time no amount of 'hands' reaching down from the spiritual realms will be able to elevate you. *You have to elevate yourself.*

...Listen to me!...

You have to elevate *yourself*.

You have to re-open your angelic mind and your angelic heart No one – not me, not the angelic host, not your God – can do it for you. At the point at which you decide to do it, *yes*, we can help, *yes,* we can harmonise with you. We will harmonise with you from that point onwards so your capability and your energy, will join our capability and our energy **...but until you open up your spiritual heart *yourself* there is no illumination. There is no ascension!** There are only the effects of the Fall going on ...and on ...and on ...and on.

What you will probably find *intriguing* is that, at the point that eventually must come, when the effects of the Fall are negated, the whole experience that you have embraced within the Fall experiment for thousands, and thousands, and thousands of years will seem like the 'blink of an eye' – as though you made a misstep in a dance but are now in harmony again. One step was a misstep and the next is back into the harmony of the dance. But for you, invested in the effects of the Fall, and for us still emerging from the cleansing spheres, this is a very real experience. It is an experience that seems to be lasting ...and lasting ...and lasting ...and lasting *forever*, but in effect **only you, as an angel, last forever**, and this experience is one of many that you will be able to fold away and just draw on through your memory.

This information has been given to the world before.

This information always comes to the world at the point where things are at their grimmest. This information has been buried. This information has been diluted. This information has been perverted.

Well, here it is *again*!

...And the reason it is here at this point in time is because you need now – more than ever in the last thousands of years – you need *now* to change your minds. You need *now* to do something.

If I have made you afraid by this final chapter – I am happy. I need to make you afraid. I need to make you see that the view you have through the filter of the Fall is inadequate; that your world you rely on is not to be relied on; that the physical senses you rely on are not to be relied on; that your world view is cloudy and distorted and that there is something *far better* waiting for you the moment that you emerge from the mistake you have chosen to invest in.

Not only that, but awaiting you outside of the effects of the Fall **is the rest of your family.** You have small glimpses of the pleasures of family on the Earth plane, when you can get past the sharp edges of personality you have solidified through the effects of the Fall, and you have glimpses of how wonderful it can be to be part of a harmonic family. You have an infinite harmonic family waiting to welcome you back into their arms beyond the effects of the Fall – a wonderful, *wonderful,* constantly blissful experience with no lack, no loss and no grieving. You are constantly with them and they with you – not in a restrictive sense but in the sense of totally, totally, *totally* belonging. That is waiting for you beyond the effects of the Fall.

You have the ability to create worlds! You have the ability to create any scenario that you can imagine. You bring it forth, you immerse yourself in it, you experience it and you put it away again. **Imagine that!** Imagine how wonderful and glorious that is to be creatively free, to be able to create *anything* you desire for the sharing, the glorification and the benefit of your angelic family ...and of your God.

That is how you got into this mess, unfortunately, in the first place... by wanting to do that, but by believing that you could manipulate the basics – the building blocks of creation – in a different way to enhance the way that creation works.

Are there questions?

Jane: I don't have any questions about this chapter, Joseph, and I would like to thank you for bringing this information through.

David: Joseph, the angelic host that are beyond the confines of the Earth – you have mentioned that most of them that have gone on have 'done their own thing', but occasionally they do 'pop in', as it were – are they guiding *you* now?

Joseph: They are guiding me and they are guiding us because they are, to a greater degree, able to communicate with us *consciously*. As we climb the ladder of cleansing through the spiritual spheres we become re-aware 'every day', as it were, of *more potential*. As we cleanse ourselves of the effects of the Fall, in the degree that we do that we restore our angelic memory and, therefore as a matter of course, are supplied with the potential of the Whole, the memory of the Whole and the understanding of the Whole.

That lives with us at heart-level constantly, but also there are times when we take ourselves, as the group soul that I am part of, into a wonderful amphitheatre or splendid arena (I wish I could show it to you). There, at a time when we are given a 'signal', we sit as family and as *one* to receive, in an individual form, a visit from one of the angelic host. You might think that we are great elevated beings (and we can understand why that would look to be the case to *you* because, by comparison, what we are capable of seems to be infinitely more evolved than what you are capable of), but when we sit and receive one of the angelic host (that, remember, we are part of), we are awed and we are humbled by the Light, by the intention, by the love and by the capability of that sweet soul in our midst.

What you also have to understand is that that sweet soul is *what we are*, and that that visitation is to bring encouragement, but also to show us what we are and where we are going. So, as we approach Infinity, we do so without fear because we can see, from the visitors who come to us, what lies ahead for us in terms of individual capability and form. There is no fear of stepping outside of the cleansing spheres; there is only a desire to one day express ourselves once again like the visitors that come to commune with us express themselves. As I said earlier in this final chapter, the whole process from you as an individual trapped in matter ...to you as an individual moving through the cleansing spheres ...to you emerging into Infinity is only *the blink of the eye*. Only the blink of an eye! But it does not seem to be so to you encased in matter, nor to us in the more evolved spheres of Creation.

So, we commune with angelic messengers, and following the Fall of civilisation there was a time when those angelic messengers were the only means of communicating with the souls that entered into stasis. You might think that we control the mechanics of the cleansing spheres, and we do to *some* extent, but they are under the greater control of our greater angelic family, and so, in that sense, we are always streaming and channelling the intents of the angelic host as they are beyond this tiny, tiny area of mistaken matter.

Does that make sense?

David: Yes, thank you.

Joseph: Is there anything else whilst we are communicating for this last time *for a while*?

Jane: The revelation that seems the most surprising in the whole book is about the angelic being splitting into two halves – the positive and the negative. I just wondered what the spiritual science behind that was and the reason why it had to split in two.

Joseph: It is because you are expressing yourself through the filter of the Fall and, in order to exist within this area where positive and negative have been disengaged from their original intent, you express yourself as one being through those *divided* channels for creation. It is an effect of the Fall and it is an effect of the redirecting of creative purpose. So, when you find yourself projected into the area of the Fall, you are already a 'house divided'. As you manifest on this level, you are already a divided consciousness because you *are* part of your creation on a physical level. You are part of a creation that has been pulled apart and has been skewed, and so you are channelled in as an angelic being and are shoehorned into a physical body, but you are split in consciousness and purpose into two parts of that physical consciousness.

Does that make it any easier to understand? It is a vast spiritual-scientific topic and we do not have the energy to deliver it as chapters. At some point we could and at some point we *hope to* but for now we have to bring together the two halves – the male and female – of this book in order that the basic message gets out there.

What happens is that the individual angelic being is pulled down into the effects of its own creation and is literally pulled apart. Are you not at this time apart from your God? Do you not exist as an individualisation and also as a part of God? But you are not conscious of being two halves, are you?

Jane: No.

Joseph: And yet you are two halves in that respect. You are *two halves*: you are the Godhead that is you and you are the individual that is you that is also part of the Godhead. You are seeing in microcosm in the area of the Fall what, in effect, your relationship with God is. The two creative forces of yourself, because of the effects of the Fall, *have to* exist separately within the matrix that you have created.

It is to do with spiritual physics; it is to do with the corruption of the way that creation works on this level. We have to envisage and foresee a time where there is a reunification, not only with the angelic host, but a reunification on Earth of the two halves of each individual member of the angelic children at a time when the Earth is 'Christed' – at a time when the Earth is reunited with the rest of Creation. Do you see?

Jane: Yes, thank you.

Joseph: Are you *sure* that you see?

Jane: I don't fully understand it.

Joseph: What don't you understand?

Jane: I can understand that with the Fall we made matter too positive and then there was a surplus of negative left over and so that unbalanced things and somehow, because we were part of our creation, we became unbalanced too ...but... no, I don't think I *can* understand it in the time we have left with this communication.

Joseph: It is certainly a mystical aspect that I am asking you to take on faith, but you are used to looking at things with regard to physical matter and from the point of view of everything being hard, being a 'shell' and being individual and isolated. I am talking about *essence*. Is it not true that you can be sitting in a room, for example, watching someone giving a lecture, but your mind is elsewhere? You are *physically* sitting in the room, but your mind is elsewhere and you are going over the past, or the present, or the future, or talking to someone in your mind's eye. Are you capable of that?

Jane: Yes.

Joseph: In being capable of that, at that point, there are two essences to you. There is the physical essence that is sitting there and still consciously listening to the lecture, and there is the spiritual essence that has decided to travel. I hope this gives you an idea of what I mean by 'essence'.

So the male and the female, or the two 'creative halves', if you like, of each angelic being are an essence that is simply placed into two vessels – in the same way that you can place yourself in that lecture and yet be outside of that lecture in your mind's eye and have very 'real' experiences away from that lecture but still be sat in it listening to it. We are not dealing with physical matter; we are dealing with you as an angelic being, and as an angelic being you have different facets and those facets normally, as part of the angelic host, operate together. They are regarded as separate facets but they are together.

On Earth, because of the effects of the Fall, those two essences are forced apart (in the way that you have forced yourselves apart from the rest of Creation) and have to inhabit different physical vessels in order to project themselves into and exist within the area of the Fall. That does not mean that there is a separation once you have elevated yourself beyond the effects of the Fall.

Once you have elevated yourself beyond the effects of the Fall, there is a *reunification*. There is a reunification of you and the rest of the angelic host, but there is a reunification of those essences of yourself that you use in order to bring through creation. And not 'creation' as you understand it *here* in taking a screwdriver and some wood and putting something together. It is infinitely more satisfying, infinitely more exquisite and delicate creation you are capable of, but not here because of the Fall. Does that help?

Jane: Yes, that does help a lot. Thank you.

Joseph: Is there anything finally?

David: No. Just to say 'thank you' Joseph.

Joseph: Please, each of you reading this book, ask for help. Ask for help in understanding the message that should strike a chord within you that has been set out in this book. But also ask for help in realising your potential, in changing this world, in having the courage to change yourself and having the courage to let go.

We are with you. Your own soul-group members are with you. The angelic host is with you, channelled through us and also through yourself.

You are a being of infinite, glorious possibility. You are a being of Infinity – you just need to remember that. And as a being of Infinity, as a being of glorious *infinite* possibility, you *create*. You create worlds ...you create solar systems ...you create universes ...you create glorious, glorious scenarios ...and you can still do that *now*.

You *need to* do that now to cleanse this region, to change this region and to bring *finally* peace on Earth, forever and ever.

Amen.

A

'a little knowledge is a dangerous thing' 95, 233

Akashic Records 158, 259

angels 18, 22, 29-31, 33, 35, 46, 48, 50, 62, 76, 90, 110-111, 113, 115, 128, 150, 169, 217

angel 22, 41, 46, 56, 76-77, 97, 103, 113-114, 129, 130, 150-153, 161, 168, 170, 173, 222-223, 231, 234-235, 238-239, 244, 249, 258, 269

  angelic being 27-28, 56, 59-61, 63, 66, 85-86, 113-114, 120-121, 127, 130, 141, 150-152, 161, 177, 186-189, 193, 195, 200-202, 204, 207, 214, 217, 220, 224, 231, 242, 245-246, 259, 262, 267, 272-275

  angelic beings 19-20, 24, 28, 30, 42, 44, 46, 55-57, 60, 62, 65, 67, 76, 86, 90, 102, 109, 112, 114, 137, 139, 142, 187, 191, 232

  angelic children 40, 75, 92-100, 104-105, 108, 111, 115-117, 127, 131-132, 136, 138, 143, 147, 155-156, 158, 164, 185, 193, 220, 223, 238, 243, 254, 259, 263, 264, 273

  angelic council 70, 73, 75-76

  angelic expression 21

  angelic facet 84

  angelic forces 23, 27-29, 55, 129, 170

  angelic fragments 85, 88

  angelic group 19, 20-22, 24

  angelic heritage 187, 220, 223

  angelic hierarchy 43

  angelic host 69, 70-72, 82-85, 87-90, 93-98, 100, 103, 105-106, 108-109, 111-112, 116, 125, 130, 136-138, 140, 142-143, 148, 151, 153, 168, 170, 188, 254, 257, 259-260, 264-

265, 269, 271-273, 275-276

  angelic intent 55-56, 208

  angelic level 29, 86, 128, 163, 208, 210, 216, 264

  angelic parent 85, 87

  angelic 'parents' 95

  angelic projections 31

  angelic vision 121

  fallen angel 113, 150, 151

animals 58, 111-112, 117-118, 131-132, 184, 225, 237, 238

ascension 80-81, 190, 198, 256-257, 259, 261, 263, 265, 267-269, 271, 273, 275

atoms 42, 47, 49-50, 55, 61, 93, 95, 117, 149, 189, 203, 232

aura 19, 58-61, 205

awakening 157, 232

B

balance 35, 46, 48, 77-78, 97-98, 102, 106, 168, 171, 173, 180, 208, 210, 226, 245, 250

beauty 36, 49, 63, 73, 74, 123, 162, 197, 247

belief 85, 98-99, 101-102, 106-107, 109, 112-116, 118, 120-121, 128, 130, 133, 136, 149-150, 243, 245, 247-248, 251, 262, 264, 266-268

  believe yourself to be right 202

Big Bang 19

Big Indian 38-39

black holes 28, 43

C

cataclysmic event 10

cells 28, 91

chakras 115

change 9-10, 13, 20, 26, 44-46, 53, 59,

148-149, 169, 179-180, 183, 189, 192, 237, 239, 249, 273

medicine 78, 206

meditations 63, 90, 151, 154, 195, 234, 244, 249

memory 42, 97, 101, 122-123, 137, 148-149, 153-154, 166, 177-178, 181, 202, 213, 215, 243-244, 264-265, 269, 271

minds 20-21, 29, 42, 65, 67-70, 90, 116, 118-119, 131-132, 134, 136, 171, 178, 187, 190-191, 215, 220, 266, 269

molecules 59, 73, 76, 117, 137-140, 148-149, 162, 183-184, 202-203, 205-206, 213-217, 219, 223, 225, 228, 232-233, 238, 258, 265, 268

moons 28

  moon 28, 31

N

no-thing 16, 35-36, 50-51, 70, 76, 125, 169, 263, 267

O

original intention 42, 45-47, 56, 71, 73, 150, 238

original sin 147-151, 153-155, 157, 159, 216

  'mistake' 51, 99, 144, 147, 149, 151, 154, 156, 183, 216, 222-223, 238, 262, 270

  sin 147-151, 153-155, 157, 159, 183, 193, 216, 223

P

paradise 100, 109, 244

permanence 79, 137, 163

Persian Gentleman 38, 39, 261

physical life 35, 98, 139, 208, 216, 218,

242-243, 251

physical matter 24-25, 30-31, 40-42, 47-48, 55-56, 59-61, 70-73, 79, 82, 88, 97-99, 101, 104, 107, 122, 134, 144, 162, 180, 210, 216, 218, 228, 238, 239, 260, 262, 264-265, 274-275

physical mind 7, 25, 27, 35, 134, 164-165, 168, 181, 190, 198, 203, 212, 218, 220-221, 226-229, 231, 245, 247, 249

physical senses 35, 56, 73, 126, 138, 164, 167, 270

physical space 30, 43

physicality 29-30, 32-33, 35-36, 46-47, 54, 56-58, 71, 84, 89, 138, 164, 173, 179, 181, 190-191, 197, 202, 204, 206-210, 212-213, 221-222, 226, 229, 239, 254, 263

physical being 53, 85, 114, 186, 188, 212-213, 239

physical body 12, 37, 51, 141, 149, 165, 188, 190-191, 196, 214, 218, 228, 233, 238, 251, 262, 273

planets 20, 28, 41-46, 48-49, 55, 69-75, 78, 86, 88-89, 94, 142, 201

  maintaining the planet 75

  planet 9-10, 13, 14, 28, 29, 32, 41, 42, 45-47, 55-59, 62, 67, 70-71, 74-75, 77-78, 80, 82-86, 88, 91, 93, 97, 99, 117, 132, 161, 169, 171, 225, 238, 251-252

  Jupiter 72

  Mars 71, 72

  Mercury 72

  Saturn 72

  Venus 71, 72

point of view of God 27

polluted 35, 38, 48-49, 53, 74, 141,

Also available in **The Joseph Communications** series:

Revelation

who you are, why you're here

...a book to change your world

In this first book of the series, Joseph invites you to understand who and what you really are, where you came from, why you are here and the miraculous things you are capable of achieving. Joseph reveals the amazing potential of the human spirit and provides a plan for changing the future of this planet before it's too late.

Intelligent, thought-provoking, non-religious and written in direct, concise language, this book will revolutionise your views through its challenging revelations about life and the nature of reality itself.

Revelation will empower you through a new awareness of the active part you play in creation and inspire you to look at your world in a whole new light.

For me, Revelation was my 'Aha!' moment – Joseph is exactly what the well-beaten spiritual path needs right now and I can't wait to hear what he has to say next!
Debbie Ann Brett, One Spirit Project – Canada.

Once I began reading Revelation I couldn't put it down and read the whole book almost in one session. Revelation will definitely change your life!
Geoffrey Keyte, Healing International – U.K.

£12.95 / $20.75
ISBN: 978-1-906625-00-9

Available from good bookshops, Amazon or direct from www.josephspeaks.com

Also available in **The Joseph Communications** series:

Illumination

change yourself, change the world

...A powerful spiritual manual for personal and global transformation.

Time is running out – Earth is heading for cataclysm. This vitally important book reveals how each of us can literally save the world ...before it's too late.

We need to change and accept personal responsibility now – or Joseph warns there are only three generations left. The Field has become so polluted by mankind's negative energy that the planet cannot sustain itself much longer ...unless radical changes are made to the way we think.

It is our responsibility to renew the Field by infusing it with sufficient Light to redress the balance and return the planet to the paradise it originally was. Illumination provides all the 'tools' to achieve personal and global enlightenment empowering the reader to direct Light and transmute our negativity into harmony, joy, love, peace and spiritual progression.

There is a great urgency to Joseph's words - we do not have an infinite number of tomorrows in which to put things right.

"The purity and essence of Light shines throughout Joseph's words - a referential handbook for daily living."
Martin Heald - Author of Destiny

"Few other messages have been so specific and as it sinks into the hearts of more and more individual lives - the planet will be transformed."
Scott Rabalais – Cornucopia of Consciousness

£12.95 / $20.75
ISBN: 978-1-906625-01-6
Available from good bookshops, Amazon or direct from www.josephspeaks.com

Also available in **The Joseph Communications** series:

Your Life After Death

...your final destination is anything but final!

Countless opportunities and wonders wait for you beyond physical death.

Authored by Joseph, a highly evolved spirit who has lived in an enlightened sphere of reality 'beyond the veil' for thousands of years, this new book delivers arguably the most comprehensive account ever written of what lies ahead for you when you leave this world behind.

An essential source of comfort and inspiration, Your Life After Death is the definitive guide to the afterlife...

... read it and you'll never look at the next life, or, indeed, this one, in quite the same way again.

Once I started reading it my own spirituality told me that what I was reading was true and I couldn't put it down. I think it's the only thing out there with real HOPE.
Meria – The Meria Heller Show

'The most amazing and authoritative account of the spiritual world'
Geoffrey Keyte - Healing International

£14.95 / $24.00
ISBN: 978-1-906625-03-0

Available from good bookshops, Amazon or direct from www.josephspeaks.com

Life in Atlantis • Spirit photography • Crop circles • What mankind can do to save the planet • Lifting our vibrations • The dangers of narrow religious beliefs • The state of *no-thing* • Getting rid of negativity from the past • Spiritual evolution • The role of workers for the Light • God • Time • How to raise the collective consciousness • Global pandemics • Jesus • The divine feminine • The Field of mankind • How mankind can prevent global cataclysm • 2012 • Ways of raising our own vibrations • Spiritual hierarchy • Who meets us when we pass over into the spirit realms • The contribution of animals to the Field • Infant mortality • The significance of seeing spiritual lights • Assisted suicide • The causes of illness • The best way to send out healing • The Earth's magnetic grids • Ascension • Listening to the inner voice • How to tune into the God-within • Effective methods of mediation • The nature of angels • Balancing materiality with spirituality • DNA theory • Dealing with dark energies • Discerning whether channelled material is true • Using intuition • Learning to use the heart-mind • The reason for accidents • Disability • What individuals can do to send Light into the world • The need for spiritual simplicity • The effect of negative thoughts on the collective consciousness • Is the Earth the only planet to experience negativity • Indigo

abuse of the planet • The imba

What will happen to mankind o

incarnation • The Fall • Previo

The nature of time • How to di

is correct • Networking points

nature of God-Light • Sacred g